BETWEEN ISRAELITE RELIGION
AND OLD TESTAMENT THEOLOGY

CONTRIBUTIONS TO BIBLICAL EXEGESIS AND THEOLOGY

SERIES EDITORS

K. De Troyer (Salzburg)
G. van Oyen (Louvain-la-Neuve)

ADVISORY BOARD

Lutz Doering (Münster)
Beverly Gaventa (Baylor)
Annette Merz (Groningen)
Jack Sasson (Nashville)
Bas ter Haar Romeny (Amsterdam)
Jacob Wright (Atlanta)

Robert D. MILLER II (ed.)

BETWEEN ISRAELITE RELIGION AND OLD TESTAMENT THEOLOGY

Essays on Archaeology, History, and Hermeneutics

PEETERS
LEUVEN – PARIS – BRISTOL, CT
2016

A catalogue record for this book is available from the Library of Congress.

© 2016 — Peeters, Bondgenotenlaan 153, B-3000 Leuven

ISBN 978-90-429-3290-6
D/2016/0602/53

All rights reserved. No part of this publication may be reproduced, stored in a retrieval system, or transmitted, in any form or by any means, electronic, mechanical, photocopying, recording or otherwise, without the prior permission of the publisher.

TABLE OF CONTENTS

Contributors VII

Robert D. MILLER II
Introduction 1

Shawna DOLANSKY
Re-Figuring Judean "Fertility" Figurines: Fetishistic Functions of the Feminine Form 5

Erhard GERSTENBERGER
The Power of Praise in the Psalter. Human-Divine Synergies in the Ancient Near East and the Hebrew Scriptures 31

Christopher B. HAYS
'Held in Slavery by the Fear of Death'. Ancient Hero Cults and the Old Testament Gospel 49

Stephen L. HERRING & Garth GILMOUR
The Image of God in Bible and Archaeology 63

Robert D. MILLER II
Iron Age Medicine Men and Old Testament Theology 87

Brent A. STRAWN
What Would (or Should) Old Testament Theology Look Like if Recent Reconstructions of Israelite Religion Were True? 129

CONTRIBUTORS

Shawna Dolansky
Carleton University

Erhard Gerstenberger
Unvisitat Marburg

Garth Gilmour
Oxford University

Christopher Hays
Fuller Theological Seminary

Stephen Herring
Oxford University

Robert D. Miller II, OFS
The Catholic University of America; University of Pretoria

Brent Strawn
Emory University

INTRODUCTION
Robert D. Miller II

In the past several decades, a number of academic studies of Israelite religion have appeared in press. These studies have used the wealth of archaeological data unearthed in the past century to reconstruct religious and ritual practices of ancient Israel and Judah independetly of the biblical text. Studies have also used comparative material from Ugarit and elsewhere in the ancient Near East to explain both the archaeological evidence and passages in the Hebrew Bible itself. The result is a much fuller picture of the daily religious practices of both the average Israelite and the official cults of Israel and Judah than has been available in the past.

At the same time, "Old Testament theologies" have continued to be published at an unslackening pace. Theologies of the Hebrew Bible or Old Testament have come from a wide variety of approaches ranging from canonical perspectives to evolutionary traditions-histories to reader-oriented theological exegesis. Were one to add to the list of monographs on Old Testament theology the myriad of articles and essays of theological interpretation, the corpus would be immense.

What has not happened is any sort of dialogue between these two corpora. That is, the majority of Old Testament theologies remain unaffected by the reconstructions of ancient Israelite religion that have appeared. This is even true of those theologies that declare themselves to be consciously invested in history, that place a value on the meaning of the biblical text for its original audiences and on the ancient religious practices described in the biblical text. The portraits of ancient Israelite religious praxis derived from archaeology and related disciplines have not significantly impacted the way in which theology of the Old Testament is done.

The present volume seeks to address this scholarly lacuna. The essays in this volume, written by a range of archaeologists and biblical scholars, bring ancient Near Eastern data and scholarly reconstructions of Israelite religion to bear on the theological interpretation of the Old Testament and on theological questions.

In her study of Judean "fertility" figurines, Shawna Dolansky begins with the archaeological realia and problematizes the initial interpretation of Judean pillar figurines as fertility goddesses or at least fertility charms. This common interpretation is not without rationale, as scholars have tied the figures to supposed state-sponsored motherhood campaigns during the reign of Manasseh. Dolansky challenges this interpretation from a historical perpespective and suggests instead a range of possibilities. Might they be a consort goddess symbolizing protection? Need they be goddesses at all? Are they votive figures at all?

In "The Power of Praise in the Psalter," Erhard Gerstenberger uses ancient Near Eastern comparative evidence to explore the Psalms for "old liturgical exaltations of the divine." He uses Mesopotamian praise texts to redefine the fuction of praise, proposing praise as a force emitted to preserve or elevate the status of the one praised. Thus in the Psalms, ongoing praise preserves the lordship of the creator.

Christopher Hays, in "Held in Slavery by the Fear of Death," addresses a broad biblical theology of both Old and New Testaments by unpacking the power over death and evil in the Old Testament, a theme quite important in the New. By examining the ubiquity and nature of the cults of dead heros in the ancient Near East, he is able to show both its connection to hope for the afterlife and its pervasive rejection in the Old Testament. The Bible's refutation of the imperial hero-cults is countercultural in the ancient context, and it also bears on modern theological questions of "quest for deathless significance."

In "The Image of God in the Bible and Archaeology," Stephen Herring and Garth Gilmour examine how ancient societies understood divine images as theophanies. Rejecting the longstanding claim that biblical authors misunderstood the function of "idols," they illustrate how familiar the authors were with the theophanic purpose of divine images that we now know were ubiquitous in ancient Israel and Judah. The biblical distinction is, they argue, more of form and not function. As we learn more about material depictions of even Yahweh, neglected aspects of the biblical portrait of God are themselves highlighted.

"Iron Age Medicine Men and Old Testament Theology," by the present author (Robert Miller), focuses on the archaeology of religion for Iron I Israel, the premonarchic highland settlement. Using current anthropological theory to interpret archaeological data as evidence of religious ideology and ritual practice, this essay proposes shamanism and totemism as explanatory frameworks for understanding early Israelite religion. The unpacking of both of these models elucidates multiple areas of the

Hebrew Bible, including not only practices the text deems heterodox but aspects of orthodox Yahwism, as well. Using these texts and more importantly using this reconstruction of early Israelite religion, several contributions to Christian systematic theology are proposed, especially in fields of missiology, sacramentality, and pastoral theology.

Finally, Brent Strawn addresses "What Would (or Should) Old Testament Theology Look Like if Recent Reconstructions of Israelite Religion Were True?" Strawn uses the work of Karel Van der Toorn as an example of a recent reconstruction of Israelite religion, a reconstruction representative of a consensus of contemporary scholarship. Since this reconstruction is in many ways at odds with the portrait of religion in the Bible, how then is one to do theology? This problem was highlighted a decade ago by Mark Smith:

> When scholars working in archaeology, biblical studies, or history of religion write explicitly or implicitly about Judaism and Christianity for audiences including Jews and Christians, their intellectual enterprise sometimes includes the unstated task of offering an alternative theology melding theology and nontheological data anchored in the culturally prestigious discourses of history and archaeology – in short, a Bible and a theology without religious experience or even belief.[1]

Clearly religious experience was more diversified in ancient Israel than mid-20th-century scholars extrapolated from Pentateuchal and Deuteronomistic parts of the Bible. But Strawn draws attention to Job as a way beyond any such facile reading of the text. Bringing a text like Job into consideration illustrates the diversity in the text itself. More importantly, the presence of Job in the context of ancient Near Eastern parallels (and some Psalms passages) raises questions about the very reconstruction of ancient Israelite religion. With Job as an one example of the "stubborn existence of the religious literature that is the Old Testament," we must conclude that "Old Testament Theology remains not only viable but crucial, even for the study and reconstruction of ancient Israelite religion." It is not only the Old Testament theologies that need to hear from Israelite religion, but the other way around as well.

SMITH, M.S.
2001. "Monotheistic Re-Readings of the Biblical God," *Religious Studies Review* 27: 25–31.

---

[1] Smith 2001, p. 31.

RE-FIGURING JUDEAN "FERTILITY" FIGURINES: FETISHISTIC FUNCTIONS OF THE FEMININE FORM

Shawna Dolansky

INTERPRETING ICONOGRAPHY

Over the last thirty years, from Holladay's seminal essay[1] to more recent works by Dever,[2] there has been a call for an explicitly archaeological approach in reconstructing biblical history.[3] We are all well aware of the problems inherent in using the biblical text to reconstruct the history of ancient Israel, and so its use has become for some, at best secondary, while archaeological artifartcts are given primacy. I would argue, however, that this has its own problems – the same issues of interpretation that cause us problems when trying to use the Bible for historical purposes plague archaeological conclusions as well, just perhaps less obviously. In other words, determining the meaning, use, and symbolism of archaeological artifacts can be (and usually is) just as problematically "interpretive." Case in point: archaeologists who see breasts on a figure and assume a fertility function are making an inference that is not necessarily warranted by the artifact itself.

Breasts on a figure from Iron Age Judah prove even more contentious to interpret. At most archaeological sites, an abundance of female figurines and relative dearth of corresponding male figurines, is often interpreted as a sign that fertility goddesses were important to the ancient culture in question. Two assumptions are inherent here: one, that female figurines have something to do with fertility, and two, that female figurines represent goddesses. In the archaeology of Iron Age Judah,

---

[1] Holladay 1987.
[2] Dever 2005.
[3] Probably one of the most successful examples of this can be found in Meyers (2007), in which the author takes an anthropological approach to the Judean Pillar Figurines, using Ucko's (1962 and 1968; see also Voigt 2000) ethnographically-based typology of anthropomorphic figurines; see further below.

however, different (though no less questionable) assumptions have prevailed. In fact, because of the strong conviction on the part of early Syro-Palestinian excavators that biblical Israel consisted of a monotheistic patriarchal society, such figurines have been understood as representing local, female-led challenges to the patriarchal elitist religion considered legitimate by the authors of the Hebrew Bible. From the earliest excavations in Judah, the so-called Pillar Figurines were considered "goddess figurines" that demonstrated the need for the prophetic condemnations of illegitimate religious practices in ancient Israel (Tell En-Nasbeh Excavation Report: I:45); excavators suggested that the figurines were part of "local worship" and manufactured chiefly by uninstructed female potters (ibid); they were evidence of the continuation of the Canaanite Bronze Age domestic cult of female nature goddesses;[4] examples that the battle of legitimate Israelite religion against the Canaanite goddesses was not always successful;[5] "charms for apotropaic or fertility purposes;"[6] or even "dumb and helpless idols"[7] and "crude playthings."[8] As Kenyon stated in her 1974 report, "The association of these female figurines with a fertility cult, abhorrent to the worshippers of Yahweh, is very obvious."[9]

Although more modern interpreters modify their language and judgments regarding the "illegitimacy" of the employment of female figurines in biblical Israel and Judah, the thrust of the argument remains the same; these figurines are commonly understood to represent a folk- and domestically-based, fertility-focused counter-cult to the priestly religion described in the Hebrew Bible and presumably practiced in state-sponsored temples and public sacred spaces.[10]

---

[4] Watzinger 1933.
[5] Galling 1937, p. 230.
[6] Hooke 1938, p. 25.
[7] Burrows 1941, pp. 220f.
[8] Tufnell 1953, p. 374.
[9] Kenyon 1974, p. 141.
[10] In this regard, Holladay (1987) concludes that the aniconic large shrines and sanctuaries at Dan and Arad represent officially-established, hierarchically organized state religion, as opposed to the "distributed" cultic remains and iconographic "clustered phenomena" – including female figurines – "which seem totally isolated from the life of the official shrines and sanctuaries, [and] are probably best explained as popular phenomena, probably dependent on traditions of folk religion stretching back into the Bronze Ages, but revitalized by foreign contacts – particularly with Phoenicia (e.g. Kuntillet 'Ajrud) – during the great age of mercantile activity which immediately preceded, and probably occasioned, the Assyrian and Babylonian takeovers of the two kingdoms" (280ff). This may be the case, but there are other possible conclusions. In later Greece and Rome, the official state religion was not in competition with domestic cults. Rather, it required a permanent priesthood, regular sacrifice, and the celebration of public state

As a historian of religion trained in literary-historical biblical criticism, I want to be able to use archeological evidence and conclusions in reconstructing biblical history. But how do I decide whose conclusions to use? Some confidently assert that the Judean pillar figurines represent goddesses and therefore contribute to our understanding of the ways in which goddesses were worshiped in ancient Israel. Others emphatically deny this is possible, but will conclude with certainty that the Judean pillar figurines represent women's religious expressions of their needs and desires and as such can tell us about women in biblical Israel. The variety of different conclusions can be accounted for by the diverse and often contradictory assumptions that each scholar brings to his/her analysis in the first place. These assumptions are rarely acknowledged, let alone examined for their validity.

In the case of biblical Judah, we have a text, albeit not one that is found along with the remains, that encourages us to understand the relative absence of male figurines not as indications of a matriarchal goddess-worshiping society, but rather as a culture that shied away from representing male figures in its iconography. In conjunction with archaeological and inscriptional data, the text also demonstrates the acknowledgment and worship of at least two goddesses in biblical Israel and Judah, raising the possibility that the figurines correspond somehow to the worship of one or the other. In light of the Deuteronomic religious reforms indicated in the Bible to be occurring precisely at the time of the proliferation of Judean pillar figurines (8th-7th centuries BCE), it is tempting to understand the figurines either in opposition to the reforms,[11] or as part of the reform program.[12] But beyond these possibilities, the text is not helpful in directly informing us as to what the figurines meant and how they were used in eighth and seventh century Judah.

The general assumptions about the figurines, discussed below, tend to lead to conclusions that the Judean pillar figurines were either: worshiped, representing a fertility goddess (usually Asherah), often understood as part of a folk movement in opposition to official religion; or they represented votive figures for women in search of fertility. These conclusions follow from a variety of assumptions regarding the meaning of breasts being offered or held. The idea that breasts are necessarily

---

holidays as a complement to domestic religious practices, not an alternative. See also Ackerman (2003) regarding the continuity between private and public religion.

[11] e.g., Dever 1994, pp. 143-68.

[12] Ryan Byrne makes a powerful argument for the JPFs as fertility figurines endorsed by the state during Judah's vassalship to Assyria (2004), but see below.

related to fertility is one that modern archaeologists tend to bring to their interpretations of these ancient artifacts. However, in ancient Judah, this motif may have meant something rather different. According to the evidence of what this motif signified in contemporary cultures, for the people of Judah the icon of the female holding her breasts may have been none of these things. Rather, it may have instead represented an apotropaic symbol of divine protection.

The Judean Pillar Figurines: Facts and Assumptions

What do we actually know about the figurines? Numbering in at least the hundreds,[13] they depict females cradling, holding, or offering their breasts. Their lower bodies are undetailed, giving way to a pillar shaped base that allows the figurine to support itself in an upright position. The earliest possible fragments appear in the tenth and ninth centuries, and the Judean pillar figurines become common in the eighth and seventh centuries, predominantly in the Judean mountains. A substantial number also appear in the Shephelah and in the Negev. Several have been discovered in Philistine contexts and in Northern Israel, but aside from these outliers, pillar figurines are almost exclusively a Judean phenomenon. Of the unbroken Judean pillar figurines, many are found in graves; others in homes, cisterns, silos, and one in a storehouse. The majority come from domestic contexts, found among domestic assemblages which many scholars have asserted are cultic in nature (but this inference may be due to the assumption that the Judean pillar figurines are cultic objects; see below). Nearly half of the provenienced Judean pillar figurines come from in or around Jerusalem,[14] but this may be because Jerusalem has been more extensively excavated than other Judean sites. Most Judean pillar figurines are found broken and in secondary contexts, indicating disposal patterns after use rather than actual use contexts.

From these basic data, scholars have arrived at a variety of contradictory conclusions regarding the function and meaning of the Judean pillar figurines, based on their different initial assumptions. The assumptions that tend to be made about the Judean pillar figurines are: (1) that they are cult objects; (2) that the Judean pillar figurines were deliberately broken; (3) that they represent the goddess Asherah; (4) that they are primarily used by women; and (5) that they are fertility figurines.

[13] Dever 2005, p. 180.
[14] Kletter 1996.

Cult Objects

Ucko's typology[15] lists "cult figures" as representations of deities and used as objects of worship usually in community contexts. However, scholars of ancient Near Eastern religions seem to use the term "cult" to also refer to objects of private piety and devotion involving rituals or magic, and not necessarily devotion to the object in question as a symbol of divinity. I will follow this latter convention, and label discussions of the Judean pillar figurines as vehicles of magic under the term "cult object" in what follows.

There tends to be two types of evidence adduced in support of the Judean pillar figurines being cult objects. The first is a claim that because they represent a female holding her breasts they must therefore either be depicting a goddess of fertility, or a worshiper seeking fertility by ritual means. However, while the ritual or cultic nature of the figurine may be inferred from this motif, we will see below that the affiliation of breasts with fertility could be more tenuous than previously assumed.

The assumption that the pillar figurines are cult objects also often follows from the assumption that they represent a goddess. For example, Keel and Uehlinger suggest that the cheap cost of the clay used for pillar figurines "carried with it the assumption that the goddess had now entered the realm of what some call a "private piety" and that the goddess was more approachable than ever before in the little cultic centers that were set up in each home."[16]

Raz Kletter, who has produced the most thorough study of the Judean pillar figurines to date,[17] is one of few scholars who question the validity of assuming that they are cult objects. He notes that "there is no clear evidence for cult in relation to the Judean pillar figurines" and further that "there is the problem of what is cult exactly and how is it expressed in the archaeological record," but concludes that all art in the ancient world "was a rigid way of expressing (mainly) royal and religious messages."[18]

The second type of evidence linking pillar figurines with cult objects has to do with the fact that some have been found with other artifacts

---

[15] Ucko 1968.
[16] Keel and Uehlinger 1998, p. 97.
[17] The present study was completed in 2008 and therefore only considers studies published prior to 2008. However, a very thorough presentation of JPFs was subsequently published as a dissertation in 2011: see Erin Darby, *Interpreting Judean Piller Figurines: Gender and Empire in Judean Apotropaic Ritual* (Dake University).
[18] Kletter 1996, p. 74, 760.

determined to be cultic in nature. For example, Meyers argues that pillar figurines have been found with ritual items at Beersheba, Tel Halif, and Tel Masos. She states that "according to data from a number of sites, the provenienced JPFs are typically part of artifact assemblages. These groups include items (such as small cuboidal altars, rattles, model chairs, miniature vessels, and lamps) that can be associated with ritual practice because they correspond with items recovered from established shrines."[19] This is the strongest argument adduced for categorizing the pillar figurines as cult objects. Certainly, the context of other artifacts with which the JPFs have been found can help us interpret the ways in which JPFs may have been understood and used.

However, the entire question of determining what constitutes "religious" or "cultic" material is itself extremely problematic.[20] The issue is whether it would even be legitimate to distinguish "religious" artifacts from non-religious ones. A cooking pot can be considered religious if it is used only for making sacred sacrificial cakes; and what of a lamp over which a blessing is recited when lit, thanking heaven for the creation of fire, but that is used functionally to provide light for women weaving textiles in the evening? I have discussed elsewhere (Dolansky 2008) the difficulty of distinguishing "religion" from "magic" for ancient Israel, so to assert that the Judean pillar figurines were non-religious artifacts employed for magical purposes (as some interpreters do) ignores the fluidity of these categories from an emic perspective. If our goal is to understand what they meant to their manufacturers and owners, it makes more sense to attempt to determine the function, symbolism, and meaning of archaeological artifacts than it does to categorise them etically: as "religious," "magical," "cultic," "secular," or otherwise.

Deliberately Broken

Because most of the figurines are broken, some have assumed that, being cult objects, they must have been deliberately damaged in magical or religious rituals.[21] Zevit, for example, concludes that "many pillar figurines were intended for single use, one prayer or one ritual – one charge of spiritual power. I hypothesise that the figurine itself was like an

---

[19] Meyer 2007, p. 125.
[20] see Barrowclough and Malone 2007; Kyriakidis 2007; Whitley and Hays-Gilpin, 2008; Insoll 2004; and C. Renfrew 1994.
[21] Meyers 2005, p. 28-9; Zevit 2001, p.271.

envelope; the image its address; the curse, blessing, prayer, or request recited over the figurine provided the contents of the message, while the act of breaking was like stamping and mailing the missive."[22]

However, after studying the breakage patterns of several hundred Judean pillar figurines, Kletter asserts that it indicates "that the Judean pillar figurines are not fundamentally different from any other assemblage of clay figurines in regard to damage patterns, and there is no real evidence for their deliberate mutilation. On the contrary, it seems that accidental breakage is a better explanation."[23] The idea that broken cult objects must have been meaningfully destroyed is further challenged when one realises that the idea that they are cult objects is itself an assumption in need of examination. If we remove this assumption, the fact that the majority are broken is no more meaningful than the fact that the majority of pottery we find is also broken. Furthermore, even if not deliberately broken, Judean pillar figurines were not buried after breakage like broken cult statues, indicating that they were not considered holy when discarded.

Asherah

But even if we allow the assumption that they are cult objects based on Meyers' argument regarding find context and ritual assemblages, should we therefore assume that they represent a goddess? For most scholars the answer is yes.[24] Such scholars usually support this assumption on the basis of synchronic and diachronic evidence linking similar art with goddess worship, and on the importance of Asherah in particular in Iron Age Judah in both inscriptional evidence and within the biblical texts. Dever states that even if the Judean pillar figurines were votive offerings, "They are better understood as images representing the goddess Asherah, used as talismans to secure her favors."[25]

Some support their assumptions and conclusions with comparative data. However, the validity of using comparative data, both diachronic (earlier/later strata) and synchronic (neighboring cultures), has itself legitimately been called into question.

---

[22] Zevit, 2001, p. 272.
[23] Kletter 1996, p. 56.
[24] e.g. Holladay 1987; Hestrin 1987; Zevit 2001; Dever 2005; Kletter 1996; Hadley 2000; Ackerman 2003; Uehlinger 1997, p.122.
[25] Dever 2005, p. 194.

For example, Zevit disagrees with presenting diachronic parallels from Late Bronze Age Canaan as context in which to understand Iron Age Israel.[26] He asserts that Iron Age archaeology demonstrates enough discontinuity with LB Canaan to demonstrate the incursion of a new ethnic group, and concludes that if Israel is not indigenous, we cannot posit continuity of ideology where we do see continuity of material culture.[27] Zevit also thinks we cannot make inferences synchronically from inscriptions at Kuntillet 'Ajrud and Khirbet El-Qom that attest to Yahweh and Asherah being worshiped as a pair: "inasmuch as neither the architectural layout nor the artifactual repertoire of these two sites are repeated elsewhere, there is no easy way to apply conclusions from the 'literate' sites to the 'illiterate' ones on the basis of syllogism."[28]

On the other hand, Dever thinks we can. He sees the Bronze Age plaque figurines of nude women (with pubic triangle, often with necklace, sometimes with lotus blossoms, snakes or animals in outstretched hands, often on back of lion) as "prototypes" of the Judean pillar figurines.[29] He notes the major differences from Judean pillar figurines (e.g. prominence of breasts only), but attributes the differences to the movement from Canaanite culture to Israelite: for Dever, the Canaanite figurines portray "the goddess" as "a rather lascivious *courtesan* of the gods, whereas the Israelite ones are much more "chaste" and portray her simply as a *nursing mother*."[30]

Although Meyers agrees that the Judean pillar figurines are votive objects, for her "the assumption that the figurines represent a goddess is problematic. Unlike small terra-cotta plaques depicting nude women holding their breasts or other more sophisticated terra-cottas that are found in Syro-Palestinian sites of the Late Bronze and Iron Ages, the pillar-figurines lack the insignia or decoration typically used to represent

---

[26] Zevit 2001, p. 84.
[27] Zevit 2001, p. 113. However, according to Holladay (1987), Philistines adapted Late Bronze Canaanite culture and syncretized very closely with it iconographically. Does this mean we cannot assume that where the Philistines adopted Canaanite/Phoenician iconography it represented even a partial assimilation of Canaanite/Phoenician ideology? Note also Dothan's (1997) observation of large differences in material culture during early phases of Philistine settlement giving way to loss of uniqueness under Egyptian and Phoenician cultural influences by the end of the eleventh century. Why should we assume that Israel and Judah were immune to this trend?
[28] Zevit 2001, p. 266.
[29] Dever 2005, p. 184-5.
[30] Dever (2005:187). Without accepting the details of Dever's conclusions, it is interesting to note the sharp decline of plaque figurines that precedes the increase in Judean pillar figurines.

deities. They wear no crowns and carry no objects that would symbolise divine power, nor do they have any of the elaborate costumes or jewelry that denote the high rank of a deity."[31]

Because only the faces, arms, and breasts are portrayed, Meyers asserts that these are nurturing figures associated with motherhood.[32] For her, "Such figures are typically used in rituals intended to deal with specific family situations, such as increasing fertility or producing healthy children. It is therefore far more likely that they are votary figures representing human females seeking the aid of a deity – any deity – in pregnancy, birth and/or lactation.... Or, more generally, these objects can be considered metaphors in material form. They are the physical expression of a woman's prayers for fertility and successful lactation; as tangible and visible objects, they represent what women seek."[33] Dever agrees with the nurturing association, further asserting that in the ancient world, breasts were associated with nursing only and were not "sex objects."[34] But for Dever, the idea that these are mothering figures only strengthens his assumption that the Judean pillar figurines represent Asherah: "the Great Mother becomes a patroness of mothers everywhere (although still possibly a divine consort)."[35]

Primarily Used By Women

Whether representing goddesses or human women, however, most interpreters agree on a fourth assumption. As Zevit states, "it is legitimate to conclude from the gender of the figurines that they represent a cult involving women primarily, though not exclusively."[36] Meyers makes an argument for this, although it is predicated on interpreting the figurines as "concrete expressions of particularly female religious life and of concern for the exclusive female role of motherhood."[37] But this assumption in itself is questionable, and is based in turn on the assumption that the Judean pillar figurines are cult objects, and that the symbolism of a female holding her breasts necessarily represents motherhood and fertility.

[31] Meyers 2005, p. 28.
[32] Meyers 1988, pp. 162-3.
[33] Meyers 2005, p. 29.
[34] Dever 2005, p. 185. However, biblical passages such as Ezek 16:7; 23:3, 21; Prov 5:19; and especially Song 4:5; 7:8; 8:10 seem to suggest otherwise.
[35] Dever 2005, p.187.
[36] Zevit 2001, p. 346.
[37] Meyers 1988, p. 162-3; cf. 2007, p. 25.

As Kletter notes, the attribution of pillar figurines to women "seems to be based on the pre-conception that female figurines belonged to female religion or the 'female house cult.' As far as the Judean pillar figurines are concerned, there is no archaeological evidence whatsoever for this view."[38]

Fertility Figurines

If there is "no archaeological evidence whatsoever" that the figurines were manufactured by, or the primary concern of women, or that they were cult objects, deliberately broken, or represented Asherah, why are all of these assumptions so readily made about them?

I would argue that all of the assumptions about the Judean pillar figurines as the basis for arguments about what they represented, how they were used, and by whom, rest on interpretations of the symbolism of the female holding, offering, or supporting her breasts.

Archaeologists of every part of the world have tended to assume that naked female figurines, or any portrayals of women that emphasise breasts, buttocks, hips, or stomachs, are necessarily fertility figures and functioned as such in a cultic way in every civilization in which they have been found. This, however, never seems to have been demonstrated or even considered critically. Feminist archaeologists, many engaged with issues of interpreting material remains from pre-literate cultures (such as Catal Huyuk) have raised the important question of whether or not portrayals of female bodies must always be symbols of motherhood or womanhood; whether, despite the striking diversity of ancient female images, they can legitimately all be characterised under the rubric of fertility or motherhood imagery; and further, whether there is a universal concept of motherhood or womanhood cross-culturally and how we can know what it was 5,000 to 20,000 years ago.[39] For pre-historic cultures, these are important questions, because we lack textual evidence for understanding the gender norms and ideologies of those societies, and thus interpreting art and iconography is a primary means by which we might attempt to reconstruct them.

For the ancient Near East, we have a variety of texts from which we can learn about goddesses and social gender norms. We know from the Hebrew Bible that procreation was important for female status; we know

---

[38] Kletter 1996, p. 49.
[39] see Bailey 2005; Joyce 2008.

that goddesses were worshiped in Israel and Judah, and we have information about those goddesses – their characteristics, attributes, and symbols – from the literature and mythologies of contemporary neighboring cultures. We know that over time, such attributes and symbols were often shared by several goddesses, and certain goddess elements were syncretised in different ways in the symbolic representations of different cultures. However, although syncretism of goddesses occurs in a variety of ways through the 2nd and 1st millennia in the ancient Near East, all goddesses do not simply become one great Mother Goddess; there are still discrete elements that remain separate and portrayed as separate goddesses. As Jo Ann Hackett has pointed out in her critique of the portrayals of the goddesses of the ancient Near East, all too often the values or attributes of syncretised goddesses are subsumed under some form of fertility function, and their individual characteristics and basic incompatibilities are overlooked or downplayed.[40] Asherah, Astarte, and Anat were known in ancient Israel, and were each understood as separate goddesses with distinct functions, and likely with separate symbols attached to them – for example, we know that Asherah was associated with sacred trees, and that the tree or pole was often used to represent her iconographically.[41]

Some scholars have regarded the pillar base of the Judean pillar figurines as potentially representative of a tree trunk, which would serve as further evidence for them that the figurines represent Asherah.[42] However, the visual association of pillar base with tree trunk is probably coincidental; there are a variety of examples of pillar bases in use throughout the ancient Near East, from Ashur in the 3rd and 2nd millennia to Philistia in the early first millennium, and there is never an acknowledged connection in these earlier figures to trees. The pillar base seems rather to be primarily a functional device that allows for a statue to be free-standing, and was used in this way for oil lamps and bird figurines in the early Iron Age, in addition to the Judean pillar figurines (see Figure 1).[43] Furthermore, it seems to have derived directly from Cypriot precedents, which were in turn adaptations of figures from Crete.[44]

---

[40] Hackett 1989.
[41] Keel 1998, p. 38; Hestrin 1987.
[42] e.g. Keel and Uehlinger 1996, p. 331.
[43] Late third millennium N. Syria pillar based figurines in Keel and Schroer 2004:74, kat 25, 26, 29.
[44] See arguments in Budin 2005; cf. also Mountjoy 1986, p. 130, fig 72; Karageorghis 1993, Pl. XVII, fig 1.

As Stephanie Budin has shown, the earliest Judean pillar figurines from the tenth and ninth centuries were found at sites known to have traded with Cyprus – Beth Shemesh, Beer Sheba, Qasile, and Lachish.[45] So it would seem that both the pillar base and the white slip wash that was found on many of the Judean pillar figurines, probably derive from earlier Aegean technologies.

Even without the connection between the pillar base and tree trunks, many scholars claim that the Judean pillar figurines must be Asherah simply because she is the most widely attested goddess worshiped in ancient Israel and Judah both textually and archaeologically. As a mother goddess, they argue, it would be natural to represent her offering her breasts as the Judean pillar figurines do. But must the image of the female offering her breasts necessarily connote motherhood or fertility? To answer this without imputing any of our modern assumptions to ancient remains, we have to try to understand what this symbol may have meant in other cultures in the ancient world.

This symbol is first used in the Neolithic Halaf culture of ancient Anatolia (6400-5800 BCE) (Figure 2; kat 2, 3, 4 p. 47 in Keel and Schroer). We have similar representations at Çatal Huyuk in Anatolia, at Samarra, and even at Harappa in Pakistan. The same portrayals arise in such diverse contexts as Middle Bronze Age Syro-Palestine (figure 3; kat 45 p. 91 in Keel and Schroer); Late Bronze Age Syro-Palestine (figure 4; kat 104 p. 135 in Keel and Schroer), Late Bronze Age Cyprus (figure 5, kat 115 p. 144 in Keel and Schroer), Iron II North Syria (figure 6, kat 153 p. 174 in Keel and Schroer), and on a Late Bronze Age cylinder seal from North Syria, where the figure standing on a lion with her hands on her breasts is identified as Ishtar/Astarte (figure 7; kat 100 p. 131 Keel and Schroer). The same motif appears on North Syrian decorated bronze horse trappings; frontlets and blinkers from a context contemporary with the Judean pillar figurines (figure 8; drawing courtesy of Paul Dion). The inner area of the frontlet shows a naked goddess holding her breasts, wearing a collar/necklace characteristic of Ishtar/Astarte, and scholars are in general agreement that this is a representation of the goddess Astarte; she is usually associated symbolically with lions, as she is here.

In a recent study,[46] Eric Gubel has argued that these horse trappings served as protective amulets; apotropaic symbols of the protective deities

---

[45] Budin 2005.
[46] Gubel 2005.

who "go before" the war horses and troops to lead them into battle and protect them from harm. Ishtar/Astarte, the naked goddess of sex and fertility, is after all, also the goddess of war. In this capacity, she is the leader and protector of her troops. And when she supports/holds/offers her breasts on war-horse frontlets, the meaning of this symbol has nothing to do with fertility, lactation, nurturing, or motherhood.

In the pre-historic contexts, we do not know what female figurines symbolized; it is simply widely assumed that they were goddess figures, and/or ritually, mythically, or magically connected to fertility. There is no evidence for this. But in historic contexts, where this figure and symbol can be positively linked to the goddess Ishtar/Astarte, we can begin to draw some inferences. We know about Ishtar from Mesopotamian mythology, and about her southwestern counterpart Astarte from Canaanite mythology. She is a goddess of sex and war, associated in Syria with horses and military campaigns. She was the main goddess of Tyre and Sidon, and central to Phoenician religion in the Iron Age. She was arguably popular in 7th century Judah as well, if we take her to be the Queen of Heaven for whom the women bake cakes in Jer 44:19.[47] She is also the most likely candidate for the goddess depicted on the Late Bronze Age terra-cotta plaques that are popular in the southern Levant before the rise of the Judean pillar figurines in Judah.[48]

Some scholars have expressed doubts that the plaque figurines represent a goddess, as they lack divine attributes. Like the later Judean pillar figurines, they are found mostly in domestic contexts, some in graves. While it is true that not all representations of naked women need necessarily depict goddesses, it is also the case that goddesses need not be represented with divine attributes. The nude female figures on models of shrines or temples, usually in pairs, sometimes three, or on clay towers and cultic stands from both Syria and Palestine, lack divine attributes, but are divine figures. Occasionally they are standing on lions, a symbol of Astarte (as on the horse frontlets). This does not make the figure on the plaque figurines, or the Judean pillar figurines, necessarily representative of deities, but it does remove the only real argument that they were not goddesses.

If the plaque figurines, and the Judean pillar figurines, representing nude or semi-nude females holding or offering their breasts, were goddesses, the question of which goddess is depicted is an important one. If

[47] see Ackerman 1992, pp. 20-35.
[48] see Moorey 2004.

the plaque figurines represent Astarte, why do many scholars assume that the pillar figurines represent Asherah?

The reason seems to be that we have much more evidence, biblical and archaeological, for the worship of Asherah in Iron Age Judah than for Astarte. Inscriptions from Kuntillet 'Ajrud and Khirbet 'el Qom attest to the inclusion of Asherah in the cult of Yahweh. The Hebrew Bible mentions Asherah, or "the asherah," some forty times. In fact, the author of 1 Kgs 18 depicts Asherah as the Tyrian goddess imported to Israel under Jezebel, when in fact extra-biblical texts confirm that the Tyrian goddess was Astarte, not Asherah. Asherah is not attested in any Tyrian text, or anywhere in coastal Phoenicia in the Iron Age. Perhaps this is a later Judahite retrojection into ninth century Israelite history, based on the fact that Asherah was the goddess worshiped in Judah at the time of authorship. If so, this conflation of Asherah with Astarte was not unique to this author. In Jdgs 3:7, "the baals and the astartes" are used to refer to foreign gods in general, but in Jdgs 2:13, 1 Sam 7:4, 12:10, the phrase that is used interchangeably for the same purpose is "the baals and the asherahs." Outside the Bible, we find the same syncretistic tendencies: in Ugaritic texts of the 2nd millennium, *rbt* (lady) is the standard title for Asherah; but in inscriptions from Sidon, Tyre, Kition, and Egypt, this epithet belongs to Astarte. In the Ugaritic texts, Asherah is called "mother;" in Phoenician inscriptions, Astarte is called "mother." Asherah is not attested anywhere in Phoenicia – but Tannit, who bears both titles of "lady" and "mother," is. In fact, Asherah is not attested anywhere in 1st millennium Canaan outside of the Hebrew Bible and the inscriptions from Judah.

Thus, identifying icons by name is almost impossible for Syria-Palestine. The Judean pillar figurines could be depictions of Astarte or Asherah. They could represent a fusion of both. Or, they could represent neither; they could be a remnant of an ancient goddess motif, used symbolically in Judah with meanings or connotations derived from their ancient symbolism. This would be analogous to the Asherah pole becoming a symbol of Yahweh's cult – whether or not it still represents a goddess, it has been subsumed by the cult of Yahweh and in that form no longer represents the worship of a separate deity in her own right.

Whether a goddess or not, what we do know about the Judean pillar figurines is that they are almost a uniquely Judean phenomenon concentrated in the eighth and seventh centuries. The people of Judah have consciously adopted the ancient motif of the female holding/offering her breasts, and we have to assume that they have done this for a reason.

They are using a particular symbol because its meaning has resonance for them, and it is a symbol that became very popular. So what is its meaning?

While a similar appearance (the female holding/offering her breasts) may not necessarily proscribe a similar set of meanings, the manufacturers of the Judean pillar figurines were not operating in a cultural vacuum. They were borrowing a symbol used for millennia throughout the ancient Near East, and adapting it for their own use. In the manufacture of the pillar base, they certainly seem to have been consciously imitating Cypriot representations of the "Goddess With Upraised Arms."[49] They simply used this foundation for portraying their own version of a long-standing ancient Near Eastern symbol of a female holding her breasts. As we have seen, in the contemporary culture of North Syria this symbolism is attached to the goddess Astarte.

While Astarte is a fertility goddess in Syria, and therefore the motif of offering her breasts could very well have a direct connection to her function as matroness of procreation, this is not necessarily the case. We have already seen her in this pose, in a context far removed from a female worshiper in search of aid in lactation or fertility. When she appears repeatedly on Syrian war-horse trappings, in the pose of the naked female holding her breasts, this motif has nothing to do with motherhood. Rather, when she rode out in front of the army on the heads of warhorses, holding her breasts, she was a warrior and a symbol of divine protection.

So why do we need to assume that the female holding her breasts is a symbol of fertility for ancient Judah? It has been suggested that fertility would have been extremely important for the people of Judah in the eighth and seventh centuries under the suzerainty of the Assyrians; that the proliferation of Judean pillar figurines is to be "understood against the ideological emphasis on social reproduction in Judah, following the Assyrian destruction of Samaria and the mass deportations of Sennacherib," as part of a state-enacted promotion of motherhood and fertility especially during the reign of Manasseh.[50] While it is true that fertility may have been of increased importance under such circumstances, it certainly would have been the case that protection would have been even more on the minds of the people of Judah at this time.

The biblical texts provide further confirmation that the Judean pillar figurines may not have had anything to do with fertility. In all of the texts

[49] Budin 2005.
[50] Byrne 2004, p. 137.

(e.g. Gen 4:1; 1 Sam 1:11), Yahweh is the one who grants fertility: from Eve's conception through Hannah's, it is consistently Yahweh who gets credit for procreation.[51] While these texts may represent only a male, elitist proscription for belief, neither contemporary texts from neighboring cultures, nor archaeological discoveries contradict this basic idea, or give us any reason to suppose that anyone in ancient Israel or Judah would credit a deity other than Yahweh with the granting of fertility; of the earth, of the animals, or of humans. Perhaps originally this motif of female offering her breasts was linked to fertility throughout the ancient Near East. But by the first millennium, with the rise of many cultures that worshiped a dominant male warrior god and increasingly focused on a male-state-god to the detriment of goddess worship everywhere,[52] perhaps the mother goddess or consort gradually became a symbol of protection.

This would explain the syncretism of Asherah and Astarte (and possibly Anat) in iconographic representations. This would also explain why Judean pillar figurines were found in homes and in graves, and how they could have existed in such numbers in Jerusalem, at the heart of the Deuteronomic religious reforms in the eighth and seventh centuries. Perhaps then, the Judean pillar figurines were not worshiped, nor were they votive figures; nor were they necessarily even understood as goddesses anymore. They didn't represent a folk movement in opposition to official religion, or women in search of fertility. According to the evidence of what this motif signified in contemporary cultures, for the people of Judah in the 8th and 7th centuries, the icon of the female holding her breasts may have become simply an apotropaic symbol of divine protection.

ACKERMAN, S.
1993. Child Sacrifice: Returning God's Gift. Pp. 20-29, 56 in *Bible Review*, Vol 9 No 3.
1992. *Under Every Green Tree: Popular Religion in Sixth-Century Judah*. HSM: Scholars Press.
2003. At Home with the Goddess. Pp. 455-468 in *Symbiosis, Symbolism, and the Power of the Past: Canaan, Ancient Israel, and Their Neighbors from the late Bronze Age through Roman Palaestina*, edited by W. G. Dever and S. Gitin. Winona Lake: Eisenbrauns.

---

[51] See further Ackerman's (1993) discussion of human fertility and infertility as the provenance of Yahweh.
[52] cf. Frymer-Kensky 1992.

BAILEY, D.
2005. *Prehistoric Figurines: Representation and Corporeality in the Neolithic.* New York: Routledge.

BARROWCLOUGH, D. and C. MALONE
2007. *Cult in Context – Reconsidering Ritual in Archaeology.* Oxbow.

BUDIN, S.
2005. Minoan Asherah? Pp.188-197 in *Archaeological Perspectives on the Transmission and Transformation of Culture in the Eastern Mediterranean*, ed. J. Clarke. UK: Oxbow.

BURROWS, M.
1941. *What Mean These Stones? The Significance of Archaeology for Biblical Studies.* New Haven: American Schools of Oriental Research.

BYRNE, R.
2004. Lie Back and Think of Judah: The Reproductive Politics of Pillar Figurines. *Near Eastern Archaeology* 67:137-51.

DEVER, W. G.
1994. The Silence of the Text: An Archaeological Commentary on 2 Kings 23. Pp. 143-168 in *Scripture and Other Artifacts: Essays on the Bible and Archaoelogy in Honor Philip J. King*, edited by M. D. Coogan, J. C. Exum and L. E. Stager. Louisville: Westminster John Knox.
2005. *Did God Have a Wife? Archaeology and Religion in Ancient Israel.* Michigan: Wm. B. Eerdmans.

DOLANSKY, S.
2008. *Now You See It, Now You Don't: Biblical Perspectives on the Relationship Between Magic and Religion.* Winona Lake: Eisenbrauns.

DOTHAN, T.
1997. Tel Miqne-Ekron: An Iron Age I Philistine Settlement in Canaan. Pp. 96-107 in *The Archaeology of Israel: Constructing the Past, Interpreting the Present*, edited by N. A. Silverman and D. Small. JSOTSup 237. Sheffield: Sheffield Academic.

FRYMER-KENSKY, T.
1992. *In the Wake of the Goddesses: Women, Culture and the Biblical Transformation of Pagan Myth.* New York: MacMillan.

GALLING, K.
1937. *Biblisches Reallexikon.* Tubingen: Mohr.

GUBEL, E.
2005. Phoenician and Aramaean bridle-harness decoration : Examples of cultural contact and innovation in the eastern Mediterranean, *pp. 111-147 in Crafts and Images in Contact, eds. Salter and Uehlinger (Orbis Biblicus et Orientalis* 210, Fribourg:Göttingen.

HACKET, J.
1989. Can a Sexist Model Liberate Us? Ancient Near Eastern "Fertility" Goddesses. *Journal of Feminist Studies in Religion*, Vol. 5, No. 1, pp. 65-76.

HADLEY, J.
2000. *The Cult of Asherah in Ancient Israel and Judah: Evidence for a Hebrew Goddess.* Cambridge: Cambridge University.

HESTRIN, R.
1987. "The Lachish Ewer and the Asherah," *Israel Exploration Journal* 37: 212-223.
1991. Understanding Asherah – Exploring Semitic Iconography. *Biblical Archaeology Review*, 17:05, pp. 50-59.

HOLLADAY, J.S.
1987. Religion in Israel and Judah under the Monarchy: An Explicitly Archaeological Approach. Pp. 249-99 in *Ancient Israelite Religion: Essays in Honor of Frank Moore Cross*, edited by P. D. Miller, Jr., P. D. Hanson and S. D. McBride. Philadelphia: Fortress.

HOOKE, S.H.
1938. *The Origins of Early Semitic Ritual.* (Schweich Lectures 1935) London: British Academy.

INSOLL, T.
2004. *Archaeology, Ritual, Religion.* New York: Routledge.

JOYCE, R.
2008. *Ancient Bodies, Ancient Lives: Sex, Gender, and Archaeology.* Thames & Hudson.

KARAGEORGHIS, V.
1993. *The Coroplastic Art of Ancient Cyprus III. The Cypro-Archaic Period: Large and Medium Size Sculpture* (Nicosia).

KEEL, O.
1998. *Goddesses and Trees, New Moon and Yahweh: Ancient Near Eastern Art and the Hebrew Bible.* Sheffield: Sheffield Academic Press.

KEEL, O. and SCHROER, S.
2004. *Eva – Mutter alles Lebendigen. Frauen- und Gottinnenidole aus dem Alten Orient.* Freiburg: Academic.

KEEL, O. and UEHLINGER, C.
1998. *Gods, Goddesses, and Images of God in Ancient Israel.* Trans. T. H. Trapp, from German. Minneapolis: Fortress.

KENYON, K.
1974. *Digging Up Jerusalem.* London: Ernest Benn Limited.

KLETTER, R.
1996. *The Judean Pillar-Figurines and the Archaeology of Asherah.* BAR International Series 636. Oxford: Tempus Reparatum.

KYRIAKIDIS, E.
2007. *The Archaeology of Ritual.* UCLA.

MEYERS, C.
1988. *Discovering Eve: Ancient Israelite Women in Context.* Oxford: Oxford University.
2005. *Households and Holiness: The Religious Culture of Israelite Women.* Minneapolis: Augsberg Fortress.

2007. Terracottas Without Texts: Judean Pillar Figurines in Anthropological Perspective. Pp. 115-130 in *To Break Every Yoke: Essays in Honor of Marvin L. Chaney*, edited by R. B. Coote and N. K. Gottwald. Sheffield: Sheffield Phoenix.

MOOREY, P.
2004. *Idols of the People: Miniature Images of Clay in the Ancient Near East.* Oxford University Press.

MOUNTJOY, P.
1986. *The Mycenaean World.* Cambridge University Press.
Pacific Institute. 1947. *Tell en-Nasbeh I: Archaeological and Historical Results.* Pacific Institute of Pacific School of Religion and American Schools of Oriental Research, Berkeley and New Haven.

RENFREW, C.
1994. "The Archaeology of Religion," in *The Ancient Mind*, eds. Renfrew and Zubrow, pp. 47-54: Cambridge University Press.

TUFNELL, O.
1953. *Lachish III: The Iron Age.* London.

UCKO, P.
1962. The Interpretation of Prehistoric Anthropomorphic Figurines. *Journal of the Royal Anthropological Institute* 92:38-54.
1968. *Anthropomorphic Figurines of Predynastic Egypt and Neolithic Crete with Comparative Material from the Prehistoric Near East and Mainland Greece.* Royal Anthropological Society Occasional Papers, 24; London: Andrew Szmidla.

UEHLINGER, C.
1997. Anthropomorphic Cult Statuary in Iron Age Palestine and the Search for Yahweh's Cult Images. Pp. 97-155 in *The Image and the Book: Iconic Cults Aniconism, and the Rise of Book Religion in Israel and the Ancient Near East*, ed. K. van der Toorn. Leuven:Peeters.

VOIGT, M.
2000. Catal Hoyuk in Context: Ritual at Early Neolithic Sites in Central and Eastern Turkey. Pp. 253-93 in *Life in Neolithic Farming Communities: Social Organization, Identity and Differentiation*, ed. J. Kuijt. New York: Kluwer Academic.

WATZINGER, C.
1933. Denkmäler Palästinas Eine Einführung in die Archäologie des heiligen Landes; Vol. I: Von den Anfängen bis zum Ende der israelitischen Königszeit; Vol. II: Von der Herrschaft der Assyrer bis zur arabischen Eroberung. Leipzig: J.C. Heinrich.

WHITLEY, D. and K. HAYS-GILPIN
2008. *Belief in the Past: Theoretical Approaches to the Archaeology of Religion.* San Francisco: Left Coast Press.

ZEVIT, Z.
2001. *The Religions of Ancient Israel: A Synthesis of Parallactic Approaches.* London and New York: Continuum.

Figure 1. Late third millennium N. Syria pillar based figurines from Keel and Schroer 2004:74, kat 25, 26, 29
By permission of the Foundation BIBLE+ORIENT, Freiburg Switzerland

Figure 2. Halaf figurines
From Keel and Schroer 2004:47; kat 2, 3, 4
By permission of the Foundation BIBLE+ORIENT, Freiburg Switzerland

Figure 3. MBA Syro-Palestine Keel and Schroer 2004:91 kat 75 By permission of the Foundation BIBLE+ORIENT, Freiburg Switzerland

Figure 4. LBA Syro-Palestine
Keel and Schroer 2004:135 kat 104
By permission of the Foundation
BIBLE+ORIENT, Freiburg
Switzerland

Figure 5. LBA Cyprus
Keel and Schroer 2004:144 kat 115
By permission of the Foundation
BIBLE+ORIENT, Freiburg
Switzerland

Figure 6. Iron II N. Syria
Keel and Schroer 2004:174 kat 153
By permission of the Foundation BIBLE+ORIENT, Freiburg Switzerland

Figure 7. LBA cylinder seal, N. Syria
Keel and Schroer 2004:131 kat 100
By permission of the Foundation BIBLE+ORIENT, Freiburg Switzerland

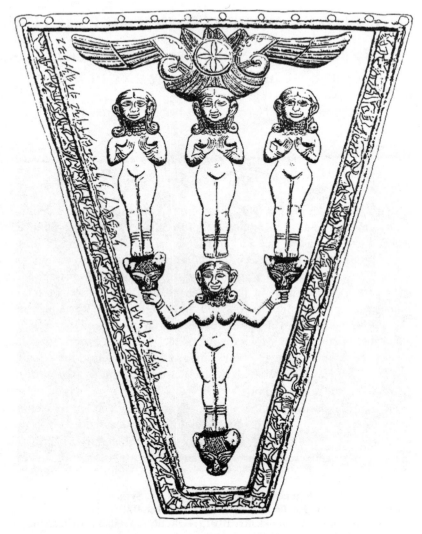

Figure 8. N. Syrian horse frontlet with Hazael inscription.
Drawing from Dion, P.-E. 1997. *Les Araméens à l'âge du fer:
histoire politique et structures sociales.*
Études bibliques, nouvelle série no 34. Paris: J.Gabalda.
By permission of Paul Dion.

THE POWER OF PRAISE IN THE PSALTER
Human-Divine Synergies in the Ancient Near East and the Hebrew Scriptures

Erhard Gerstenberger

HYMNS AND THEIR DYNAMICS:
ANTHROPOLOGY OF DIVINE SERVICE

Gerhard von Rad, eminent Old Testament theologian of the past century, put hymnic praise as the first and foremost answer of Yahweh-believers over against the saving acts of their God.[1] His understanding of praise was wide and deep: Eulogies comprised unconditional acknowledgement of Yahweh's deeds in nature and history, recognition of cosmic agitation (cf. Ps 19A), absorption in theophanic beauty, articulation of potent human life.[2] The question to be asked in the light of Old Testament and Ancient Near Eastern evidence is this: Is that circumscription exhaustive or are there perhaps other ingredients visible in the old liturgical exaltations of the divine? Some OT observations should alert us to the possibility that praise may be a force all by itself emitted to build up or preserve the status of the addressed one.

There are, indeed, a number of passages and incidents in the Hebrew Scriptures which may point into that direction. Twice in the Psalter superhuman beings viz. all the nations are challenged to "bring to Yahweh glory and strength, bring to Yahweh the glory due to his name" (*kabod wa'oz / kebod šemo*, Ps 29:1-2; 96:7-8 = 1Chr 16:28-29). Save for the entities called upon the wording is exactly the same in both psalms. The three-partite formula does sound like a liturgical shout. Its verb (*yahab*, "give", "bring") occurs mostly in imperative forms and has a strongly demanding tone (cf. Gen 29:21; 30:1; 47:15-16; Ps 60:13; 108:13; 1 Sam 14:41). Close parallels of the liturgical summons are Deut 32:3, "Give [*habu*, plural] greatness to our God!" and Ps 68:35,

---

[1] Von Rad 1957, pp. 353-367.
[2] Von Rad 1957, p. 367. "To praise is the form of existence most appropriate of human beings. To praise and not to praise are opposing each other like Life and Death."

"Give [*tenu*, plural] power to God". The objects cited in all examples amount to veritable manifestations of the Divine: *kabod* is that majestic authority which may be clad in tremendous radiance of numinous energy deadly for human beings but on the other hand absolutely necessary for life and world-order (cf. Exod 19:9-22; 24:15-17; 33:18-23; 40:34-35; Ezek 1:26-28; 10:4; 43:2; Ps 19:2; 72:19; 113:4-5; 115:1; 145:11-12).[3] *'oz*, on the other hand, signifies a broad spectrum of physical, political, mental strength and the protection these powers offer (cf. Ps 8:3; 28:8; 61:4: 62:8; 74:13; 89:11; 90:11).[4] The third gift to God, demanded from some adorer, is *godäl*, "greatness" (Deut 32:3). This expression is rather unspecific for praise contexts occurring eight times in regard to God only (cf. Deut 3:24; 5:24; 9:26; 11:2; Ps 150:2). These designations of might and potency touched upon but briefly do not simply constitute qualities of the revered Lord but seem to have, at times, a certain autonomy. Yahweh acts "in his greatness" (Deut 9:26; Ps 79:11; 150:2) just as "according to his righteousness/loving-kindness/forgiveness/patience/love" etc. (cf. Ps 65:6; 143:11; 5:8; 6:5; 13:6; 21:8; 25:5-7; 103:11, 17; cf. also adjectival formulaic expressions: Exod 34:6; Ps 86:15; 103:8; 145:8; Joel 2:13). The prepositions used to denote such potencies include *ke*, *be*, *le*, and frequent possessive suffix of the 2nd person singular establishes a relationship with Yahweh. In some significant contexts, however, the impersonal numinous powers seem to move around and act on their own (cf. Ps 85:11-12), or appear as separate energies carrying out their own purposes in alliance with the divine person (wrath and anger: Ps 2:5; 21:10; 69:25; 90:7; 102:11; vengeance: Ps 94:1; Isa 59:18; Jer 50:28; Mic 5:14; peace: Ps 29:11; 34:15; Isa 26:12; 54:10; Mic 5:4).

The issue at stake, therefore, is wider than the functions or dimensions of eulogy. It does imply the very notions of the Divine in relation to the world and to humans as well as vice versa. Furthermore, we are confronted with the fact that our own theological thinking is taking place in determined cultural and religious patterns which western Christian tradition has formed through two thousand years of debate and indoctrination. In fact, Christian faith in western cultures is mainly based on doctrine rather than on spiritual practice. This difference alone makes for huge

---

[3] Cf. Weinfeld 1982. *kabod*

[4] Cf. Wagner 1987, 6. *'zz*; *'oz* etc. Commenting on the admonition to "bring" or "give" potencies to God Wagner emphasizes that "nobody is able to give anything to Yahweh that he would not possess already."

incongruences between Scriptural and modern parameters of religion. One important consequence for Christian exegesis is this: Whoever reads the Old Testament without feeling here and there irritated in his or her coordinates of faith (determined by one's own denominational tradition) has not really understood the ancient texts.

Pre-Israelite Antecedents: Sumerian Praise-Concepts

We know full well today that Hebrew psalmody has been part of Ancient Near and Middle Eastern ways of celebrating the presence of divine beings and superhuman powers. Happily, written evidence for this broad and deep stream of liturgical traditions goes up into the 2nd and 3rd millenniums B.C. as far as Mesopotamian and Egyptian hymnology is concerned. An astonishing number e.g. of Sumerian literary writings contain articulations of praise. The Oxford ETCSL-edition[5] brings together near 400 literary texts, of which more or less 10% are too fragmentary to be useful for any investigation. Of the remaining 360 specimens at least 200 are showing some kind of expression connoting eulogies to divine entities.

To delve deeper into this treasure of praise-affirmations it may be advisable to catch on to a special formulaic expression which occurs 64 times in Sumerian hymnic texts of ETCSL: "[Divine Name = DN; sum.: ^{d}DN zà-mí]! Hail!"[6] In its most simple form, in fact not a grammatical phrase but rather an elementary shout or exclamation, it impulsively puts side by side the name of the eulogized deity or object and the noun zà-mí. "Praise!" or "Hail!" would be a proper translation. To give a couple of examples:

> 34: "O king, honeyed mouth of the gods! Praise be to Enki [^{d}en-ki zà-mí].
> 35: Ninĝišzida, son of Ninazu!
> 36: Praise be to Father Enki [a-a ^{d}en-ki zà-mí].
> 37: A balbale of Ninĝišzida." [Colophon; ETCSL 4.19.1, l. 34-36]

---

[5] The Electronic Text Corpus of Sumerian Literature = ETCSL (free accessible in the internet, see bibliography) is the most extensive body of Sumerian literature available in transcription and English translation; it has been accumulated until 2006 (and unfortunately left unfinished) in Oxford, Great Britain.
[6] Cf. Gerstenberger 2014.

The context of the euphoric outburst is quite clear: Ningišzida (possibly: "Lord of the Good Tree") is being celebrated in l. 1-33 as a very powerful numen, both in mythological and political terms (l. 1-24), who once had received his extraordinary prowess from higher deities like Enki in the depths of Abzu (l. 25-33). The double summons to the congregation or choir, then, to honor Enki, the power-font (l. 34, 36) comes out of that very logic of praise: The source of strength is to be extolled in order to maintain the flow of energy to the beneficiary. The last line (l. 37) is a scribal colophon, marking the poem – for archival purposes? – as a special song for Ningišzida, not Enki.

Inana, the goddess of love and war, is well represented in Sumerian praise literature. One of the poems dedicated to her tells the story of Enheduana, the Accadian priest installed at the ancient city of Ur and her victory over local lords.[7] The final words are: "Praise be to the destroyer of foreign lands, endowed with divine powers by An, / to my lady enveloped in beauty, to Inana!" (ETCSL 4.07.2, l. 153-154). The Sumerian text reveals the real impact of the final "hail", being the very last word of l. 154: ^{d}inana zà-mí. The epithets of the goddess ("destroyer of foreign lands, endowed ... enveloped ...") all precede the empowering shout. The zà-mí- cheer at the end seems to summarize what has been going on throughout the hymnic poem. The adorer, nominally Enheduana, "recites" the powers of Inana in order to give her strength for the political battle at hand (l. 63-65, cf. l. 139-141; 150-152). All these passages do not use the expression zà-mí but specify clear enough synonyms like "holy song" (šir kug) and "divine power" (me).

There are, to be sure, some instances in the large corpus of hymnic texts which directly speak about "applying zà-mí" to a worthy recipient corroborating the reading of the Inana hymn above. A most significant example is found in the ancient hymn for Keš, archaic city with a legendary sanctuary. Enlil, the most traditional and influential deity of Sumer, lord of Nippur and its temple Ekur ("Mountain House") is described in the Keš poem as the founder of sanctuary and city. "Enlil spoke in praise of Keš" (ETCSL 4.80.2, l. 9; cf. l. 38-39). Unfortunately, the translation is hiding somewhat the original meaning of the phrase. The Sumerian wording is: ^{d}en-líl-le kèš^{ki} zà-mí àm-ma-ab-bé „Enlil spoke a zà-mí to Keš", this means to say something like: "he endowed her with power". The widely used formula zà-mí dug-ga$_4$, "spoken/performed/delivered

---

[7] Cf. Zgoll 1997.

'hail'", furthermore, in its various shades of meaning supports the performative meaning of uttering praise.[8]

zà-mí along this line becomes a synonym of other expressions denoting anonymous powers or energies, like e.g. "destiny" (*nam-tar*), "authoritative word" (*inim*), "divine potencies" (*me*), "holy rites" (*ĝarza*), "numinous auras" (*melem*), "law", "justice" (*si sá*), "order", "plan" (*ĝiš ḫur*) and others. All these forces, according to Sumerian understanding, did work in their own ways and settings. The "praise" element had its "Sitz im Leben" in liturgical ceremonies where groups of worshippers could voice their admiration and support. Interestingly, *zà-mí* and its companions never were employed in a technical sense designating genres of texts, postures, or actions. They all have been conceptualized in the Sumerian tradition as spiritual and impersonal powers wielded by gods and goddesses, but, in fact, semi-independent and silently influencing beings and courses of events.

How did *zà-mí* work, then? The addressees of eulogies be they personal entities, sacred objects like temples, musical instruments, or other cultic paraphernalia, were trusted to hold important positions of influence within the spiritual structure of world- and social order. They were considered champions of all the right and wholesome developments on earth or in certain locals of the world. The spiritual quality inherent in *zà-mí* is articulated in adjectival attributions: "Great Mountain, Father Enlil, your praise is sublime!" (ETCSL 4.05.1, l. 171: *kur gal a-a* ᵈ*en-líl zà-mí-zu maḫ-àm*; cf. ETCSL 1.3.5, segm. D, l. 62; 2.6.9.2, l. 56). The lexeme *maḫ* signifies „greatness", „majesty", „power", paralleled by *gal* (ETCSL 2.4.2.03, segm. A, l. 20 etc. [refrain]; 2.5.4.01, l. 403). For the most part, however, the dynamics of praise in Sumerian hymnic texts is expressed by the adjective *dùg*, "good", "effective", "beautiful", "sweet" (43 occurances in ETCSL).[9] Considering the dynamic character of "hail-shouts", and "hail-songs" (both: *zà-mí*) a mere emotive / aesthetic event or an exclusive description of static qualities we may read all adjectival attributions as indications of live manifestations of power. "Your praise is effective" (*zà-mí-zu dùg-ga-àm*; ETCSL translates:"… is sweet") is a standard affirmation (29 times in ETCSL) addressing various entities (ETCSL 1.3.4, segm. C, l. 37 [Inana]; 2.5.4.03, l. 13 [Nippur]; 2.5.6.2, l. 47 [Enki]; 4.12.1, l. 59 [Martu] etc.).

---

[8] Cf. Gerstenberger 2014, pp. 197-205. Pascal Attinger discusses the most relevant occurrences of that phrase, cf. Attinger 1993, pp. 756-759.
[9] Cf. Gerstenberger 2014, pp. 65-69, 177-185.

Further Old Testament Testimony

Israel's faith from the beginning has been embedded in the experiences of Ancient Near Eastern cultures and religions. We have to recognize and acknowledge this fact. With the appearance, at the latest, of the Dictionary of Deities and Demons in the Bible in 1995[10] it should have become clear that biblical theologies through the ages cannot be separated from contemporary theologies and rites of that pluralistic world Israel and beginning Christianity were living in. To focalize on the Old Testament: There are dozens or even hundreds of coincidences in theological and ethical conceptions making ancient Israel's faith a special variation of religious creed within a common stream of Ancient Near Eastern world views. So far, experts working in the field of Ancient Near Eastern religions (including Old Testament varieties of faith)[11] are pretty much in accordance when it comes to accept an intricate relationship of the relevant theological and ethical paradigms.

What has been largely neglected in academic theology, however, is the existence throughout the Ancient Near East of a good number of impersonal forces which hardly can be denominated as gods or spirits. They are incommunicable yet do constitute semi-autonomous beings. There are no odes addressing these bundled energies directly. But our own religious tradition in general postulates personality as an essential condition for all higher beings. Clear enough, because we want to communicate with the numina. Even the Dictionary mentioned above concentrates on personalized Deities and Demons allowing little space for entries on anonymous i.e. impersonal forces or potencies.

As already indicated there are numerous examples of impersonal entities which participate in Yahweh's actions or do obeisance to Him. At this point we do not want to go into the countless cosmic beings which are summoned to praise him (cf. Ps 148) because they still pertain in some ways to the category of personalized superhuman authorities. We rather want to examine those faceless energies which nevertheless play such important roles in the world. To name but a few: "Justice / righteousness / order" (*ṣedeq, ṣedaqah*); "solidarity / care / truth" (*ḥesed, 'emet*); "word / saying / instruction" (*dabar, torah*). In some passages such potencies are nothing but direct actions of the Lord. Other

---

[10] Cf. Toorn 1999.
[11] There is some justification in using the plural form of OT theologies, cf. Gerstenberger 2002.

affirmations allow for a certain distance between God and a self-enacting power. To look somewhat more closely at these texts:

The concept of "justice / righteousness / (world)order" was known and cherished throughout the Ancient Near East. Sumerian kings (e.g. Urnamma of Ur) try to comply with their divine obligation to establish equity, and famous Hammurabi of Babylon boasts in the epilogue of his "law-code" of realizing God's will in this regard. The Old Testament has much to tell about this same intercultural phenomenon of justice and world order.[12] *ṣedeq, ṣedaqah*, although frequently linked to Yahweh with possessive pronouns, have their own extension and being (cf. Ps 71:19; Isa 51:8 [NRSV ambiguously "my deliverance" for *ṣidqati*]). God maintains a relationship with "his just order" (Isa 45:24; Dan 9:7; Job 37:23) which seems less personal than his ties to wisdom in Prov 8 but nevertheless is a bipolar affair.

> [Yahweh] loves righteousness and justice [*ṣedaqah umišpaṭ*] / the earth is full of [his] steadfast love [*hesed*]. (Ps 33:5; NRSV)

He even "puts *ṣedaqah* on his body "like a breastplate" (Isa 59:17). The passage enumerates neatly other powers in the vicinity of Yahweh to be used by him, maintaining an own identity:

> He put on righteousness [*ṣedaqah*] like a breastplate / and a helmet of salvation [*ješu'ah*] on his head;
> He put on garments of vengeance [*naqam*] for clothing / and wrapped himself in fury [*qin'ah*] as in a mantle. (Isa 51:17; NRSV)

The imagery seems profusely military (cf. Ex 15:3; Isa 63:1-6). It certainly does not present to us objective facts of a re-constructible spiritual world. But it reflects the way our forefathers and -mothers conceptualized their encounter with the superhuman world. For them, Yahweh was the personal side of the world order. He carried with him or commanded over countless forces of edification and destruction which, for their part, emitted their inherent power, for better or for worse. In this context we remember the sad news of some Deuteronomists stating: "Still, Yahweh did not turn from the fierceness of his great wrath ..." (2 Kings 23:26), in spite of Josiah's perfect performance according the prescriptions of the Torah (2 Kings 23:25). Wrath supersedes loving-kindness in this case. The positive forces acting in favor of the people of Yahweh need to be acknowledged and even praised and proclaimed by the community of believers (cf. Ps 22:32; 40:11; 51:16; 71:15-18; 88:13).

---

[12] Cf. Botterweck, et al. 1989, pp. 898-924.

> The might of your awesome deeds [*nora'ot*] shall be proclaimed, / and
> I will declare your greatness [*gedullah*].
> They shall celebrate the fame of your abundant goodness [*ṭub*], / and
> shall sing aloud of your righteousness [*ṣedaqah*]. (Ps 145:6-7; NRSV)

Hebrew possessive pronouns and genitive-constructs are capable to signify a broad range of relationship between the "proprietor" and the "possessed". In our contexts they are likely not to denote personal qualities as may be expected in church dogmatics: The sovereign Lord in our mind acts solely on his own voluntary impetus. Obviously, in those ancient cultures of the Middle and Near East things looked different. If this be true, the last quoted passage may be read as testifying to the solemn endorsement of divine powers by the individual singer and the congregation, culminating in "singing aloud your righteousness". (Ps 145:7; "singing ... of your righteousness" [NRSV] is an adaptation to current theological misconceptions).

The second couple of rather independent spiritual forces in the OT pointed out above is *ḥesed* and *'emet*.[13] There are a good number of antecedents, analogies and parallels in Ancient Near Eastern religious and ethical texts. The basic social level where the concept of solidarity in its wider sense is frequently alluded to is that of intimate human relations (cf. Ps 27:10; 35:13-14; 133; Gen 20:13; 21:23; 34; Ex 20:12; 23:1-13; Lev 19; 25:25-55; Deut 24:6-21; Jos 2:12; 2 Sam 9:7; 16:17; 1 Kings 20:31-34; 2 Kings 4:13; Isa 49:15; Jer 7:1-10; Mic 7:1-6; Zech 7:9-10; Prov 19:22). *ḥesed* and related ideas of solidarity in most diverse situations are the glue of small social groups. Their presence is praised, their loss lamented in the Hebrew Scriptures. Quite understandably these energies have been lauded as special gifts and rather independent dynamic forces.

"Loving-kindness" and "fidelity", as the terms we focalize on are sometimes translated, truly are markers of good social relationship. To "do *ḥesed*" is tantamount to leave aside mere egoistic or economic motivations and help or support the less fortunate or weaker fellow being (cf. Gen 19:19; 20:13; 21:23; 24:49; 47:29 etc.). This does not preclude the expectation of a future reward for helpful behavior (cf. 2 Sam 2:5-6; 9:1-13). Quite often the solidarity concept is articulated by formulaic *ḥesed we'emet* to emphasize the trustworthy, solid, and lasting relationship. Proverbial sayings recommend living by the two virtues: "Whoever pursues righteousness [*ṣedaqah*] and kindness [*ḥesed*] / will find life

---

[13] Cf. Botterweck, et al. 1982, pp. 48-71. Botterweck, et al. 1973, pp. 313-348.

[*ḥajim*] and honor [*kabod*]." (Prov 21:21). "Do not let loyalty [*ḥesed*] and faithfulness [*'emet*] forsake you; / bind them around your neck, / write them on the tablet of your heart. / So you will find favor [*ḥen*] and good repute [*śekel ṭob*] / in the sight of God and of people." (Prov 3:3-4). Small wonder, that a basic note for all human life such as *ḥesed we'emet* becomes a living, imagined force in social affairs. As already indicated, they – together with other spiritual entities – gain a quasi-independent existence. The ruling king is being addressed in Ps 89:15:

> Righteousness [*ṣedeq*]and justice [*mišpaṭ*] are the foundations of your throne; / steadfast love [*ḥesed*] and faithfulness [*'emet*] go before you. (NRSV)

> God will send forth his steadfast love [*ḥesed*] and his faithfulness [*'emet*]. (Ps 57:4; NRSV)

> [God] does not retain his anger ['*ap*] forever, / because he delights in showing clemency (NRSV) [*ḥesed*; literally: ... because he regards kindness / solidarity highly]. (Mi 7:18)

These and many more examples reveal a detached functioning of the cited spiritual powers. They are in a way serving the purposes of divine command, but they certainly also fulfill their tasks by essential drive or innate capacity. Being forces of social cohesion and well-being they are transferrable to the community of humans. A spirit of alliance between the people and God can be established by their work of common trust and help. Interestingly, Yahweh once is called an *'el 'emet* (Ps 31:6), apparently being classified according to known categories of deities. Trustworthiness may have been the renown of family or clan gods (cf. Gen 28:20-22).[14] Yahweh, along this line, adopted the prime capacity of those lower deities, or, more adequately to our subject, he affiliated with that spiritual force so characteristic of protective numina.

In the third place we opted for the concepts of "Word" (*dabar*) and "Torah" (*torah*) as further specimens of impersonal powers very influential in Old Testament theological thinking. Of course, the former has a long pre-history in ancient Near and Middle Eastern religions, while the latter seems to be unique in Biblical faith and very characteristic of emerging Judaism during the Persian period.[15] The Word of high deities already was believed to be a means not only of communication with their

---

[14] Another type of deity in the Bible is the *'el gibbor* (Isa 9:5; 10:21), *'iš milḥamah* (Exod 15:3), *'el neqamot* (Ps 94:1), *'el qanna'* (Exod 20:5) – all pointing to the warrior God of clan and state contexts.

[15] Cf. Gerstenberger 2011.

clients but also an effective force of its own to create and maintain good living conditions as well as to destroy adverse potencies and check negative developments. Word and (loud) voice usually go together to connote the authority and might of God and his solemn announcements (cf. Ex 19:19; Deut 5:25-27; Am 1:2). In the Hebrew Scriptures the topic of Yahweh's Word-Voice-Command-Orientation-Denouncement-Verdict apparently has been greatly elaborated through Israel's history (cf. 2 Kings 22-23; Jer 36). There are really countless references to his speaking which finally were crowned by due reverence to the Torah, that Pentateuchal and subsequent Prophetic collection of divine testimonies. There are hardly any analogies for the genesis of sacred writings in Mesopotamian religions. But Old Persian Zoroastrianism seems to have developed in a similar fashion towards conceptions of revelation, mediation, and execution of divine commandments, admonitions, and promises.[16]

To give but a few examples of the extraordinary growth of Word- and Torah-theologies within the Old Testament.[17] The idea of God speaking through signs and chance constellations goes back to pre-Biblical belief. The Babylonians e.g. cultivated an extensive system of watching and interpreting of *omina* of various types (natural phenomena; dreams; liver-investigation; oil on water configurations etc.). Experts would observe and interpret such phenomena and give counsel as to what ritual was appropriate to contain and overcome the announced calamities.[18] Known mostly from the David story is solicitation of a divine decision (cf. 1 Sam 23:10-12). A priest apparently shakes a breast-bag containing two checkers ("urim"; "tummim"), one signifying "yes" the other "no". The first one to jump out of the case is the answer of God. This means: Pure accident is made the medium of divine communication. 1 Sam 28:6 mentions other ways of "asking" the Lord and receiving answers. All these avenues count on intermediate techniques of accessing the will of God. A side glance at more personal mediation helps to understand the pluriform conceptions of divine-human relations.[19]

The "Word of Yahweh" in more recent layers of the Old Testament ever more becomes an institution all by itself. God speaks as the creator, and there is the intended object as if made by magic (Gen 1:3-27):

---

[16] Cf. Gerstenberger 2011, pp. 68-76, 429-434.
[17] Cf. Botterweck, et al. 1977, pp. 89-133. Botterweck, et al. 1995, pp. 597-637.
[18] Cf. Heeßel 2000.
[19] Various ways of conceiving God as the president of a divine council are present in the OT: 1 Kings 22:19-28; Ps 82:1-4; Job 2:1-6.

> By the word of Yahweh [*debar yhwh*] the heavens were made, / and all their host by the breath of his mouth [*ruaḥ piyo*]. (Ps 33:6; NRSV, except for "Yahweh")

"Word" and "breath/spirit" seem to function like inspired instruments in the creative act (cf. also Ps 33:4-5, 9 for more subsidiary implements in creation). The "Word of Yahweh" turns a preferred entity in late layers of the Pentateuch. Moses is the exclusive receptor of Yahweh's ordinances and communicator to the people starting with Ex 19 through Num 36. Deuteronomy in its last redactions ostensibly poses as a repetition of Moses' singular mission. Yahweh speaks from Mount Sinai itself or from the Tent of Meeting to hand over that most precious divine "Instruction" (*torah*) for the congregation. In some traditions it is immediately written down into a "book" or "scroll" thus assuming a visible, tangible, recitable treasure of tradition and symbol of divine presence. The Words of Yahweh assume a physical body and a spiritual force. They even fertilize the ground:

> For as the rain and the snow come down from heaven, / and do not return there until they have watered the earth / ... so shall my word be that goes out from my mouth; / it shall not return to me empty / but it shall accomplish that which I purpose / .... (Isa 55:10-11; NRSV).

And they may have a terrible destructive force:

> Is not my word like fire, says Yahweh, and like a hammer that breaks a rock in pieces? (Jer 23:29; NRSV except "Yahweh")

The last quoted saying comes from a context trying to clarify the difference between right and false prophecy (Jer 23:9-40). We may understand that legitimate prophesy has a convincing power of its own. It is self-fulfilling because of its divine strength. Many of the introductory and legitimizing introductions of prophetic words presuppose such potency in simply stating: "The word of Yahweh that came / happened to N.N." (cf. Jer 7:1; 11:1; 30:1; 34:1; 35:1 etc.). Prophets in this manner are put on an equal footing with Moses (cf. Deut 18:15-18, in contrast to Deut 34:10). They receive the mighty Words of Yahweh filled with divine strength and mysteriously identical with the original Mosaic Torah of which the later prophets are true interpreters (cf. Jer 26; 36). Small wonder that already in some traditions of the OT the written Torah receives some sort of veneration.

A key passage is the first reported reading of Torah by Ezra in the time of Nehemiah (Ne 8:1-8). The book of the "Law of Moses" is the central piece of worship. Ezra brought the scroll, "opened [it] in the sight of all the people ...; and when he opened it, all the people stood up." (v. 5). We are witnessing the beginnings of synagogue worship revolving around the Torah. "... the ears of all the people were attentive to the book of the law." (v. 3). The Levites present "helped the people to understand the law, ... So they read from the book, from the Law of God, with interpretation. They gave the sense, so that the people understood the reading." (vv. 7-8). Holy Scripture becomes an agent of sorts in the cultic ceremonies of Judaism, Christianity, and Islam. In consequence, we find hymnic praises of the Torah in the Psalter:

> The law (*torah*) of Yahweh is perfect, / reviving the soul;
> the decrees (*'edut*) of Yahweh are sure, / making wise the simple;
> the precepts (*piqqudim*) of Yahweh are right, / rejoicing the heart;
> the commandment (*miṣwah*) of Yahweh is clear, / enlightening the eyes;
> the fear (*yir'ah*) of Yahweh is pure, / enduring forever;
> the ordinances (*mišpaṭim*) of Yahweh are true / and righteous altogether.
> More to be desired are they than gold; / sweeter also than honey,
> and drippings of the honeycomb. (Ps 19:8-11; NRSV)

The word *torah* and five synonyms open up the first six lines of this artful poem. (In Ps 119 with its blocks of eight lines beginning with the same letter of the alphabet we find seven synonyms in each block). Adjectives and participles of each line correspond with the *nomen regens*, that is with *torah* and its equivalents. They – the ordinances, decrees, precepts etc. – are the acting parts in the hymn. That is why they are so "desirable" and "sweet" (v. 11) which, really, must not be said of God. In short, the Word of Yahweh and the canonized collection of His sayings are to be acknowledged as spiritual forces *sui generis*.

God and Impersonal Energies

Exegetical work with ancient texts implies a consciousness of historical and mental differences. We cannot presuppose that our accustomed patterns of thinking and believing were operative already in the minds and hearts of Biblical witnesses or any other people of the Ancient Near East in spite of a good number of anthropological constants. (Behavioral science discovers patterns of comportment going far beyond the human race into the animal kingdom). But there have been so many ruptures and changes in societal and scientific development that basic axioms have shifted over the millennia.

This is particularly true for "reading" and understanding the world including all theological theories and doctrines. Whoever seeks in the Bible an endorsement of his or her modern world views and spiritual fixations certainly misses ancient outlooks, convictions, and sentiments. To say it more bluntly: Exegesis of Biblical texts necessarily implies experiences of clashing civilizations and modes of believing. Some parameters of antiquity simply do not coincide with modern constructions of reality and values. The reason of such incongruence is bipolar: We are living in our "proven" intellectual shell just as our forbears had their "trusted" capsule of rules and insights. There is no such thing in human mental history as an absolute truth. Each society works out contemporary half-truths and tries to live in harmony with them. Therefore, it is the responsibility of exegetes to discover the proprieties of ancient thinking and believing and at the same time become aware of the fundamentals of one's own time and society. Otherwise there will be no way of dialoguing with Biblical witnesses in order to learn from them.

As to our subject "God and impersonal energies" we are seriously blocked by our traditional conceptualization of the Divine to fully come to grips with Biblical views of deities and powers which permeate the world. In particular, we are caught with Christian doctrines of the One and Only God who can be visualized only, e.g. under the mathematical figure of Unity and Exclusiveness (against a plurality of prime causes) and the psychological grid of personality (against impersonal energy). For us it is necessary to postulate God – against all Old Testament prohibitions of imagining Yahweh in the likeness of any earthly object or idea – as the sole source of all being, history, and religion. There must not be a second cause, influence or goal in this world. And secondly, this One Deity must be a regular person like ourselves, endowed with care, perspicuity and guidance. Truly, we want God to exist in our own image. Deviations from a basic module of the Divine are not permissible. If Biblical witnesses are able to open our eyes for their ancient perspectives on the Numinous we may come back to evaluate "praise" as another form of impersonal power in this pluriform and wondrously mysterious world.

Oneness and Plurality of the Divine

The theological concept of one and only one divine will governing all affairs throughout the universe and the entire history is a logical construct which satisfies our desire for clarity and rationality. We cannot admit a plurality of causes because this would do away with other presuppositions of our tradition: The one and same Deity is thought of to be all-present, all-mighty, all-knowing, permeating macro- and micro-cosmos. Some Old Testament texts, notably the book of Isaiah laid the ground for this mode of thinking:

> Listen to me, O Jacob, / and Israel, whom I called:
> I am He; I am the first, / and I am the last.
> My hand laid the foundation of the earth, / and my right hand spread out the heavens;
> when I summon them, / they stand at attention. (Isa 48:12-13, NRSV; cf. Gen 1)

> Thus says Yahweh, the King of Israel, / and his Redeemer, Yahweh Zebaoth:
> I am the first and I am the last; / besides me there is no god.
> Who is like me? Let them proclaim it, / let them declare and set it forth before me. (Isa 44:6-7; NRSV, except Yahweh)

> I am Yahweh and there is no other. / I form the light and create darkness,
> I make weal and create woe; / I, Yahweh, do all these things. (Isa 45:6-7; NRSV, except Yahweh)

The "all but one" principle of world interpretation has been perfected in due course to exclude whatever other agents. In some (Protestant) churches it led to the extreme of a "doctrine of strict predestination" insisting in the all-encompassing authorship of all things by the one supreme deity. Splitting off the bad agents as satanic forces helped to maintain mono-causal thinking. Still, theologies of the one and exclusive deity always ran into great trouble with their own axioms. If there is a sole mover and decision-maker behind all things that happen, the discrepancies and inequalities of humankind and the natural habitat cannot be explained away by human free will nor by unpacified satanic opponents. The age old question of theodicy raises its head and irritates without end (cf. the book of Job).

Old Testament and Ancient Near Eastern faith is far removed from doctrinal narrowness of any kind. Sure, there are attempts to affirm the uniqueness and oneness of Yahweh (or other deities like El Elyon, El Šaddaj). Nowhere in the Hebrew Scriptures do we find the notion of a mathematical oneness, not even in the famous *Šema' Yisrael* of Deut 6:5: "Listen Israel, Yahweh is our God, Yahweh one" (or: "Yahweh alone"; own translation). Many more witnesses, however, count on a plurality of divine figures and they include, as we have seen, impersonal forces attributing to them a certain range of effectiveness free of divine supervision. To reduce divine guidance, sustenance, restoration to an effort of one single "super-brain" (like an immense computer) to the ancients would have been an absurd idea. They rather acknowledged the impenetrable tangle of causes, side-causes, counter-causes, and, most of all, the strict prohibition of imagining God in human terms as the one brain of the universe. Therefore, they often left Him with the authorship of good and evil events, with a staff of heavenly assistants, and a good number of impersonal forces acting out divine purposes on their own account. The thematic example for this will be presented below.

Personal and Impersonal Forces

We now have to focus on another feature of Christian doctrine which seriously narrows down Biblical witness. The personification of God in the likeness of human personality (in the Bible mostly the masculine brand) is a common characteristic at least in Western thought. Jewish, Christian and Muslim Theologies, all of them, with the exception of any mystic currents throughout the ages and regions, adamantly cling to the concept of the Divine being a personal being. How else could we communicate with Him or Her? Humans have felt the dire need to speak to God and hear Him/Her talk to them. The Deuteronomist, fully aware of the prohibition of idols,[20] thought of Yahweh as a male speaker throughout. Wasn't this an act of idolizing God? Sure enough, humans want to talk to God (except for mystics who may find a higher way of communication in spiritual immersion). They need to do so. But they have to remain conscious of the fact, that such conceptualizations are products of our human brains which in no way can capture the full reality of God. Every theological affirmation is a highly risky and always an inadequate portrayal of the Supreme Being. All the *ipsissima verba* of God in the Bible at the same time are formulated in precarious human language be it Hebrew, Aramaic, Greek, Latin, English or any other tongue. To force God into a personality-frame like we know it from our experiences with ourselves and other persons may be a dangerous fault of every theological discourse. Presumably, however, we cannot do without personifications of God. We should know, at the same time that the personal scheme is by far inadequate for a full description of the Ground of Being.

---

[20] Cf. Deut 4:15-16: "... take care and watch yourselves closely, so that you do not act corruptly by making an idol for yourselves, in the form of any figure – the likeness of male or female ..."

It is not needless to point to the fact that our life today is to a large part carried by impersonal thinking. Modern science and techniques are built on mechanical ways of thinking and constructing. Machines, electrical and electronic equipment, medical procedures, agriculture etc. cannot be directed by magic or prayers. Few people would try to do just that. What we want is to know and apply impersonal physical and chemical laws, causal chains without personal interferences. Unbelievable as it seems to be, our spiritual life appears to be untouched by the daily mechanisms. We mostly do not even try to live our faith within that ordinary world of science and techniques. Rather, Christians normally flee back into the realm of ancient myths and personality cults.

Ironically, it is the old Biblical world which reminds us not to disdain impersonal manifestations of power. They do have their own potential of realizing the good and just society. They are effective, they are to be cherished and lauded, they deserve recognition side by side with God. Of course, our problem is what these impersonal assistants of the Unconditional Challenge are like in our present context. Justice and righteousness, mercy and love, forgiveness and solidarity are good companions also today. There may be newcomers among the impersonal powers which were less known in ancient times. Should Christians not officially welcome Human Dignity, Democratic Procedures, Gender-, Race-, Religious Equality among the divine energies?

Praise – The Power of Believers

A special mention is due to personal and communal praise as another example of spiritual strength in which each confessing congregation has a large stake. Traditionally, sacred eulogies have been understood as due offerings to the saving God who benignly governs the whole world putting the adorers on lower levels of existence. Ancient Near Eastern evidence, including Hebrew Scriptures, is different. Praise surely is an offering to deities and sacred beings. But it also constitutes energy on its own grounds, imbued with its own force. On the other hand, the addressees are in want of such support. Praise maintains and increases the potencies even of the highest God. Yahweh, at least, is demanding shares of might and glory from other heavenly beings (cf. Ps 29:1-2; 96:7-8). Psalm 148 implements this desire in grand style. It is a compact summons to praise Him issued to everything from the highest to the lowest beings.

> Praise Yahweh!
> Praise Yahweh from the heavens; / praise him in the heights!

> Praise him, all the angels; / praise him, all his host!
> Praise him, sun and moon; / praise him all you shining stars!
> Praise him, you highest heavens, / and you waters above the heavens!
> ....
> Praise Yahweh from the earth, / you sea monsters and all deeps,
> fire and hail, snow and frost, / stormy wind fulfilling his command!
> Mountains and all hills, / fruit trees and all cedars!
> Wild animals and all cattle, / creeping things and flying birds!
> Kings of the earth and all peoples, / princes and all rulers of the earth!
> Young men and women alike, / old and young together! (Ps 148:1-4, 7-12; NRSV except Yahweh)

Ongoing praise keeps up the Lordship of the creator. This is the meaning also of the liturgical formula "Blessed be Yahweh" (*baruk yhwh*; cf. Gen 9:26 [against NRSV, cf. Gen 14:20]; 24:27; Ex 18:10; 1 Sam 25:32, 39; 1 Kings 1:48; 5:21; Ezek 3:12 [*kebod yhwh*!]; Pss 18:47; 28:6; 31:22 and 12 more times in the Psalter). Praise as well as blessings transmits power from the side of the eulogists to the side of the recipient of the homage. In this fashion Gerhard von Rad was quite right with his notion that praises had to be sung continuously to Yahweh the saving God who figuratively was "enthroned over the hymns of Israel" (Ps 22:4).

ATTINGER, P.
1993 *"Eléments de linguistique sumerienne. La construction de du_{11}/e/di "dire"*, (OBO Sonderband), Fribourg / Göttingen.

BOTTERWECK, G. J., RINGGREN, H., HEINZ-JOSEF, F.
1973 *Theologisches Wörterbuch zum Alten Testament.* Vol 1. Stuttgart: Kohlhammer.
1977 *Theologisches Wörterbuch zum Alten Testament.* Vol 2. Stuttgart: Kohlhammer.
1982 *Theologisches Wörterbuch zum Alten Testament.* Vol 3. Stuttgart: Kohlhammer.
1984 *Theologisches Wörterbuch zum Alten Testament.* Vol 4. Stuttgart: Kohlhammer.
1989 *Theologisches Wörterbuch zum Alten Testament.* Vol 6. Stuttgart: Kohlhammer.
1995 *Theologisches Wörterbuch zum Alten Testament.* Vol 8. Stuttgart: Kohlhammer.

GERSTENBERGER, E. S.
1988 *Psalms* (Forms of Old Testament Literature. Vol. 14) Grand Rapids: Eerdmans.
2001 *Psalms* (Forms of Old Testament Literature. Vol. 15) Grand Rapids: Eerdmans.

2002 *Theologies in the Old Testament.* Translated by John Bowden from the original *Theologien im Alten Testament*, 2001), Minneapolis/London: Fortress/ T&T Clark Continuum 2002.
2011 *Israel in the Persian Period* (transl. by Siegfried Schatzman from the original *Israel in der Perserzeit*, 2005), Atlanta: SBL 2011.
Macht des Lobens. Die Theologie sumerischer Hymnen seit dem 3. Jahrtausend v.u.Z., doctoral dissertation handed in at Marburg University, Institute for Near and Middle East Studies (Jan. 2014).

HEESSEL, N. P.
2000. *Babylonisch-assyrische Diagnostik.* Münster: Ugarit-Verlag.

The *Electronic Text Corpus of Sumerian Literature* (ETCSL), Oriental Institute of Oxford University until 2006 (http://etcsl.orinst.ox.ac.uk).

VAN DER TOORN, K., BECKERING, B., and VAN DER HORST, P. W. eds.
Dictionary of Deities and Demons in the Bible (1995), Leiden / Grand Rapids: Brill / Eerdmans 1999.

VON RAD, G.
1957 *Theologie des Alten Testaments*, vol. 1: *Die Theologie der geschichtlichen Überlieferungen Israels.* München: Kaiser Verlag.

ZGOLL, A.
1997 *Der Rechtsfall der En-ḫedu-Ana im Lied nin-me-šara* (Alter Orient und Altes Testament 246), Münster: Ugarit-Verlag.

'HELD IN SLAVERY BY THE FEAR OF DEATH'

Ancient Hero Cults and the Old Testament Gospel[1]

Christopher B. Hays

I.

One of the classical Christian ways of understanding atonement is that Christ saves humankind by overcoming the power of death and evil. That model has been prevalent for centuries within Eastern Orthodoxy, and it gained popularity among a wider variety of Christians in the wake of Gustaf Aulén's 1930 book, *Christus Victor*. It is less often remarked that the *Christus victor* view of atonement is organically linked to a different view of sin, a view that reverses the emphasis of the classical western idea that "the wages of sin is death" (Rom 6:23). Instead, the Orthodox have noticed more than other traditions the significant biblical witness to the idea that death is the cause of sin, not the other way around.

One of the primary proof texts for this view of sin and death is Heb 2:14-15:

> Since ... the children share flesh and blood, he himself likewise shared the same things, so that through death he might destroy the one who has the power of death, that is, the devil, and free those who all their lives were held in slavery by the fear of death.

Drawing on that passage, John Chrysostom preached, "He who fears death is a slave and subjects himself to everything in order to avoid dying... [But] he who does not fear death is outside the tyranny of the devil." (*Homily 4 on Hebrews*) Although recent works such as John Romanides' *The Ancestral Sin* have encouraged the recovery of this

---

[1] For the inspiration to write this essay and the explanation that follows, I am deeply indebted to the work of Richard Beck (2014). I am also grateful to Brad Strawn for the opportunity to develop the ideas presented here in preparation to respond to Prof. Beck's lecture at the 50th anniversary celebration for the Fuller Theological Seminary School of Psychology.

understanding,[2] it remains distinctly undervalued among Western Christians, especially Protestants.

In his recent book *The Slavery of Death*, Richard Beck helpfully observes that the Eastern view of death and sin described above accords well with psychological accounts of the human condition: a neurotic reaction to death is in fact the root of many problems for the human race. He goes on to show how the example and gospel of Jesus Christ teach a different view of life and death that leads its adherents to greater goodness and flourishing. The project of this essay will be to indicate the ways in which the Old Testament also explicitly espouses overcoming the slavery of death as a key to righteousness.

Beck begins with the distinction between basic anxiety and neurotic anxiety. Basic anxiety is "the anxiety of biological survival, the anxiety of our fight-or-flight response."[3] It emerges in response to immediate threats to one's life, e.g., starvation or physical attack. By contrast, neurotic anxiety emerges in connection with more abstract threats; it is "characterized by worries, fears, and apprehensions associated with our self-concept."[4] If we grant that survival is a minimal goal for human beings, then basic anxiety is not something to be eradicated; it helps keep us alive. However, when mere threats to self-concept are met with the same violent reactions as threats to life, we are dealing with neurotic anxiety, which brings with it moral and ethical dangers. We might think of a banker who obsessively hoards much money than he needs to survive, with no thought of fairness to the workers who produce the profits he reaps. Says Beck: "Slavery to the fear of death often manifests in the form of neurotic anxiety."[5]

Neurotic anxiety may function at the level of societies, as well. It is often noted that modern western cultures try to hide death away; with our emphasis on youthful appearance, our sometimes fanatical attempts to prolong life through medical technology, and our outsourcing of funerary preparations, we try to hold death at arm's length. In his seminal essay, "The Pornography of Death," Geoffrey Gorer notes that as the "natural processes of corruption and decay have become disgusting," and the "ugly facts are relentlessly hidden."[6]

---

[2] Romanides 2002.
[3] Beck 2014, p. 28.
[4] Beck 2014, p. 28.
[5] Beck 2014, p. 29.
[6] Gorer 1955, p. 51.

Beck observes that we are even prone to look away from those whose sickness or disability *reminds us* of our mortality and fragility, and he cites Arthur McGill:

> Why is there this passion to gather people into the arena of true life and to remove from them all marks of sickness and disability? Because many Americans have to create a society which does not cause or require debility and death. Life, life, and more life – that is the only horizon within which these Americans want to live.[7]

Societies also deny death indirectly by seeking meaning that transcends the limits of a human life. Ernest Becker famously wrote that "cultures are fundamentally and basically styles of heroic death-denial."[8] That very large claim is likely to require explanation. The term "heroic" refers to activity that is "larger than life," that seeks to associate the finite human being with something that is deathless. Becker expands:

> The fact is that this is what society is and always has been: a symbolic action system, a structure of statuses and roles, customs and rules for behavior, designed to serve as a vehicle for earthly heroism. Each script is somewhat unique, each culture has a different hero system. ... It doesn't matter whether the cultural hero-system is frankly magical, religious, and primitive or secular, scientific, and civilized. It is still a mythical hero-system in which people serve in order to earn a feeling of primary value, or cosmic specialness, or ultimate usefulness to creation, of unshakable meaning. They earn this feeling by carving out a place in nature, by building an edifice that reflects human value: a temple, a cathedral, a totem pole, a skyscraper, a family that spans three generations. The hope and belief is that the things that man creates in society are of lasting worth and meaning, that they outlive or outshine death and decay, that man and his products count.[9]

As Beck summarizes Becker: "Basically, for a hero system to 'work,' for it to give us a sense of security and permanence in the face of death, we need to experience it as absolute, unassailable, true, eternal, transcendent, and ultimate."[10] This leads us to a final point: "heroic death denial" is not all bad, because the products of human cultures have much in them that is beautiful and worthwhile. But the lurking risk of neurotic anxiety about our cultures does bring danger with it. For example, Americans may justly be proud of certain aspects of our society, but when we

---

[7] McGill 1987, p. 35.
[8] Becker 1973, p. 11.
[9] Becker 1973, pp. 4-5
[10] Beck 2014, p. 41.

feel our values and security threatened even far from our borders, patriotism can and does harden into jingoism and aggression.

Beck argues that the Christian Gospel is an antidote to the fear of death, and the sin to which that fear leads. More specifically, it is the example of Jesus that serves as a model for his followers. Jesus' relationship to death, and the fear of death, is a significant theme throughout the New Testament. In the Temptation (Matt 4), Jesus rejects worldly power, and even self-preservation. And in the Sermon on the Mount, he emphasizes righteousness instead of personal glory:

> "Do not store up for yourselves treasures on earth, where moth and rust consume and where thieves break in and steal; but store up for yourselves treasures in heaven, where neither moth nor rust consumes, and where thieves do not break in and steal. For where your treasure is, there your heart will be also." (Matt 6:19-21)

Eventually, at Gethsemane, Jesus faces the terror of his own impending death, and he experiences "basic anxiety" as any human would. He asks, "remove this cup from me." But in the end he masters the fear of death – "yet, not what I want, but what you want" (Mar 14:36, Matt 26:39; cf. Heb 5:7-10).

The Pauline witness to Jesus similarly emphasized focus on the other instead of oneself:

> Do nothing from selfish ambition or conceit, but in humility regard others as better than yourselves. Let each of you look not to your own interests, but to the interests of others. Let the same mind be in you that was in Christ Jesus, who, though he was in the form of God, did not regard equality with God as something to be exploited, but emptied himself, taking the form of a slave, being born in human likeness. And being found in human form, he humbled himself and became obedient to the point of death – even death on a cross. (Phil 2:3-8; also Rom 5:6-8)

At the risk of stating the obvious: Death on a cross was the antithesis of a good and glorious death in Roman Palestine (Gal 3:13: "Cursed is everyone who hangs on a tree"; see Deut 21:23). For Paul and the gospel writers, this final act by Jesus was his ultimate rejection of glory on the world's terms. His life of love and service to the world was not complete until this final act.

Followers of Christ are explicitly called upon to imitate him, and participate in his death and resurrection. Galatians 2:19-20 puts this in somewhat mystical terms ("I have been crucified with Christ; and it is no longer I who live, but it is Christ who lives in me."), while other passages are more explicit:

- "If any want to become my followers, let them deny themselves and take up their cross and follow me." (Matt 16:24)
- No one has greater love than this, to lay down one's life for one's friends. (John 15:13)
- We know love by this, that he laid down his life for us – and we ought to lay down our lives for one another. (1 John 3:16)

For Jesus and his earliest followers, the courageous willingness to die without any worldly glory or enduring fame was the path of righteousness, the antidote to sin. And – to bring the analysis full circle – this allows the believer to participate in Christ's victory in resurrection, as 1 Cor 15:54-57 celebrates –

> When this perishable body puts on imperishability, and this mortal body puts on immortality, then the saying that is written will be fulfilled: "Death has been swallowed up in victory." "Where, O death, is your victory? Where, O death, is your sting?" The sting of death is sin, and the power of sin is the law. But thanks be to God, who gives us the victory through our Lord Jesus Christ.

II.

This essay extends Beck's analysis farther back into the history of religion, showing how the Gospel that combats the sinful reflexes of the fear of death is in fact present in the Old Testament as well as the New. In *The Slavery of Death*, Beck alludes only briefly to the Old Testament, drawing on Walter Brueggemann's *The Prophetic Imagination* to emphasize the importance of envisioning God as free from one's preconceived notions and ideologies in order to be free oneself. But in fact, significant parts of the Old Testament explicitly espouse the gospel of freedom of fear from death, and from the cults of heroic death denial that characterize that fear.

To recognize the presence of that gospel in the Old Testament, one must first understand something about the way ancient Near Eastern people generally thought about death. There was no "common theology"[11] of death and afterlife in the ANE – that claim would invite misunderstandings and oversimplifications – but certain facets of beliefs about the afterlife were widely shared among those who wrote most of the surviving texts and authorized most of the surviving monuments.

---

[11] Smith 1952, pp. 135-47.

Some of the most striking examples of ancient Near Eastern beliefs about the afterlife come from Egypt. Death was a central concern of Egypt's culture, such that the Egyptologist Jan Assmann has commented: "the theme of death can . . . constitute an introduction to the essence of all of ancient Egyptian culture." [12] An oft-quoted passage from the New Kingdom text "The Instruction of Any" emphasizes the central position that the tomb occupied in Egyptian thought:

> *Do not leave your house*
> *without knowing your place of rest. . . .*
> *Furnish your station in the valley [of the dead]*
> *the grave that shall conceal your corpse.*[13]

Every day, then, the Egyptian was told to focus on his death and afterlife, and to make preparations for it.

All of this preparation for death was meant to work much like preparations for other types of journeys: it was meant to ensure success and enjoyment. It would be easy to conclude that the Egyptians had a positive view of death; in their texts and art, they often presented a happy afterlife which was an idealized form of this life. Tomb paintings are full of images of the deceased enjoying bounty in the afterlife. Mortuary texts portray the deceased flourishing in every way. And tombs were provisioned with items intended to allow the person to continue to live happily in the "blessed West." In the case of elite burials, this included not only food, jewelry, and tools or weapons, but furniture, games, chariots, even *shabti*s – small-scale sculptures of servants meant to magically attend to the dead in the next world.

Did the ancient Egyptians fear death, then? The eminent Egyptologist Alan Gardiner saw them as "pathetic"; all their lavish preparations for the afterlife, both material and magical, only showed them to be "panic-stricken as to what might be done or might happen to them after their deaths."[14] There is a tension here: The Egyptians can be portrayed as morbidly obsessed with death, but from another perspective, they wanted nothing to do with it. They were only interested in life. In this way they were much like many present-day Americans; to paraphrase McGill: *Life, life, and more life – that was the only horizon within which those Egyptians wanted to live.*

---

[12] Assmann 2005, 2.
[13] Lichtheim 1976, vol. 2, p.138.
[14] Gardiner 1935, p. 20.

The tension between these portrayals can be resolved if one surveys Egyptian texts and art more thoroughly; then it becomes quite clear that the happy images masked a fear of death equal to any culture's. They feared the destruction of their corpses, the afterlife judgment, and ultimately the so-called "second death" which represented total and final annihilation. "If we wish to learn something about the experience of death in Egypt," wrote Assmann, "we must turn these [positive] images [of the afterlife] inside out."[15] Only by great human exertions in the realms of magic and the divine was the happy afterlife possible. To say that a blessed afterlife was the natural state of death to an Egyptian would be akin to saying that a rose garden is the natural state of a field.

> [The happy afterlife] was the distant goal of countless efforts, without which death would be an absolute opposition: isolation, termination, end, disappearance, darkness, filth, defectiveness, distance from the divine, decomposition, dismemberment, dissolution, in short, all that constitutes the opposite of those radiant images of a transfigured existence. The Egyptian experience of death was not, overall, much different from that elsewhere in the world, except for the astonishing, and in this respect probably unique, attitude that the Egyptians assumed toward this experience, an attitude based on trust in the power of counterimages, or rather in the power of speech, of representation, and of ritual acts, to be able to make these counterimages real and to create a counterworld through the medium of symbols.[16]

By the period of the Hebrew Bible's composition, in the first millennium BCE, pessimism and skepticism about the happy afterlife increasingly crept into the cultural discourse in Egypt. Some of the guides to the underworld from that period include compendia of the horrors of the afterlife as the Egyptians perceived them – horrors that were not surpassed even by medieval Christian portrayals of hell.[17]

The Egyptians' fear of death and focus on it was not all negative, however; for one thing, it impelled much of the enormous cultural productivity for which Egypt is famous. As Siegfried Morenz wrote, "The Egyptian was not crushed by death, which he experienced so pervasively and to which he attached such negative connotations. Instead he was inspired by it to splendid creative accomplishments."[18] Perhaps the most famous example is the pyramids, which were none other than massive

---

[15] Assmann 2005, p. 18.
[16] Assmann 2005, 18. On this tension, see also Burns, 1972.
[17] Hornung 1994, pp. 133–56.
[18] Morenz 1973, pp. 197–98.

tombs for the pharaohs. Egypt quite naturally developed a cultural system of "heroic death-denial" of the sort that Becker described. Cults of dead kings and sages sprung up, and with them the practice of necromancy, the consultation of the dead for knowledge and wisdom.[19] Even the common dead could speak from the afterlife, as the Letters to the Dead show.[20] Insofar as Beck describes our "cultural lifeways" as "cultural containers of immortality that we can pour our lives into," is it too literalistic to think immediately of sarcophagi, *actual* containers of one's life for immortality? All of these reflexes of the terror of death were meant to offer their owners the experience of the "absolute, unassailable, true, eternal, transcendent, and ultimate" – precisely what Beck says hero systems should do.

Despite its magnificence, Egyptian culture came with fairly obvious costs. Prof. Beck asks, "How is death creating selfishness and violence in … situations of relative abundance?"[21] And he concludes that in "affluent societies where self-preservation is not a pressing concern, we begin to worry about living a meaningful and significant life in the face of death."[22] In the case of Egypt, it is not even as abstract as the recognition that the wealth of elites is almost always extracted from the labor of others. It is clear from both archaeology and from the Bible that great building projects such as the pyramids were literally built by slave labor. Although some of the skilled craftsmen were middle class, essentially the pharaohs built these huge tombs by crushing fellow human beings. So the focus on their quest for personal meaning and enduring significance did in fact lead to a loss of regard for others, and to selfishness and violence.

To reiterate, Egypt was only one of many ancient Near Eastern nations that practiced a cult of dead heroes. In fact, there is no amply-attested ANE culture that lacks indications of such a cult. Ancient Israel and Judah were not exceptions. Some theologians, seeking to assert the uniqueness of the cultures that produced the Bible, have cited the prohibition of Deut 18: "No one shall be found among you … who consults ghosts or spirits, or who seeks oracles from the dead."[23] And it is indeed the case that in the form of Yahwism that came to be normative, as propagated from the central shrine, the belief

---

[19] Ritner 2002, p. 89-96.
[20] Lesko, 2000, p. 1765; also, Gardiner and Sethe 1928.
[21] Beck 2014, p. 28.
[22] Beck 2014, p. 60.
[23] E.g., Johnston 2002, pp. 150-66.

in the powers of the dead was discouraged. But as for most times and places in the nations' history, cults of the dead were probably well known. Rarely do people bother to ban something that isn't happening. Even King Saul is portrayed as seeking out a medium to consult the deceased Samuel (1 Sam 28).[24]

Cults of the dead were a problem for the authors of the Bible because opinions attributed to the dead could and did come into conflict with knowledge of God derived from other sources. We see this plainly in the book of Isaiah, for example. Isaiah (who is frustrated that his advice is not being heeded, as 7:10-13 indicates) fumes in 8:19-20 that those who advocate consulting the dead will be accursed and "have no dawn."

Isaiah condemns hero cults in other ways as well. In 22:15-19, he brings a message of condemnation to a royal steward named Shebna. As with many of Isaiah's oracles, this one is delivered in an unusual place: at a tomb which Shebna is having carved for himself in a cliff. Such an exalted tomb was meant to be "unassailable, true, eternal, transcendent, and ultimate," and interestingly it is possible that archaeologists have found the tomb where this scene took place. It is an unusual tomb. Typically, ancient Judeans were buried in communal tombs shared with their families; the deceased would be laid out until his or her body decomposed, and then the bones would be swept aside to make way for the next person who died. So when you read that someone in the Bible "was gathered to his people," he really was. In ancient Israel and Judah, regular people didn't put their names on a tomb, because it didn't belong to one person. It was a house for all the dead of a family, and sometimes more than one family.[25] By contrast, Shebna's tomb, like a few others of its time, was Egyptian in style. It was meant to be an eternal resting place for one person only, never to be disturbed. It had a stone coffin for one; the name of the inhabitant was carved in stone above the door; and it even had a *pyramidion* (a miniature pyramid) on top of it. The owner was making himself into a little pharaoh.

Isaiah is offended by all this. He cries out, "What are you doing here? And whom do you have here, that you have cut for yourself a tomb here?" But why is Isaiah offended? Is Shebna just betraying that he has a poor sense of aesthetics? No – Isaiah rightly perceives what the tomb

---

[24] The author of that text is interested in discrediting Saul, but he did so in terms that his readers understood from their own cultural milieu (and probably their own experience).

[25] See, e.g., Osborne (2011) and literature cited there.

symbolizes: excessive self-esteem, and forgetfulness of others in the face of the fear of death. Again, he says, *whom do you have here?* That is to say: "Where are your *people*? Where are *they* buried?" Shebna has left them all behind; he is self-invented, and trying to create for himself his own hero-system through his wealth and his cultural mastery. But Isaiah says *no* – *no* to self-glorifying burial practices, *no* to wasting money and energy on self-regard, *no* to the cult of dead heroes. And *yes*, instead, to a God who calls his people "to do justice, and to love kindness, and to walk humbly with your God (Mic 6:8).

The rejection of the cult of dead heroes and its excesses is a core message of the Old Testament's gospel. The people of God are called to remember the suffering the Egyptian hero cult caused them, and not to repeat it.[26] That constant refrain was one of Israel's most important confessions: "the LORD your God... brought you out of the land of Egypt, out of the house of slavery" (Exod 20:2; Deut 5:6). Indeed, Deuteronomy says over and over again: "*Remember* that you were a slave in the land of Egypt" (Deut 5:15, etc.). Presumably some Israelites did remember – they remembered that the cause of their slavery was the cult of heroes, and they rejected it.[27] The memory of slavery, paradoxically, offered freedom from slavery to sin and the fear of death.

The rejection of hero cults is actually quite pervasive in the Hebrew Bible, both explicitly and implicitly. Absalom is subtly mocked for setting up a monument to himself out of a fear of being forgotten (2 Sam 18:18), and Qohelet reflects in this way on his pursuit of riches and success:

> I became great and surpassed all who were before me in Jerusalem. ...
> Then I considered all that my hands had done and the toil I had spent in doing it, and again, all was vanity and a chasing after wind, and there was nothing to be gained under the sun. (Eccl 2:9-11)

Admittedly, the Hebrew Bible's approaches to death are rarely as radical as Jesus' when he said, "Follow me, and let the dead bury their own

---

[26] Parenthetically, it is surely not accidental that pessimism and skepticism about traditional hopes for the afterlife tended to grow in Egypt during the so-called "intermediate" periods, when the nation's power and influence were on the wane. A hero-system is more vulnerable to doubts when it is not functioning optimally.

[27] Some will object that, because there is little proof that this message made much impact on the religious situation on the ground in Israel and Judah, referencing it pulls one away from Israelite religion toward biblical theology. In reality, it is both; it is profoundly unlikely that Deuteronomic theology and the repeated confessions that are associated with it arose suddenly, out of nowhere, in a late period.

dead" (Mat 8:22), but it is the source of the radical idea that the Lord "will swallow up death forever" (Isa 25:8). This is *Christus victor* before the Incarnation, if you will. These are the first voices in our Bible that preached faithfulness to YHWH as freedom from fear of death.

Current readers can only marvel in gratitude that the Bible preserves these authors' witnesses. Their countertestimony against the imperial hero-cults of antiquity is unusual and important. Out of their history of suffering came some of the world's earliest and most powerful voices for justice, which inspired Martin Luther King Jr. and others: "Let justice roll down like waters, and righteousness like an ever-flowing stream!" (Amos 5:24).

III.

The study of Israelite religion will probably always have to justify itself in the context of theological education – to say nothing of the life of the Church. Because of its resolutely historical focus and its specialized data, it is easily misunderstood as antiquarian and recondite in an atmosphere that emphasizes "relevance" and "applicability" more than ever. In reality, however, the historical study of Israelite religion is one of the most useful case studies for those interested in theology in practice. It takes authoritative scriptures and asks, *How did these function in their own times?* Or, to put it in more confessional terms, How did God first speak, and how were those words received?

Israelite religion brings ancient cultural contexts to life in a way that makes connections with our own present cultural contexts easier and more natural. In the case of hero cults, a study of ancient cultural contexts makes it clear that the biblical texts surveyed above were just as countercultural in the ancient Near East as they are in our own times.

Today, the quest for deathless significance is more likely to be undertaken through careers, families, and possessions than through building monumental tombs for the veneration of the dead. But at worst, the pursuit of personal meaning that will endure after death still creates structures of oppression akin to those of the ancient Egyptian elites.

The recognition of ancient contexts and the way the Bible interacts with them makes biblical theology more colorful and effective. Humankind are not simply fearful of death; like Shebna, we often act like little pharaohs, trying to overcome death through our own success, wealth, and power. But the Bible, from beginning to end, calls all the little pharaohs to forget themselves for a while, and live for others: the poor, the widow, the orphan, the resident alien, and the slave. It presents the reader with a God who swallows up death, and in whom is life everlasting.

ASSMANN, J.
2005   *Death and Salvation in Ancient Egypt,* Translated by D. Lorton. Ithaca, N.Y.: Cornell University Press.

BECK, R.
2014   *The Slavery of Death.* Eugene, Ore.: Cascade.

BECKER, E.
1973   *The Denial of Death.* New York: Free Press.

BURNS, J. B.
1972   "Some Conceptions of the Afterlife In Ancient Egyptian Thought," *The Philosophical Journal* 9: 140–49.

GARDINER, A. H.
1935   *The Attitude of the Ancient Egyptians to Death and the Dead.* Cambridge University Press.

GARDINER, A. H. and SETHE, K.
1928   *Egyptian Letters to the Dead, Mainly from the Old and Middle Kingdoms.* London: Egypt Exploration Society.

GORER, G.
1955   "The Pornography of Death," *Encounter* 5: 49-52.

HORNUNG, E.
1994   "Black Holes Viewed From Within: Hell in Ancient Egyptian Thought," *Diogenes* 42: 133–56.

JOHNSTON, P. S.
2002   *Shades of Sheol: Death and Afterlife in the Old Testament.* Downer's Grove, Ill.: InterVarsity.

LESKO, L. H.
2000   "Death and Afterlife in Ancient Egyptian Thought," in *Civilizations of the Ancient Near East,* edited by Sasson, J. M., pp. 1763-1774. Peabody, Mass.: Hendrickson.

LICHTHEIM, M.
1976   *Ancient Egyptian Literature.* Berkeley: University of California Press.

MCGILL, A. C., WILSON, C. A. and ANDERSON, P. M.
1987.   *Death and Life: An American Theology.* Philadelphia: Fortress Press.

SIEGFRIED MORENZ,
        Egyptian Religion (Ithaca, N.Y.: Cornell University Press, 1973).

OSBORNE, J. F.
2011   "Mortuary Practice and the Bench Tomb: Structure and Practice in Iron Age Judah," *Journal of Near Eastern Studies* 70: 35-53.

RITNER, R. K.
2002 "Necromancy in Ancient Egypt," in *Magic and Divination in the Ancient World,* edited by Ciraolo, L. and Seidel, J. Vol. 2: pp. 89-96. Leiden: Brill.

ROMANIDES, J.
2002 *The Ancestral Sin,* Translated by Gabriel, G. S. Ridgewood, NJ: Zephyr Publications.

SMITH, M.
1952 "The Common Theology of the Ancient Near East," *Journal of Biblical Literature* 71: 135-47.

THE IMAGE OF GOD
IN BIBLE AND ARCHAEOLOGY

Stephen L. Herring and Garth Gilmour

In the ancient Near East, gods and goddesses were manifested by means of material objects. How, exactly, these ancient cultures understood this conceptualization is difficult to determine with absolute certainty. Multiple problems exist.[1] Chief among them is our ability to adequately explain ancient concepts of representation by means of modern terminology. There have been some helpful investigations into this area that apply various philosophical theories in the attempt to clarify the ancient belief.[2] Yet, while these authors themselves admit that such systems tend to "collapse" and "fall short" when applied to the evidence,[3] their research has demonstrated that a great divide exists between the ancients' understanding of representation and our own, which tends to see a representation as a mere copy of a real object. Yet, this ancient understanding is not entirely foreign to modern conceptions. For example, T. Jacobsen's groundbreaking article, "The Graven Image," explains the cult statue as:

> ...a foreshadowing of and a stage in divine presence, a theophany... the statue mystically becoming what it represents...the statue ceases to be mere earthly wood, precious metal and stones, ceases to be the work of human hands. It becomes *transubstantiated*, a divine being, the god it represents.[4]

As Jacobsen hints, then, there are some modern analogies that may enable us to understand the ancient conception. Other scholars have made this analogy more explicitly, comparing the ancient conceptualization to that of the Christian (specifically, Roman Catholic and Orthodox) sacrament of the Eucharist, in which bread and wine become the actual body

---

[1] See, e.g., Bottero (2001, pp. 21-28) for a short, convenient, discussion.
[2] See, e.g, Mettinger 1995, pp. 21f.; Berlejung 1998; Bahrani 2003.
[3] For discussion, see Herring 2013, pp. 14-21.
[4] Jacobsen 1987, pp. 22-23; *italics ours*.

and blood of the divine Jesus through a ritual of prayer and invocation.[5] Regardless of the analogy used, though, what seems clear is that many in the ancient Near East did not recognize a simple, distinct separation between a representation and its referent. In other words, for them the cultic image became the god.

Some of the clearest examples of this type of belief come from ancient Mesopotamian cult-image induction rituals of "mouth-washing" (*mīs pî*) and "mouth-opening" (*pīt pî*).[6] These rituals detail the procedures one had to undertake in order to make a human-made statue into a living god. The purpose of these rituals can be summed up in the first line of one incantation: "On the day when the god was created (and) the pure statue was completed" (STT 200:2).[7] According to A. Berlejung, the rituals were designed to purify the statue, by ritually separating the statue from its profane origin, to imbue the statue with powers and, then, to activate these powers.[8] The divine nature of the consecrated statue is made explicit by the texts. So, for example, the Ninevite Ritual Text (lines 165-68) prescribes the following:

> Into the ear(s) of that god you speak as follows:
> "You are counted among your brother gods…
> From today may your destiny be counted as divinity;
> With your brother gods you are counted…"[9]

This text obviously implies that the ritual imbued the image with the ability to hear as well. The rituals, however, were thought to activate more than just hearing in the image. After the ritual, the image was thought alive and, thus, animated to function as a living being. In contrast, before the ritual, the image was considered inanimate: "This statue

---

[5] See, e.g., Dick 2005, p. 51; Herring 2008, pp. 480-94. For other modern analogies, see Freedberg 1989; Waghorne 1999, pp. 211-243.

[6] References to the ritual go back to the third millennium. For the history of the ritual, see Berlejung 1998, pp. 191-192. For the growth and development of the ritual, see Walker and Dick 2001, pp. 18-20. For text and translation of these texts, see Walker and Dick 2001, pp. 33-245; 1999, pp. 55-122; Berlejung 1998, pp. 422-73. For recent discussions of these texts, see Jacobsen 1987, pp. 15-32; Berlejung 1998, pp. 191-283; 1997; Walker and Dick 1999; Herring 2013, pp. 25-48. On the influence of the rituals on biblical texts, see, e.g., Schüle 2005; Strine 2014; Herring 2013.

[7] For translation and discussion of the Sutlantepe tablet 200, see Walker and Dick 1999, pp. 96-100.

[8] A. Berlejung 1997, p. 45; cf. Berlejung 1998, 281.

[9] For text, translation and discussion of the Ninevite Ritual Text, see Walker and Dick 1999, pp. 84-97. On how the accompanying signs and terminology in these texts also indicate the divinized nature of the statue, see Herring 2013, p. 28; cf. Sommer 2009, pp. 20-21.

without its mouth opened cannot smell incense, cannot eat food, nor drink water" (STT 200:43-44). It was empowered to hear, speak, see, smell, eat, drink and act. It was the god on earth. Indeed, the relationship between a deity and his/her image meant that it was cared for (e.g. fed, bathed, clothed) and protected. The "abduction" of a divine image was, thus, described in terms of divine abandonment (often self-initiated), while the statue's return as the return of divine presence.[10]

In this somewhat complicated ontological belief, the "real" presence of the one represented is "transubstantiated" into the representation with the result that the representation exists as a valid substitute – or rather, "extension" – of the referent.[11] Thus, the image should not be understood as a mere statue, relief, or sculpture, at least not in the way these terms are used today, since they, in modern use, imply a separation between the represented and the representation.[12] In contrast, the image in Mesopotamia "has the potential of becoming an entity in its own right, a being rather than a copy of a being."[13]

This concept is prominent in the practice of making substitute figurines for imitative or sympathetic magic.[14] In these contexts, the blurred distinction between the represented and the representation allows the figurine "to represent, more or less accurately, either an enemy to whom one wanted to pass on the evil one suffered, or another carrier who could even be the bearer of the evil himself, if needed."[15] The best example of the latter case is the so-called ritual of the substitute king, wherein another human was ritually made the substitute of the king, when the king's life was threatened by omens. The substitute was given the king's name, his clothes, and his insignia.[16] The substitute became a valid representation of the king and any evil was thereby transferred to the former.

Kings were also represented by images in cultic settings. So, for example, the royal images of Gudea of Lagash (ca. 2100 BCE) and his son, Ur-Ningirsu, were dedicated to particular deities, placed in a temple or shrine, and received regular offerings.[17] These statues were "provided

---

[10] Bahrani 2003, pp. 174-84.
[11] For in-depth discussions of this point, see Bahrani 2003; Herring 2013.
[12] Winter 1992, p. 36 n. 5; Bahrani 2003, pp. 121-148; Berlejung 1998, pp. 64-65; Herring 2013, pp. 14-21, 25-48.
[13] Bahrani 2003, pp. 124-125.
[14] For a discussion on sympathetic magic, divination and the "substitute king" in this context, see Herring 2013, pp. 32-37.
[15] Bottero 1992, p. 142; cf. Garr 2000, pp. 140-141.
[16] Bottero 1992, pp. 138-155.
[17] Winter 1992, p. 15; cf. Hallo 1988, p. 58.

with messages to be communicated to the god through direct discourse."[18] Likewise, the 8th century BCE statue of Hadduyitî of Guzana was set up before the god Hadad-Sikkanu to allow continual communication between the king and the god. Like the image of a god, the image of the king is "not just some well crafted art object essentially detached from what it expresses" but "is part of the person of the king."[19] It is the presence of the king extended, or manifested, continually before his god.

This sort of conceptualization, then, clarifies the real fear of having one's image fall into the hands of an enemy. Images of deities and kings were abducted and assaulted on a regular basis. Kings were tried and even punished by means of their images.[20] Consequently, precautionary measures were taken to ensure their wellbeing. The addition of curses against anyone harming the king's image invoked the well-known Near Eastern paradigm of *lex talionis* in which the punishment selected is the one most fitting for the crime. So, curses on these images consistently called for the ending of progeny and the sterilization of the attacker, "thereby not only ending his existence but making any survival through his offspring impossible."[21] The image was on par with progeny.[22] To destroy the image of the king was equivalent to the denial of lineage, both meant to immortalize the referent.

Therefore we may conclude that an image has a functional component in the ancient world that is difficult for many of us today to understand. As Garr states, the image served "to express its divine or human referent in its particular setting."[23] Yet, as we have seen, the image went beyond merely expressing its referent. It actually made manifest the presence of its referent; it became what it represented. It functioned as a valid "substitute" of the referent when the referent was not physically present. Therefore, the image did not merely symbolize power or dominion; it was actually empowered to accomplish tasks.

---

[18] Winter 1992, p. 15; cf. Hallo 1988, p. 58 and n. 25.
[19] Schüle 2005, p. 10; Bahrani 2003, pp. 138-145.
[20] On the psychological and magical aspects of the abduction and assault on a king's image, see Bahrani 2003, pp. 174-182; Freedberg 1989, pp. 246-282, 378-428; Herring 2013, pp. 31-37.
[21] Bahrani 2003, p. 170.
[22] Garr's emphasis on the language of the cultic image induction rituals is important here: "Because it is 'born', the 'image' is not a strictly manufactured product. Instead, it is a ritually induced descendent of its referent. In a certain sense, the 'image' is the referent's child", 2000, p. 143; cf. Bahrani 2003, pp. 165-171; Hehn 1915, p. 43.
[23] Garr 2000, p. 155.

Conception in the Hebrew Bible

A similar conceptualization of cultic images can be found in the Hebrew Bible. Although there are no explicit expressions of such a belief in the form of ritual texts or consecration ceremonies,[24] the presence of this type of conceptualization must be demonstrated by inferring the belief through other means, i.e., the widespread presence of images and an intimate familiarity with the conceptualization itself.

Research into the narrative descriptions of early Israelite cult found in the Pentateuch has suggested that these religious conceptions took final shape only in the post-exilic period and that they were heavily influenced by the religious reforms of the late pre-exilic, exilic and post-exilic periods. Constructing an ideal period before the state served the religious aims of these later reform movements who sought to make illicit some of the cultic features of early Israel, of which the prohibition against images is perhaps the most prominent (Exod 20:4-6; Deuteronomy 5:8-10; Exod 20:20-23; 34:17; Leviticus 19:4; 26:1; cf. Deuteronomy 27:15).[25]

This does not mean, however, that the early YHWH cult was not *"de facto* aniconic"[26] or, at least, contained aniconic tendencies. Yet, as the expanding prohibitions indicate,[27] cultic images *were* prevalent in the Israelite cult, so that a growing number of scholars now believe that pre-exilic YHWH worship was never based on an aniconic cult.[28]

The traditional response points to the absence of any references to anthropomorphic statuary of YHWH in ancient texts, and to the archaeologists' inability to find any such representation. But representations of deities should not be confined to anthropomorphic statuary. Indeed, as recent studies have demonstrated, there is very little to distinguish

---

[24] There are however a few scholars who see reflections of these consecration ceremonies in the biblical text. See note 6 above.

[25] See Albertz 1994, pp. 60-66; Dohmen 1985, pp. 237-277; Herring 2013, pp. 49-54.

[26] Mettinger (1995, p. 18) distinguishes between *de facto* aniconism and 'programmatic' aniconism, where the latter is formal and prescribed, while the former relates to 'the existence, prior to that, of a much older *de facto tradition* of aniconism in which aniconism was perhaps a conventional observance but not the subject of theological reflection and hardly linked with iconophobia or iconoclasm'. Mettinger's *de facto* aniconic tradition is characterised by 'an indifference to icons', 'a mere absence of images', and 'tolerant aniconism', while the programmatic aniconic tradition that developed later is identified with a 'repudiation of images', 'iconophobia' and even 'iconoclasm.'

[27] Uehlinger 2006, p. 84.

[28] For convenience, see the multiple essays in Van Der Toorn (1997), esp., pp. 73-95, 97-156, 157-72.

between the function of an anthropomorphic statue and any other divine representation.[29] In other words, whether or not YHWH had an anthropomorphic statue is not a decisive factor in determining whether or not Israel shared the belief that cultic representations functioned to make YHWH present.[30]

YHWH's Representations in Text and Archaeology

Despite the polemical nature of the biblical texts that present practices and beliefs associated with other ancient Near Eastern cults as foreign and, therefore, beyond the bounds of legitimate YHWH worship, there is ample evidence that many of these practices were approved elements of the cult of YHWH. So, according to the biblical text, high-place worship was a traditional and, often legitimate, feature of the early YHWH cult.[31] Furthermore, this type of worship included representations of divine presence: standing stones and stylized trees.

While standing stones have a long history in Israel and the Levant stretching back millennia before the biblical period,[32] they are not unique to the region nor even the wider ancient near east; their use as ritual objects is a cultural phenomenon in ancient societies all over the world.

Biblical sources appear to reserve positive judgment for those standing stones that serve "non-cultic" functions. They are universally early, and function as legitimate elements of Israelite tradition from the time of the Patriarchs until the period of the Judges. Jacob set up a stone at Bethel after his dream of angels descending from heaven, and anointed the stone with oil (Genesis 28:18-21; see also Genesis 35:14-15). Moses set up an altar and twelve stone pillars at the foot of Mt Sinai to commemorate the covenant with YHWH, and the Israelites offered burnt offerings there (Exodus 24:4-5). Twelve stones again are set up on the west bank of the Jordan at Joshua's command after the successful crossing of the river, as a memorial of the event (Joshua 4). Later, after celebrating the renewal of the covenant at Shechem, Joshua set up a 'large stone' under the sacred tree 'near the holy place of the Lord', probably in front of the Canaanite temple that had stood there for several hundred years (Joshua

---

[29] Uehlinger, 1996, pp. 543-547; cf. Mettinger 1995, p. 22.
[30] Herring 2013, pp. 49-85.
[31] See, e.g., 1 Sam 9f.;1Kgs 3:4, etc.; cf. Albertz 1994, pp. 84-86; Larocca Pitts 2001; Provan 1988, pp. 57-90.
[32] Avner 1984, pp. 115-119; 1990: 133-136; 1993.

24:25-26).³³ The last explicit reference to standing stones in the Hebrew Bible comes at the coronation of Abimelech in Judges 9:6, which again takes place on the forecourt of the temple at Shechem, at the stone under the sacred tree.

In a seminal study in 1969, C. Graesser discerned four main functions of standing stones based on the biblical text: 1.) Memorial stones, which marked the memory of a dead person; 2.) legal stones, which marked a legal relationship between two or more individuals; 3.) commemorative stones, which commemorated an event and called to mind the participants (whether human or divine); and 4.) cultic stones, which marked the "sacred area where a deity may be found" and "the exact point where the deity is immanent".³⁴ However, the nice distinction between cultic and non-cultic stones that emerges in Graesser's categorisation is not easily maintained, nor are the categories mutually exclusive, but frequently overlap. So, for example, the twelve stones erected by Moses and Joshua respectively may be memorial and legal and commemorative representing, at least for the authors of these passages, the twelve tribes. But they are also cultic, celebrating and solemnly marking the presence of YHWH at the events they represent. The single stones, on the other hand, set up at Bethel and Shechem, are more clearly representational of the deity (note Jacob's anointing of the stone with oil), and mark the immanence of YHWH – in Jacob's dream, at the renewal of the covenant, and at the coronation of Abimelech. YHWH was present both as a participant and as a witness to these events, so that the stone in each case represents YHWH and serves both legal and commemorative roles.

More recently, E. Bloch-Smith has sought to move away from Graesser's four separate functions, more appropriately describing the purpose of the stones as to render implicit criteria explicit, and to signal the divine presence as witness or participant in the ceremony, whether it is a commemoration of the dead, the witness of an agreement, or the worship of the gods.³⁵

There are now numerous archaeological examples of standing stones, or masseboth, in the southern Levant from the biblical period. A row of ten monoliths at Tel Gezer, some over three meters high, dominated the middle of the site; they date to the Middle Bronze IIC, in the middle of

---

³³ Stager 1999, 2003; Gilmour 2005b, p. 891.
³⁴ Graesser 1972, p. 37; this paper is a summary of Graesser's unpublished 1969 Harvard doctoral dissertation, *Studies in Maṣṣēbôt*.
³⁵ Bloch-Smith 2005, 2006.

the second millennium BCE.³⁶ From the same period comes a small shrine defined by approximately thirty small standing stones in a circle that was recently discovered on the main tell below the courtyard of the later Late Bronze Age palace/administrative building at Hazor, in the northern Galilee.³⁷ Also on the main tell at Hazor, in Area A, a large rectangular temple dating to the early Late Bronze Age was destroyed and covered over toward the end of the period, but that the sanctity of the area was retained was evidenced by the presence of standing stones in stratum XIII of the thirteenth century, the most regular of which had an offering bowl in front of it.³⁸ In area C, on the lower tell, a small shrine with 11 small stelae was found, also dated to the thirteenth century. The middle stone had two hands raised towards the moon – an offering to the moon god.³⁹

At Shechem in the central hill country a Middle Bronze Age Temple that probably stood until Iron Age I (12th or 11th century BCE) dominated the ancient city. In the large open space in front of the temple, perhaps originally situated on either side of the entrance, were bases for two large standing stones, one of which was recovered. Nearby was a large gray brick altar with white marl curbing. Another altar, dated to the 12th century BCE, was also found in the forecourt alongside the socket for a third massive standing stone. Now broken but still preserved to a height of 1.45 m, this stone is likely to have originally stood twice as high. It is quite possible that this is the stone referred to in the biblical passages cited above that stood alongside a sacred tree near the holy place of the Lord where Joshua renewed the covenant, and later where Abimelech was crowned (Joshua 24:25-26, Judges 9:6).⁴⁰

While the biblical references to standing stones, or the legitimate use of them, ceases with the Abimelech story, archaeological research has shown that they continue in use down into the Iron Age, the period of the Israelite and Judahite monarchies. At Hazor, again, in stratum XI,

---

³⁶ Dever 1973: pp. 68-70; Dever et al. 1971, pp. 120-124; see most recently, Dever and Seger 2014, p. 12.
³⁷ Ben-Tor 2002, p. 256, fig. 2; 2013, pp. 82-83, fig. 22.
³⁸ Yadin 1972, pp. 127; Yadin et al. 1961: pl. IX. The interpretation of the finds from the Late Bronze II levels is controversial and uncertain, particularly as to when the temple went out of use. In the last final report to deal with this matter it is suggested that the temple was destroyed at the end of Late Bronze IIA, and in strata XIVA and XIII (Late Bronze IIB) only the small cult corner with the stelae and bowls near the entrance of the destroyed temple continues to exist (Ben-Tor and Bonfil 1997, pp. 108).
³⁹ Yadin et al. 1958, pp. 83-92, pls XXIX, XXX
⁴⁰ Stager 1999, pp. 240, 245-246; Gilmour 2005b, pp. 890-891.

dated to the 12th and 11th centuries BCE, a small short-lived pit-and-hovel settlement was established on the main mound. The only structural building excavated in this settlement contained a room identified by Yigael Yadin, the excavator, as an Israelite High Place. While his identification may have been over-enthusiastic,[41] the structure did contain a number of cultic artefacts, including a basalt stone ignored by Yadin which has lately been restored as a *massebah* and which was probably the religious focus of the building.[42]

During the University of Chicago expedition to Megiddo in the Jezreel Valley in the 1920s and 30s a large domestic structure was excavated near the city gate in what later became known as stratum VA-IVB, dated to the tenth century BCE. The size of the building and the thickness of its walls suggest that it was the house of an important official, perhaps the governor of the city. In the front of the house was a courtyard with a corner given over to the storage of cultic paraphernalia. Among these items were several pairs of artefacts, including standing stones, incense altars, limestone offering stands and fenestrated stands, and in each case one of the objects was larger than its pair.[43] This pairing is significant, and is a repeating pattern in Iron Age religious activity in Israel and Judah. It occurs again in slightly different guise at the southern site of Lachish where a storeroom for cultic equipment was excavated in stratum V, also dated to the tenth century. Nearby in the same level a large standing stone was uncovered alongside a circle of ash a few centimetres deep, which the excavator interpreted as the remains of a sacred tree that stood next to the stone.[44] There are clear similarities between the interpretation of the massebah and associated sacred tree at Lachish and the sacred stone at Shechem referred to in the biblical passages above, that stood alongside and in the shade of a sacred tree.

One further incidence of sacred stones is worth mentioning, at Arad in the northern Negev desert where again there is evidence of pairing. At the Judahite military fortress at this site, a shrine was excavated within the walls. The importance of the shrine to the fortress was underscored by the discovery of a number of ostraca at the site that referred to the shrine and the priests that served there.[45] The small raised niche that was the focus of attention in the shrine was approached by three steps;

---

[41] Gilmour 1995, pp. 23-34; 2005a, p. 364.
[42] Ben-Tor 1996, pp. 266-268.
[43] Gilmour 1995, pp. 59–60; Zevit 2001, pp. 220–225, 247–249, 312–313.
[44] Aharoni 1975, pp. 28–32; Bloch-Smith 2006, p. 73.
[45] Aharoni 1981; Herzog et al. 1984, p. 22.

flanking the steps were two incense altars, one large and one small. There were also three *masseboth* in the niche, two of flint and one larger one of limestone that may have been painted. The recording at the time of the excavation was not clear, and the finds have been the subject of some disagreement over the years. It appears that when they were first excavated the two altars and the large limestone *massebah* were found laying on the steps and on the floor of the niche respectively. Built into the niche's back wall and right hand wall were the two flint *masseboth*. While there are different opinions about the use sequence of the different features in the niche, the most widely accepted view is that originally the two flint *masseboth* served as the focus of attention, and later the single limestone *massebah* either replaced them, or stood alongside them.[46] For our purposes, the presence of one or two or even three standing stones in a Judahite shrine in a military base is significant. This was not a group of rebels who ran off into the desert to practise their unorthodox religion in secluded safety. Rather, this was the kingdom's principal military base and administrative centre in the northern Negev; the longevity of the shrine (over a century, eventually dismantled by Hezekiah in the late eighth century BCE) and the status of the site clearly indicate that these features were recognised and accepted as state-sponsored elements in the national cult.

The pairing of standing stones and other cultic objects that is evident at these sites leads us to consider the role of Asherah as the consort of YHWH in ancient Israelite society and religion.[47] Inscriptions from the eighth century BCE site of Kuntillet 'Ajrud in the Sinai are critical to our understanding of the relationship between YHWH and Asherah. Of the many inked graffiti found at the site, three are particularly relevant: one on Pithos A, referring to 'YHWH of Shomron and Asheratah', and two inscriptions on Pithos B referring to 'YHWH Teman and to Asheratah'.[48] At another site, Khirbet el-Qôm in the hill country of Judah, near Lachish, an inscription carved into the wall of a burial cave also refers to YHWH and Asherah together.[49] In the light of these written testimonies, and the

---

[46] Gilmour 2009, p. 97 n. 7.

[47] The literature on this subject is vast. Mentioned forty times in the Hebrew Bible, Asherah not only played an important role in the biblical narrative but also occurs in texts from neighbouring cultures and appears in archaeological inscriptions. Hadley 2000 is a major recent scholarly review, and studies by Becking 2001 and Ackerman 1992 are also important. Dever 2005 offers a more popular overview of the subject.

[48] Hadley 2000, pp. 121–129, 137–152; Zevit 2001, pp. 390, 393–399.

[49] Zevit 1984, p. 39; 2001, p. 361.

many biblical injunctions against Asherah or her image, it seems reasonable to conclude that the pairing of standing stones and other objects is evidence of the veneration of YHWH and Asherah together in ancient Israel and Judah.

Asherah has long been associated with sacred trees. On a jar from Lachish in the Late Bronze Age II the goddess Elat is associated with a sacred tree flanked by two quadrupeds. The tree represents growth and revival and is seen as a source of life in the ancient near east. Ruth Hestrin has pointed out that the easy interchange in iconography between the tree and the pubic triangle indicates that both sets of imagery must be indicative of the goddess Asherah, and that sacred trees in the context of ancient Israel and Judah should be seen to refer to this goddess.[50] The injunction in Deuteronomy 16:21, "You shall not plant any tree as an Asherah beside the altar of YHWH your God," is further indication of the imagery associated with both deities.

The presence at Shechem of the large standing stone alongside and in the shade of a sacred terebinth should, in this light, be seen as a manifestation of the divine couple of YHWH and Asherah, just as they are manifested later at Lachish, Megiddo, Arad and elsewhere.

Another indication of the prevalence of Asherah may be found in the large number of pillar figurines found largely in domestic contexts in Judah following the destruction of Samaria. Many scholars interpret these figurines as images of the goddess Asherah,[51] possibly small copies (for private, domestic use) of the larger Asherah statue פסל האשרה that evidently was placed in the Temple by Manasseh (2 Kings 21:7), and may even have been there since before the time of Hezekiah (2 Kings 18: 4), until it was removed in the reforms of Josiah described in 2 Kings 23.

The recent publication of a sherd from Jerusalem that was excavated in the 1920s has added significantly to the literature on YHWH and Asherah in the eighth and seventh centuries.[52] The sherd is incised with a design showing two humanoid characters, male and female, each with distinctive characteristics identifying them as deities. The male image has the conical headdress of Canaanite deity figurines, and the

---

[50] Hestrin 1987.
[51] Holladay 1987, pp. 276–278; Kletter 1996, pp. 76–77; see also Moorey 2003, p. 60, who rejects the association with Asherah, suggesting that they represent 'mourning' figures, and now Darby 2014, who suggests they have to do with rituals associated with healing and protection.
[52] Gilmour 2009.

female has the prominent pubic triangle so typical of Canaanite plaque figurines from the Late Bronze and early Iron Ages. The sherd itself comes from a late Iron Age pottery vessel that was broken before the images were incised.

The cultic significance of the incised design, the characteristics identifying the two figurines as deities, the clarity of the dating to the late eighth or early seventh centuries, and the findspot in Jerusalem's City of David all strongly advocate that the sherd should be understood to represent YHWH and Asherah. If this conclusion is correct, the images on the sherd must be a reflection of concepts of these deities held by the inscriber(s) of the design. For our purposes in this paper this is critical, for it demonstrates that whoever carved and used the sherd had a concept of YHWH and Asherah that is here portrayed pictorially. Therefore, there were representations of both deities that the artist drew on. For the first time, we have a pictorial representation of this sacred pair which was drawn or carved at the time the Temple stood in Jerusalem.

Other types of imagery that occur during this period include large numbers horse and rider figurines, many of which have lost their riders by the time they are found by the archaeologist's trowel. Most scholars agree that they relate to the influx of Assyrian culture during the eight and seventh centuries, and are probably related to Assyrian astral cult, representing the sun god Shamash.[53] The presence of discs on the foreheads of the horses and the biblical references to horses and chariots of the sun in 2 Kings 23:11 support this interpretation.

It is clear from both the archaeological and biblical records that the use of imagery, from figurines to pictures to altars to trees to standing stones and much more besides, was not unfamiliar to the people of Israel and Judah in the period of the monarchy. Much of this took place in private or domestic ritual, and certainly the presence of the Assyrians influenced the religious life of both Israel and especially Judah, opening the door to all sorts of practices that are referred to in the biblical text or implied in the archaeological finds: rooftop shrines, oracles of the dead, worship of Shamash the sun god and the moon and the stars, and altars for incense and libations. While they may have been seen as foreign practices, they were very much part and parcel of life in Israel and Judah, sufficiently so for them to be the targets of prophetic attack.

---

[53] Kenyon 1974, p. 142; Keel and Uehlinger 1998, p. 343; see also Holland 1995, pp. 184–187; *contra* Moorey 2003 (who says they have no religious significance) and Cornelius 2007 (who proposes they represent cavalry).

Prominent among these are representations of Asherah and YHWH as standing stones, sacred trees, figurines, pairs of sacred objects and now, with the sherd from Jerusalem, even as humanoid figures strongly influenced by Late Bronze Age Canaanite precedents. Prophetic opprobrium from the period of the monarchy only confirms what the archaeology so clearly demonstrates, that Israel and Judah were no different from their neighbours in their familiarity with and use of imagery in cultic practice.

In addition to this specific evidence from text and archaeology for the presence of anthropomorphic imagery in ancient Israel, some scholars have argued that there are a "whole series of locutions, rituals and prophetic visions" in the bible that are "incomprehensible" if a divine image is not assumed.[54] For example, just as the anthropomorphic statues of other ancient Near Eastern deities are fed and clothed, so also does YHWH receive nourishment (Exodus 25:30), clothing (Ezekiel 16:8) and jewelry (Exodus 24:10). Furthermore, literary formulae that are often suggestive of a personal confrontation with a cult statue in other ancient Near Eastern literature are also quite prominent in the bible ("seeing/beholding" the divine face, glory, form, etc.).[55] While this sort of evidence is often swiftly dismissed as stemming from metaphorical language typical of dreams and visions that, at the most, might be taken as some sort of "mental iconography,"[56] the parallel use of these tropes in neighboring cultures that did use deity images and statues tends to promote the presence of similar imagery in ancient Israel and Judah.

It is less easy to dismiss the conceptualization of the ark in the so-called Ark Narrative (1 Samuel 2:12-17, 22-25; 4-6; 2 Samuel 6).[57] Although certainly "aniconic," the ark in this narrative functions *exactly* as any other iconic cult statue. The ark is presented here as the localized presence of YHWH, recognized by both the Israelites (1 Samuel 4:3, 21a-22) and the Philistines (vv. 7-8). The Philistines treat the captured ark in a manner consistent with captured (statues of) gods in the ancient Near East, presenting the ark before (the statue of) their god Dagon (5:2).[58] YHWH

---

[54] Niehr 1997, p. 81
[55] On the expression and its origin in the personal confrontation with a divine image, see Nötscher 1924; Seow, 1995, pp. 609-610; cf. Niehr 1997, pp. 81-85; Bunta 2007, pp. 233-234.
[56] E.g. Smith 1988, pp. 171-183; Mettinger 1995, p. 187; Williamson 2013, pp. 32-34.
[57] There are multiple interpretations of the "ark" in the biblical text. For a brief summary including bibliography, see Seow 1992. On the Ark Narrative, specifically, see Miller and Roberts 1977; Levtow 2008, pp.132-143; Herring 2013, pp. 67-74.
[58] On this practice in the ANE, see Cogan 1974.

refuses subjugation, forcing Dagon to pay homage to the ark (vv. 3-4) and, then, mutilating him by cutting off his head and hands (v. 4). Or, as N. Levtow has described it, YHWH renders Dagon powerless, depriving Dagon of all sensory organs.[59] In other words, YHWH turns the tables, reversing the effects of the induction ritual that animated the Dagon statue, so that he has "a mouth, but cannot speak, eyes but cannot see; he has ears, but cannot hear, a nose, but cannot smell" (mod. Psalm 115:5-6).

There is also some evidence for a Yahwistic bull image in ancient Judah. The evidence comes primarily from two, related, narratives: 1 Kings 12:25-33 and Exodus 32.[60] According to 1 Kings 12, Jeroboam son of Nebat established alternatives to the Jerusalem cult in Bethel and Dan by making and consecrating two bull-calf images, one for each shrine. Although the relationship of the images to YHWH is not explicitly stated in the text, Jeroboam's aim to mimic the YHWH cult at Jerusalem (vv. 31-32) and the presentation formula that describes the images as "your gods...who brought you up from Egypt" (v. 28) makes such a relationship highly probable.[61] The identical presentation formula occurs in the related narrative in Exodus 32:4, where the relationship between the image and YHWH is made clearer by the explicit dedication of the feast to YHWH (v. 5).

The conceptualization of the calf is further clarified in this same narrative.[62] Aaron's description of the creation of the calf ("I threw [the gold] into the fire, and this calf came out," v. 24) is completely in line with the common understanding of cultic image origins. Aaron's words are, in fact, comparable to the ritual amputation of the Mesopotamian craftsmen in the cult induction rituals previously discussed. After a priest pretends to amputate the craftsmen's hands, they swear out loud: "I did not make him (the statue)..." (BM 45749 line 52).[63] Thus, the common interpretation that Aaron was lying is only true up to a point, since after the construction and consecration of an image it would have been thought sufficiently separated from human origin.[64] Furthermore, the presentation

---

[59] Levtow 2008, p. 117.
[60] The literary relationship between the two passages is almost universally recognized. See also Deut. 9:8-21; Hos. 8:6, 13:2
[61] On the calves as cultic images and not mere pedestals, see Herring 2013, pp. 148-149.
[62] For a fuller discussion of the following points, see Herring 2013, pp. 139-150.
[63] Babylonian Ritual Tablet BM 4579. Text and Translation in Walker and Dick 1999, pp. 72-83.
[64] Loewenstamm made this same point in 1975, but compared the divine origin of the calf to that of Baal's palace in the Baal cycle (CTA 4 vi 16-40) (1975).

formula and the proclaimed feasts and sacrifices dedicated to YHWH described in this passage (vv. 5-6) are hints that a consecration ritual may have occurred.[65]

Likewise, that the bull-image was thought to function as cult images do elsewhere is underscored by the response of YHWH and Moses, even though it is not stated overtly. Moses, for example, does not simply destroy the calf, but orders its complete annihilation: "[Moses) took the calf...burned it...ground it to powder...scattered it upon the waters and made the people drink it" (32:20). A glance at the history of interpretation of this passage reveals a preoccupation with harmonizing these activities with the material make up of the calf.[66] This trend changed with scholars such as Loewenstamm, who compared the destruction of the calf with destruction of Mot in the Ugaritic Baal cycle.[67] In two separate passages, Mot's remains are treated in exactly the same way.[68] Further, these actions correspond to the destruction of other cult images in the Hebrew Bible (Deuteronomy 7:5; 12:3; 2 Kings 23: 6, 15), as well as wider ancient Near Eastern practice of mutilation and destruction of divine images.[69]

As recent studies have demonstrated, these types of actions aimed at images had more than just a political or religious(-political) aim. Given the very real relationship between the represented and the representation, the abduction, mutilation and destruction of a divine image should also be seen in psychological and theological terms – "as clear evidence for the superiority of the victor's god."[70] In the case of Exodus 32, whatever the calf was it was deemed enough of a threat to the role of YHWH (and, more directly, Moses) to be taken as seriously as one would a captured deity.[71]

Ironically, however, the best evidence that the ancient Israelite authors were immersed in ancient, cultic conceptualizations comes from the denials.[72] These denials take many forms in the Hebrew Bible (prohibition, condemnation, parody, etc.), and challenge the belief that raw, profane

---

[65] For discussion, see Faur 1978, pp. 1-15; Herring 2013, pp. 123 n. 201, 139-145.
[66] Begg 1985, pp. 208-251; Hahn 1981, pp. 208-212; Herring 2013, pp. 143-145.
[67] Loewenstamm 1967, p. 485.
[68] Anat is said to "burn," "grind," and "scatter" Mot (CTA 6 ii 4-37; v 7ff).
[69] See Begg 1985, pp. 211-229; Herring 2013, pp. 144-145.
[70] Miller and Roberts 1977, p. 10. For further references, see above n. 20.
[71] For a fuller treatment on the divinity of the calf and its relation to YHWH and Moses in Exodus 32-34, see Herring 2013, pp. 127-164.
[72] For a fuller discussion on the following points, see also Dick 1999; Levtow 2008, pp. 40-85, 143-152; Herring 2013, pp. 74-84.

and, above all, lifeless material objects could ever become a divine being. While denying the possibility, these polemics demonstrate an intimate knowledge of the conceptualization and a willingness to participate in the broader rhetoric and ritual of cults centered on divine images.

The principle arguments made by the biblical authors against the fashioning and worship of cultic images are centered on identifying the deity with the raw materials and human craftsmanship that make up the cultic image.[73] In some cases this can be as simple as the use of the root 'āśā ("to make") plus an explicit mention of the human origin and/or the raw materials.[74] So, for example, in the passage describing the migration of the tribe of Dan to the north, Micah confronts the Danites who stole his cultic image with ironic words: "You have taken my gods, which I have made!" (Judges 18:24; cf. vv. 27, 31).[75]

Other passages, however, go to much greater effort in the attempt to point out the ludicrous notion that a product of human hands and profane materials could be a god. This sentiment is expressed clearly in Jeremiah 10: 1-16, where YHWH is shown to be more powerful than the deities of Mesopotamia, identified with their cult images: the foreign images are made from "a tree from the forest" that has been "worked with a chisel by the hand of a craftsman" (v. 3), thus "their instruction is nothing but wood" (v. 8). Humans "decorate them with silver and gold" and "fasten them with hammer and nails" (v. 4), so that they cannot speak nor can they walk; they must be carried (v. 5). They are "scarecrows" (v. 5), "insubstantial," a "work of mockery" (v. 15), both "stupid and foolish" (v. 8). They cannot breathe (v. 14). They are not alive but dead, so that that they are powerless to do anything, whether good or evil (v. 5). In contrast, YHWH is "true" and is, indeed, alive (v. 10). He is powerful (v. 10). His voice is heard: it brings forth the storm and the flood (v. 13); it even controls the "wind" (v. 13). Thus, he is to be feared (v. 7). Although, the craftsmen of cultic images are "skilled" (v. 9), YHWH "established the world" (v. 12). The craftsmen make lifeless, powerless statues (vv. 8-9), but YHWH makes heaven, earth, and all things (vv. 12, 16).

Habbakuk 2:18-19 compares YHWH and cultic images (and their makers) on similar grounds:

---

[73] Dick 1999, p. 30.
[74] cf. Dick 1999, p. 16 n. 39, 35; Weinfeld 1992, p. 324.
[75] Preuss argues that this text is an early attempt to mock cultic statues, noting the combination of explicit human origin, the Deuteronomistic cliché ("wood and stone" [see also Weinfeld 1992, p. 324]) and the reference to the craftsman (1971, p. 65).

> Of what profit is an idol? For its sculptor shapes it, a metal-covered image and a teacher of falsehood; for the shaper trusts in its shape, to make mute idols. Woe to the one who says to wood, "Wake up!" To a mute stone, "Get up!" Will it instruct? Look, it is plated with gold and silver, there is no breath in it at all. But YHWH is in his holy temple. Be silent before him, all the earth!

Similar examples are found in great abundance in the Hebrew Bible.[76] These authors reveal an intimate knowledge of the necessary materials, the manufacturing process and the conceptualization of cult images. There is an abundance of rare and technical terminology, describing craftsmen, tools and materials.[77]

Interestingly, it is precisely this focus on the origin of cultic images that led previous scholars to declare ancient Israel's ignorance of the cults surrounding them.[78] According to these scholars, Israel showed themselves ignorant of the true nature and, thus, power of the foreign cults – the mythologies. Yet, as we have seen, these rituals were extremely important to the conceptual framework of the iconic cults. By targeting the very same weaknesses that the consecration rituals were meant to eliminate, the Israelite authors demonstrate, at the very least, that they understood the importance of these ceremonies by which a statue became a god. They document the various stages, means and materials of the production of the divine image and rhetorically (re)connect the cult statue with profane material, negating the efficacious nature of the ritual. They capture the divine images and, much like the Philistine statue of Dagon, render them powerless and deprived of their senses (Psalm 115:5-6; cf. Jeremiah 10:5).[79]

Conclusion

In ancient Israel/Judah, YHWH did have cultic representations that functioned in the same way that cultic representations functioned elsewhere in the ancient Near East: they were thought to manifest the divine presence.

---

[76] E.g., Hosea 8:4-6; 13:2; 14:4; Isaiah 40:18-20; 41:6-7; 44:9-20; Psalms 115:3-9; 135:15-18. On these and other texts in this context, see Levtow 2008, pp. 40-85, 130-163; Dick 1999; Herring 2013, pp. 74-85.

[77] See Herring 2013, p. 81 n. 157-59.

[78] See, e.g., Kaufmann 2005. On Kaufmann's error in this context, see, esp., Levtow 2008, pp. 23-24.

[79] "This statue without its mouth opened cannot smell incense, cannot eat food, nor drink water" (STT 200 lines 43-44).

Whether as standing stones, stylized trees, various theriomorphic images or the ark, YHWH had a "body," through which his presence was manifested. Admittedly, this conclusion rests in large part on the assumption that the, likely widespread, use of iconic and aniconic cultic imagery implies similar conceptualizations as are found elsewhere in the ancient Near East. As we have seen, this assumption is furthered by the conceptual parallels that indicate that the biblical authors were very familiar with the function of cultic images to manifest the presence of deity.[80] If there is a difference between ancient Israel/Judah and other Near Eastern culture then it likely exists on the level of form and not function. But even if we allow that assumption, caution is needed. The traditional stance that YHWH was never represented by an anthropomorphic image is being slowly undermined by a number of recent investigations, both archaeological and textual. The more we find, the better our understanding.

ACKERMAN, S.
1992   *Under Every Green Tree: popular religion in sixth-century Judah.* Atlanta, Ga: Scholars Press.

AHARONI, Y.
1975   *Investigations at Lachish: the sanctuary and the residency (Lachish V).* Tel Aviv: Gateway.
1981   *Arad Inscriptions.* Jerusalem: Israel Exploration Society.

ALBERTZ, R.
1994   *A History of Israelite Religion in the Old Testament Period*, 2 Vols. Translated by J. Bowden. Louisville, KY: Westminster/John Knox Press.

AVNER, U.
1984   "Ancient Cult Sites in the Negev and Sinai Deserts," *Tel Aviv* 11(2):115-131.
1990   "Ancient Agricultural Settlement and Religion in the 'Uvda Valley, Southern Israel," *Biblical Archaeologist* 53: 125-141.
1993   "*Masseboth* Sites in the Negev and Sinai and Their Significance," in *Second International Congress on Biblical Archaeology in Jerusalem, 1990*, edited by J. Aviram, pp. 166-181. Jerusalem: Israel Exploration Society.

BAHRANI, Z.
2003   *The Graven Image: Representation in Babylonia and Assyria.* Philadelphia: University of Pennsylvania.

---

[80] This familiarity is found most often in the negative commentary regarding "foreign" cultic practices. There are, however, a few positive expressions of the belief that a material image could re-presence god on earth. These positive attestations were limited to a certain type of material image – humans. See, e.g., Genesis 1:26-7; 5:1-3; 9:6; Exodus 34:29-35; Ezekiel 36-37. This is a subject that I (SH) have explored further in my book *Divine Substitution* (2013).

BECKING, B. M.
2001   *Only One God?: Monotheism in Ancient Israel and the Veneration of the Goddess Asherah*. Sheffield: Sheffield Academic Press.

BEGG, C. T.
1985   "The Destruction of the Calf (Exod 32,20/Deut 9,21)," In *Das Deuteronomiom: Entstehung, Gestalt und Botschaft*, edited by N. Lohfink, pp. 208-251. Leuven: Leuven University.

BEN-TOR, A.
1996   "Tel Hazor, 1996," *Israel Exploration Journal* 46(4): 262-269.
2002   "Tel Hazor, 2002," *Israel Exploration Journal* 52 (2): 254-257.
2013   "The Ceremonial Precinct in the Upper City of Hazor," *Near Eastern Archaeology* 76 (2): 81-91.

BEN-TOR, A. and BONFIL, R.
1997   *Hazor V. An Account of the Fifth Season of Excavation, 1968*. Jerusalem: Israel Exploration Society and the Hebrew University of Jerusalem.

BERLEJUNG, A.
1997   "Washing the Mouth: The Consecration of Divine Images in Mesopotamia," in *The Image and the Book: Iconic Cults, Aniconism, and the Rise of Book Religion in Israel and the Ancient Near East*, edited by K. van der Toorn, pp. 45-72. Leuven: Peeters.
1998   *Die Theologie der Bilder: Herstellung und Einweihung von Kultbildern in Mesopotamien und die alttestamentliche Bilderpolemik* (Orbis Biblicus et Orientalis 162). Freiburg: Vandenhoeck & Ruprecht.

BLOCH-SMITH, E.
2005   "Maṣṣēbôt in the Israelite cult: an argument for rendering implicit cultic criteria explicit," in *Temple and worship in biblical Israel*, edited by J. Day, pp. 28-39. London: T&T Clark.
2006   "Will the Real *Masseboth* Please Stand Up," in *Text, Artifact, and Image: Revealing Ancient Israelite Religion*, edited by G. Beckman and T. J. Lewis, pp. 64-79. Providence: Brown Judaic Studies.

BOTTÉRO, J.
1992   *Mesopotamia: Writing, Reasoning, and the Gods*. Chicago: University of Chicago Press.
2001   *Religion in Ancient Mesopotamia*. Chicago: University of Chicago Press.

BUNTA, S.
2007   "Yhwh's Cultic Statue after 597/586 B. C. E.: A Linguistic and Theological Reinterpretation of Ezekiel 28:12," *Catholic Biblical Quarterly* 69: 233-234.

COGAN, M.
1974   *Imperialism and Religion: Assyria, Judah, and Israel in the Eighth and Seventh Centuries B.C.E*. Missoula: Scholars.

CORNELIUS, I.
2007   "A Terracotta Horse in Stellenbosch and the Iconography and Function of Palestinian Horse Figurines," *Zeitschrift des Deutschen Palästina-Vereins* 123(1): 28-36.

DARBY, E.
2014 *Interpreting Judean Pillar Figurines. Gender and Empire in Judean Apotropaic Ritual.* Tübingen: Mohr Siebeck.

DEVER, W. G.
1973 "The Gezer Fortifications and the 'High Place': an Illustration of Stratigraphic Methods and Problems," *Palestine Exploration Quarterly* 105(1): 61-70.

DEVER, W. G. and SEGER, J. D.
2014 "A Brief Summary of the Stratigraphy and Cultural History of Gezer," in *Gezer VI. The Objects from Phases I and II*, by G. Gilmour, pp. 8-17. Winona Lake, IN: Eisenbrauns.

DEVER, W. G., LANCE, H. D., BULLARD, R. G., COLE, D. P., FURSHPAN, A. M., J. S. HOLLADAY JR., SEGER J. D., WRIGHT, R. B.
1971 "Further Excavations at Gezer, 1967-1971," *Biblical Archaeologist* 34(4): 93-132.

DICK, M. B.
1999 "Prophetic Parodies of Making the Cult Image," in *Born in Heaven Made on Earth: The Making of the Cult Image in the Ancient Near East*, edited by M. B. Dick, pp. 1-54. Winona Lake, IN: Eisenbrauns.
2005 "The Mesopotamian Cult Statue: A Sacramental Encounter with Divinity," in *Cult Image and Divine Representation in the Ancient Near East*, edited by N. Walls, pp. 43-67. Boston: ASOR.

DOHMEN, C.
1985 *Das Bilderverbot: Seine Entstehung und seine Entwicklung im Alten Testament.* Bonn: Athenäum.

FAUR, J.
1978 "The Biblical Idea of Idolatry," *Jewish Quarterly Review* 69:1: 1-15.

FREEDBERG, D.
1989 *The Power of Images: Studies in the History and Theory of Response.* Chicago: University of Chicago.

GARR, R.
2000 "'Image' and 'Likeness' in the Inscription from Tell Fakhariyeh," *Israel Exploration Journal* 50: 227-234.

GILMOUR, G. H.
1995 *The Archaeology of Religion in the Southern Levant: an Analytical and Comparative Approach.* Unpublished DPhil diss. University of Oxford.
2005a "Hazor," in *Dictionary of the Old Testament: Historical Books,* edited by H. G. M. Williamson and B. T. Arnold, pp. 360-366. Downers Grove, Ill.: InterVarsity Press.
2005b "Shechem." in *Dictionary of the Old Testament: Historical Books,* edited by H. G. M. Williamson and B. T. Arnold, pp. 889-893. Downers Grove, Ill.: InterVarsity Press.
2009 "An Iron Age II Pictorial Inscription from Jerusalem Illustrating Yahweh and Asherah," *Palestine Exploration Quarterly* 141(2): 87–103.

GRAESSER, C. F.
1972 "Standing Stones in Ancient Palestine," *Biblical Archaeologist* 35(2): 34-63.

HADLEY, J. M.
2000 *The Cult of Asherah in Ancient Israel and Judah. Evidence for a Hebrew Goddess.* Cambridge: Cambridge University Press.

HAHN, J.
1981 *Das "Goldene Kalb": Die Jahwe-Verehrung bei Stierbildern in der Geschichte Israels.* Bern: Lang.

HALLO, W. W.
1988 "Texts, Statues and the Cult of the Divine King," in *Congress Volume: Jerusalem, 1986,* edited by J. Emerton, pp. 54-66. Leiden: Brill.

HEHN, J.
1915 "Zum Terminus 'Bild Gottes'," in *Festschrift Eduard Sachau: zum siebzigsten Geburtstage gewidmet von Freunden und Schülern,* edited by G. Weil, pp. 36-52. Berlin: Reimer.

HERRING, S. L.
2008 "A 'Transubstantiated' Humanity: The Relationship between the Divine Image and the Presence of God in Gen. i 26f," *Vetus Testamentum* 58: 480-494.
2013 *Divine Substitution: Humanity as the Manifestation of Deity in the Hebrew Bible and the Ancient Near East.* Göttingen: Vandenhoeck & Ruprecht.

HERZOG, Z., AHARONI, M., RAINEY, A. F., and MOSHKOVITZ S.
1984. "The Israelite fortress at Arad," *Bulletin of the American Schools of Oriental Research* 254: 1–34.

HESTRIN, R.
1987 "The Lachish Ewer and the 'Asherah'," *Israel Exploration Journal* 37 (4): 212–223.

HOLLADAY, J. S.
1987 "Religion in Israel and Judah Under the Monarchy: An Explicitly Archaeological Approach," in *Ancient Israelite Religion,* edited by P.D. Miller, P.D. Hanson and S.D. McBride, pp. 249-299. Philadelphia: Fortress.

HOLLAND, T. A.
1995 "A Study of Palestinian Iron Age Baked Clay Figurines, with Special Reference to Jerusalem: Cave I," in *Excavations by K. M. Kenyon in Jerusalem 1961–1967, Volume IV: The Iron Age Cave Deposits on the South-east Hill and Isolated Burials and Cemeteries Elsewhere,* edited by I. Eshel and K. Prag, pp. 159-189. Oxford: British School of Archaeology in Jerusalem and Oxford University Press.

JACOBSEN, T.
1987 "The Graven Image." in *Ancient Israelite Religion,* edited by P. D. Miller, P. D. Hanson and S. D. McBride, pp. 15-32. Philadelphia: Fortress.

KAUFMANN, Y.
2005 *Religion of Israel*. London: Allen & Unwin.

KEEL, O. and UEHLINGER, C.
1998 *Gods, Goddesses, and Images of God in Ancient Israel*. Edinburgh: T&T Clark.

KENYON, K. M.
1974 *Digging up Jerusalem*. London: Benn.

KLETTER, R.
1996 *The Judean Pillar Figurines and the Archaeology of Asherah*. Oxford: Tempus Reparatum.

LAROCCA PITTS, E.
2001 *"Of Wood and Stone": The Significance of Israelite Cultic Items in the Bible and Its Early Interpreters*. Winona Lake, IN: Eisenbrauns.

LEVTOW, N.
2008 *Images of Others*. Winona Lake, IN: Eisenbrauns.

LOEWENSTAMM, S.
1967 "The Making and Destruction of the Golden Calf – A Rejoinder," *Biblica* 48(4): 481-490.
1975 "The Making and Destruction of the Golden Calf – A Rejoinder," *Biblica* 56(3): 330-343.

METTINGER, T. N. D.
1995 *No Graven Image? Israelite Aniconism in Its Ancient Near Eastern Context*. Coniectanea biblica: Old Testament series 42. Stockholm: Almqvist & Wiksell International.

MILLER, P. D. and ROBERTS, J. J. M.
1977 *The Hand of the Lord: A Reassessment of the "Ark Narrative" of 1 Samuel*. Baltimore, MD: Johns Hopkins University.

MOOREY, P. R. S.
2003 *Idols of the People. Miniature Images of Clay in the Ancient Near East*. Oxford: Oxford University Press.

NIEHR, H.
1997 "In Search of YHWH's Cult Statue in The First Temple," in *The Image and the Book: Iconic Cults, Aniconism, and the Rise of Book Religion in Israel and the Ancient near East*, edited by K. Van Der Toorn, pp. 73-95. Leuven: Peeters.

NÖTSCHER, F.
1924 *"Das Angesicht Gottes schaun" nach biblischer und babylonischer Auffassung*. Würzburg: Becker.

PREUSS, H. D.
1971 *Verspottung fremder Religionen im Alten Testament*. Stuttgart: Kohlhammer.

PROVAN, I.
1988 *Hezekiah and the Books of Kings*. Berlin: De Gruyter.

SCHÜLE, A.
2005 "Made in the Image of God: The Concepts of Divine Images in Gen. 1-3," *Zeitschrift für die alttestamentliche Wissenschaft* 117: 1-20.

SEOW, C. L.
1992 "Ark of the Covenant," in *The Anchor Bible Dictionary*, volume 1, edited by D. N. Freedman, pp. 386-393. Garden City, NY: Doubleday.
1995 "Face," *Dictionary of Deities and Demons in the Bible*, edited by K. Van Der Toorn, pp. 608-13. Leiden: Brill.

SMITH, M. S.
1988 "'Seeing God' in the Psalms: The Background to the Beatific Vision in the Hebrew Bible," *Catholic Biblical Quarterly* 50: 171-183.

SOMMER, B. D.
2009 *The Bodies of God and the World of Ancient Israel*. Cambridge: Cambridge University.

STAGER, L. E.
1999 "The Fortress Temple at Shechem and the 'House of El, Lord of the Covenant'," in *Realia Dei: Essays in Archaeology and Biblical Interpretation in Honor of Edward F. Campbell, Jr. at His Retirement*, edited by P. H. Williams Jr. and T. Hiebert, pp. 228-249. Atlanta: Scholars Press.
2003 "The Shechem Temple: Where Abimelech Massacred a Thousand," *Biblical Archaeology Review* 29(4): 26-35, 66, 68-69.

STRINE, C. A.
2014 "Ezekiel's Image Problem: The Mesopotamian Cult Statue Induction Ritual and the Imago Dei Anthropology in the Book of Ezekiel," *Catholic Biblical Quarterly* 76: 252-72.

UEHLINGER, C.
2006 "Arad, Qitmīt – Judahite Aniconism vs. Edomite Cult? Questioning the Evidence," in *Text, Artifact, and Image: Revealing Ancient Israelite Religion*, edited by G. M. Beckman and T. J. Lewis, pp. 80-114. Providence: Brown Judaic Studies.
1996 "Israelite Aniconism in Context," *Biblica* 77: 540-9.

VAN DER TOORN, K. (editor)
1997 *The Image and the Book: Iconic Cults, Aniconism, and the Rise of Book Religion in Israel and the Ancient Near East*. Leuven: Peeters

WAGHORNE, J. P.
1999 "The Divine Image in Contemporary South India: The Renaissance of a Once Maligned Tradition," *Born in Heaven, Made on Earth: The Making of the Cult Image in the Ancient Near East*, edited by M.B. Dick, pp. 211-243. Winona Lake: Eisenbrauns.

WALKER, C. and DICK, M. B.
1999 "The Induction of the Cult Image in Ancient Mesopotamia: The Mesopotamian *Mīs Pî* Ritual," in *Born in Heaven, Made on Earth: The Making of the Cult Image in the Ancient Near East*, edited by M. B. Dick, pp. 55-122. Winona Lake: Eisenbrauns.
2001 *The Induction of the Cult Image in Ancient Mesopotamia: The Mesopotamian Mīs Pī Ritual: Transliteration, Translation, and Commentary*. Helsinki: Neo-Assyrian Text Corpus Project.

WEINFELD, M.
1992 *Deuteronomy and the Deuteronomic School*. Winona Lake, IN: Eisenbrauns.

WILLIAMSON, H. G. M.
2013 "Was There an Image of the Deity in the First Temple?" In *The Image and its Prohibition in Jewish Antiquity*, edited by S. Pearce, pp. 28-37. Oxford: Journal of Jewish Studies

WINTER, I.
1992 "Idols of the King: Royal Images as Recipients of Ritual Action in Ancient Mesopotamia." *Journal of Ritual Studies* 6: 12-42.

YADIN, Y.
1972 *Hazor*. (Schweich Lectures 1970.) London, The British Academy.

YADIN, Y., AHARONI, Y., AMIRAN, R., DOTHAN, T., DUNAYEVSKY, I. and PERROT, J.
1958 *Hazor I*. Jerusalem, Magnes Press.
1961 *Hazor III-IV, Plates*. Jerusalem, Magnes Press.

ZEVIT, Z.
1984 "The Khirbet el-Qôm Inscription Mentioning a Goddess," *Bulletin of the American Schools of Oriental Research* 255: 39–47.
2001 *The Religions of Ancient Israel: A Synthesis of Parallactic Approaches*. New York: Continuum.

IRON AGE MEDICINE MEN AND OLD TESTAMENT THEOLOGY

Robert D. Miller II, OFS

Several important histories of early Iron Age Israel have appeared in recent years.[1] These provided archaeologically-based reconstructions of early Israelite society and economics. Yet the "relatively few, highly complex and ambiguity-ridden concepts around which the social organization of a culture revolves and the emotional and intellectual energy of its members is largely spent"[2] have been largely ignored.[3] That is, religion, broadly defined, has been for the most part left to the study of the biblical text alone.[4]

Archaeology, as the study of artifacts (including structures), is keenly poised to explore the mental representations pertaining to artifacts that are tied up with the practices for which they were used.[5] The most obvious example is archaeology of ritual, defined with Rappoport as "the performance of more or less invariant sequences of formal acts and utterances not entirely encoded by the performers."[6] But there is more. All artifacts have a symbolic, ideological side – distinct according to context in most cases (ideology does not exist independently of material culture) – that can sometimes be seen in morphological analysis of those artifacts.[7] Sacred memory is regularly abetted by non-linguistic artifacts, in

---

[1] E.g., Liverani 2005. Throughout this essay, I freely attach the label "Israel" to the Iron I highlands of Palestine, for reasons presented thoroughly in Miller (2004), and reiterated in Kletter (2005, pp. 581-82). For dissenting views, see Faust 2005, pp. 494, 496.
[2] Polanyi 1981, p. 99.
[3] This reflects a similar avoidance of religion by archaeologists of other regions and cultures; Whitley, et al. 2008, p. 12.
[4] Exceptions include Zevit (2001) and Barton and Stavrakopoulou (2010) but these are focused on the Iron II period. Were archaeologists to eschew biblical texts because they are often highly scholastic products of the religious elite, a reticence found also in archaeologists of India, this would be equally problematic; Fogelin 2007, pp. 23-42.
[5] McCauley and Lawson 2007, pp. 3, 7.
[6] Rappoport 1999, p. 24; McCauley and Lawson 2007, p. 2. We must recognize, however, that most religious activity in small-scale societies may be informal behavior; Culley 2008, p. 68.
[7] Romain 2011, p. 33; Bard 1992, pp. 3-4; Morris 1991, p. 26. Ezra 1994, p. 189.

both oral and textual cultures, and archaeology is also able to examine this aspect of artifacts.[8] Archaeology, therefore, can be a key resource in reconstructing early Israelite religion.

The archaeology of religion will include both architecture of special places and the artifacts associated with such places,[9] although "There are very few, if any, locations that categorically exclude either ritual or mundane activities."[10] Significant also will be mortuary information.[11]

Rather than simply catalog, we must explain the religion from the artifacts. One could easily assume the biblical text provides such an interpretation; it would be most difficult to prove that it does not. Such information, however, is inextricably bound with thick cultural concepts, intentions, and concerns of the author's own period and of many others before his time.[12] The biblical text cannot be used as a direct source for reconstructing cultural concepts. Given the near impossibility of identifying texts of a specific timeframe, let us explain the artefactual evidence by ethnographic analogy.[13] "The comparative approach does not entail, a priori, any identification, full or partial, of the phenomena or developments which are being compared."[14] But, "reconstructions cannot be achieved without the help of the comparative method,"[15] We cannot simply "attempt, by inductive, empiricist research to infer the religion of early Israel from supposedly objective archaeological data; ... no matter how 'objective' a researcher tries to be or how well he or she knows the data, the method produces only an illusion of objectivity and inevitability."[16]

Ethnographic analogy will provide explanation of the archaeological realia. One should accept these analogies not merely because of multiple

---

[8] McCauley and Lawson 2007, p. 9.
[9] Renfrew 1994, p. 49.
[10] Kyriakidis 2007, p. 17.
[11] O'Shea 1984, p. 18; Bard 1992, p. 3. I will avoid labeling this "popular religion," a term rightly rejected altogether (Davis 1982, p. 322; Nunn 2006, p. 58). After all, is the designation "popular" used because this was the religion of the common person or because it shows non-normative local particularity (Chartier 1984, pp. 230, 233)? "Religion must always be studied as the religion of certain groups in a given time and place" (Davis 1982, p. 322). At the same time, all archaeology of religion is bound to unpack only artifacts attesting to the beliefs of an elite whose material produce was of a durable material; Emerson and Pauketat 2008, p. 171.
[12] Dever 1997, p. 298.
[13] McCauley and Lawson 2007, p. 8.
[14] Gelb 1980, p. 32.
[15] Gelb 1980, p. 35.
[16] Lewis-Williams 1991, p. 149.

areas of correspondence and sheer weight of parallels. "The piling up of common attributes cannot be said to make one analogy more probable than another."[17] Rather, the merit of the analogies derives from seeing the same causal/determining mechanism in both societies, Israel and the comparand, the same behavioral systems that produce particular artefactual patterns.[18] In what follows, then, I will outline the artefactual evidence, and then use ethnographic analogy to explain Early Israelite religion in terms of two recurring patterns of religious representation found throughout human groups, shamanism and totemism.[19] After this, true to the purpose of this volume, I will explore what the presence of these shamanic and totemic patterns in early Israel means for biblical theology.

Archaeology of Religion in Early Israel

Since the archaeology of religion includes architecture of special places and associated artifacts, let us first catalog ritual space in Iron I Israel. The site of el-Burnat Sitti Salaamiyya, conveniently called for several decades now "Mt. Ebal," a site on the eastern slope of Mount Ebal, has three strata dating from the Late Bronze Age to the mid-12th century B.C.E. What makes the site most interesting and the focus of questions regarding its function, is a rectilinear structure from Stratum IB (1200-1140 BCE) of 30.0 m^2 with corners oriented to the compass points, having no floor or entrance, filled with bones of bulls, sheep, goats, and deer, ash, and pottery.[20] On the southeast side of the structure is what may be a ramp, and there are well-paved, rectangular courtyards around the structure on three sides.[21] The percentage of pithoi and jugs in the site's pottery assemblage is higher than most Iron I highland sites, and the percentage of cooking pots lower, while sickle blades are completely absent.[22] There is a large quantity of bones, especially of deer bones.[23] Most of the bones were burnt, with 44 per cent of the burned remains coming from the central structure, and 63 per cent of the deer bones

---

[17] Lewis-Williams 1991, p. 152.
[18] Lewis-Williams 1991, p. 152-53
[19] Cf. McCauley and Lawson 2007, p. 8.
[20] Hawkins 2012, pp. 9, 39.
[21] Hawkins 2012, pp. 9, 43.
[22] Hawkins 2012, pp. 10, 57, 60.
[23] Hawkins 2012, pp. 64-65.

coming from it.²⁴ Deep cut marks on antlers and a disproportionate amount of deer crania illustrate the intentional removal of antlers.²⁵ It all seems to add up to a large permanent altar. Mt. Ebal's "structure" is oriented to compass points and has a ramp like non-Iron I altars,²⁶ but has no altar horns, and no other altars have bone or ash fill.²⁷ So, acknowledging that ritual locations often host a variety of rituals for the same group of people,²⁸ Mt. Ebal is a cultic site of some sort, albeit not a very "biblical" one in light of the compass orientation, the ritual use of deer (kosher, but illicit for sacrifice), and some sort of liturgical(?) use of their antlers.

There may have been a Secondary Public Cult Room at Ai.²⁹ At end of a street in Site D, there is tiny room #65 (8.5m × 2.5m), with a bench at the foot of its wall all the way around, where a four-tiered, 80cm tall fenestrated incense burner with paws as a base was found.³⁰ Analogous pieces are Megiddo P6055 and others, two at Tell Qasile, and three at Beth Shean.³¹ Inside the burner was a clay animal figure (#1091) of either a greyhound dog or a jackal (not a mouse), similar to one found at Taanach.³² Also in the room were a bowl for a cult stand, having a chalice profile with a tang (#1054), a bovine figurine, and a bowl (#1055) with flat base and a row of breasts around the carination.³³ The form of this room suggests, on the basis of ethnographic analogy, "a focus on transformation via small group communitas performance rituals; strong smells in smoky, enclosed spaces; and rites of initiation and myth telling."³⁴

The building at Tell el-Farah North/Tirzah (Level VIIa) that Chambon called a temple in J6 (squares 487-491)³⁵ is an Iron I house of a type with a rectangular space bordered with rooms on three sides, the sides set off by pillars and the end by a wall, although it is paved, has an additional vestibule, and lies directly over the Middle Bronze Age temple.³⁶ There

---

²⁴ Hawkins 2012, pp. 10, 65.
²⁵ Hawkins 2012, p. 64.
²⁶ Hawkins 2012, p. 148. Such compass orientation is common worldwide; Malone 2007, p. 26.
²⁷ Hawkins 2012, pp. 149-50.
²⁸ Kyriakidis 2007, p. 15.
²⁹ Gilmour 1995, pp. 173, 427.
³⁰ Marquet-Krause 1935, p. 340.
³¹ Allen 1980, pp. 38, 60.
³² Allen 1980, pp. 11-13.
³³ Gilmour 1995, pp. 172-73; P. Thomsen 1936/37, p. 95.
³⁴ Hastorf 2007, p. 86.
³⁵ Chambon 1984, p. 20.
³⁶ de Vaux 1957, p. 575; Braemer 1982, p. 71.

was a statuette made of bell bronze or Corinthian brass (silver-bronze alloy) found in the building in the shape of an anthropomorphic goddess (#1.491).[37] Such larger spaces, ethnographically, "were gathering points for a group to participate in sensory, communal performances of music... (sound), incense (smell), and food (taste)."[38]

An Iron I altar, 60×60×40 cm, was found in 2013 at Shiloh on the southern edge of the site, but information is still sketchy.

The so-called "Bull Site" is not an Iron I shrine.[39] The pottery and the flint assemblages are those of domestic habitations,[40] although it did produce an incense burner – we will return to the "Bull" below. However, its dating is a serious concern. Although the excavator[41] always referred to the site single-period Iron I,[42] an independent survey of the site found only *five percent* of the sherds collected to be Iron I.[43] And if Finkelstein's redating of "Einun" pottery to the Middle Bronze Age is correct, then 90 per cent of the pottery found at the site is Middle Bronze.[44] Lawrence Stager is correct that the "Migdal Temple" of Shechem is not from the Iron I period.[45]

Overall, this amounts to few cult sites.[46] This is especially clear in comparison to clearly cultic Iron I buildings at Dan (Room 7082), Tell Abu Hawam (T.30), Beth Shean (ST and NT), and Tel Qasile (XII, XI, and X). But these, along with much of the data outlined by Albertz and Schmitt in their *Family and Household Religion,* are all outside of the central hill country to which most scholars would limit early Israel.[47]

Moving from locations to objects, the same artifact can be both household cookware and a ritual vessel, depending on the cultural context in which a person uses it.[48] So to focus our gaze, "... [o]bjects can and do manifest a religious function of one sort or another when they appear in other identifiable cultic contexts such as temples, shrines, and sanctuaries."[49]

---

[37] Chambon 1984, p. 20.
[38] Hastorf 2007, p. 93.
[39] Contra Dever (2005, p. 464).
[40] Mazar 1982, p. 41.
[41] The entire excavation of this site took one day; Mazar 1997.
[42] Mazar 1982.
[43] Zertal 1996.
[44] Finkelstein 1995, p. 97.
[45] Stager 1999, pp. 228-49; Zwickel 1994, p. 76.
[46] On the lack of Iron I cultic sites in Benjamin specifically, see Langston (1998, pp. 72-179).
[47] Albertz and Schmitt 2012, pp. 496-98.
[48] Anderson 2012, p. 168
[49] Schmidt 2013, p. 281; Anderson 2012, p. 169.

As for cult objects, beginning with things found in shrines or tombs, note that the famous "bull" of the "Bull Site" was not found by archaeologists but was a chance surface discovery by a soldier.[50] It cannot be reliably included. The Bull site did produce a ceramic incense burner (if it is analogous to ones from Megiddo and Beth Shean) or model of a shrine (if analogous to one at Tell el-Farah North)[51] – unless these are Middle Bronze.

From a tomb at Dothan come two animal figurines and an anthropomorphic lamp (#P1344) with a prone male human figure with arms outstretched as if flying, wearing a crown of five clay globules, stuck on the underside. There are no parallels. It is 16 cm long, made with applied clay in the imitation of a giant clam's shell. Dothan tombs also produced two jugs shaped like bulls (#P1237 and #P1232). We have already listed a number of figurines from Ai Site D.

If we expand the list to include figurines found outside of securely cultic contexts, we will include Shiloh's Iron I Building 335, with a stand decorated with a leopard killing a deer, a figurative applique of a horse, the head of a lion on a cooking pot, and a ram's head on a krater handle.[52] At Ai's Area B South Bench House, locus 1801.4, a figurine of a goose 7.5cm long was found, similar to ones at Beth Shean.[53] A horse figurine was also found in the South Bench House.[54] Two figurines of horses' busts come from Bethel (#1054 from Room 308 and #1112 from uncertain locus) and a human figurine (#328 from locus 44).[55] An "Astarte" plaque (#104) was also found there, although lacking the divine symbols common on Late Bronze age equivalents.[56] An identical plaque was found at Dothan.

---

[50] Mazar 1982; Contra Dever (2005, p. 464). Additional reason for not considering the bull is the possible redating of most of the site's pottery to the Middle Bronze age, parallels to similar bulls from MB contexts could assign the Bull Site's bull to that period, as well; Finkelstein 1995, p. 97; but cf. Mazar 1999, pp. 146-47.

[51] Mazar 1982, pp. 36-37, fig. 10.

[52] Albertz and Schmitt 2012, p. 169.

[53] "Denyer 1976" Report in Nicol Museum.

[54] Albertz and Schmitt 2012, p. 75.

[55] Albertz and Schmitt 2012, p. 84.

[56] Zevit 2001, p. 270. The goddess Astarte is the most likely candidate for the goddess depicted on the Late Bronze Age terra-cotta plaques that are popular in the southern Levant before the rise of the Judean pillar figurines in Judah (see Moorey 2004). Some scholars have expressed doubts that the plaque figurines represent a goddess, as they lack divine attributes. They are found mostly in domestic contexts, some in graves. While it is true that not all representations of naked women need necessarily depict goddesses, it is also the case that goddesses need not be represented with divine attributes. The nude female figures on models of shrines or temples, usually in pairs,

Some conclusions obtain. There was very little in the way of permanent cultic facilities in early Israel, if these existed at all. Incense burners and their stands were quite common.[57] These stands and the associated figurines and chalices do not present "elevated levels of sensory pageantry," so much as suggest regular use.[58] This would suggest "frequently-performed rituals accompanied by comparatively low levels of sensory pageantry."[59] There is possible evidence of altars for the sacrifice of caprovids and a ritual use of deer antlers. There is no ritual use of antlers in the Bible, and antlers do not appear in Pardee's list of ninety-two different objects mentioned as offerings in Ugaritic texts.[60]

Searching the entire known ethnographic world for ritual use of antlers shows they are always connected with "Shamanism."[61]

Shamanism in Early Israel

Shamanism is not easily defined. Mircea Eliade's definition of a shaman as one who enters an altered state of consciousness to journey to other worlds was once widely accepted in anthropology.[62] Yet we cannot rely on Eliade's 1951 *Chamanisme*, translated into English in 1964. Although it greatly stimulated the study of shamanism, it relied overmuch on one Yakut ethnographer and attempted to squeeze Yakut ideas about souls, initiation, and torture by spirits into a comparative framework, overgeneralizing and simplifying even for northern Asia, much less for all the world.[63] Yet the term "Shamanism" allows the "rendering, as faithfully and subtly as possible, into a lingua franca of scholarly discourse, where

---

sometimes three, or on clay towers and cultic stands from both Syria and Palestine, lack divine attributes, but are clearly divine figures. Occasionally they are standing on lions, a symbol of Astarte (as in the horse frontlets). This does not make the figure on the plaque figurines, or the Judean pillar figurines, necessarily representative of deities, but it does remove the only real argument that they were not goddesses. See Dolansky in this volume.

[57] Haran (1993; 1995) argues that these were not incense altars but altars for small-scale vegetable offerings, but the comparative ancient Near Eastern evidence, cited below, does not support Haran's view. Seymour Gitin's (2002) study of incense altars is primarily about Iron II Israelite, Judahite, and Philistine examples.

[58] McCauley and Lawson 2007, p. 35.

[59] McCauley and Lawson 2007, p. 34.

[60] Pardee 2002, pp. 224-25.

[61] Fletcher 2001; Edson 2009, p. 83.

[62] Harner 1987, p. 3.

[63] Balzer 1996, p. 309.

analytical terms are employed which on the one had are arguably applicable to the case under study, but which at the same time have a wider range of applicability, involving other cultures, other settings in time and space."[64] Shamanism is not a religion itself, but a relatively autonomous segment of various religions.[65] Roughly, shamanism is a complex of beliefs and practices based in the idea that spirits pervade the universe and that these spirits can be deliberately contacted for specific purposes by specific persons through altered states of consciousness.[66]

Masks are an essential element of shamanism.[67] In most shamanic cultures, the masks represent the animal spirits and enhance the connection with them.[68] Mongolian shamans of the Genghis Khan period, however, wore antlers in their headwear as a symbol of the struggle against Buddhism.[69] Other shamans wore masks of animals they intended to hunt, to ensure an adequate take for the community.[70]

While some deer-spirit masks are completely theriomorphic, it is also possible to affix real or artificial antlers to an anthropomorphic mask, and there are examples from Siberia, the Q`eqchi Maya, Hopewell (200 BCE-400 CE), and at Spiro Mound in Oklahoma (1200-1450 CE).[71]

Masks are a common artifact found in temples and graves throughout Syria, Mesopotamia, and Iran.[72] There are Humbaba masks from Old

---

[64] Van Binsbergen and Wiggermann 1999.
[65] Edson 2009, p. 8.
[66] Cf. Romain 2011, pp. 7-10.
[67] DuBois 2009, pp. 182-84.
[68] Romain 2011, pp. 193-94; King 1987, p. 192; Edson 2009, p. 24.
[69] Purev and Purvee 2004, 181.
[70] Edson 2009, p. 34.
[71] Romain 2011, pp. 41-42; Edson 2009, p. 236. Deer shamanism often accompanies bear shamanism; Romain 2011, pp. 39-42. There is bear shamanism in Neolithic Anatolia; Türkcan 2007, p. 260. No bear bones have been found in Iron I Israel. But in the Late Bronze Age, there exist seventeen bear bones from Lachish (LB II-III), and there are a few Iron II examples each from Tel Dan (9th/8th century), Hazor (1 bone, 9th century), and Tel Qiri. We should be surprised to see that there are seventeen bear bones from LB Lachish, plus two additional undated specimens. Wild animals of any sort are relatively rare on post-Neolithic sites in the Near East, and carnivores other than dogs are even rarer. Hunting was uncommon, and carnivore populations were never high. Because of the skeletal elements present in the Lachish examples and the cut marks on them, they most likely came with bear skins and thus may have been traded in that form from wherever the animals were killed. The biblical text describes Elijah, an erstwhile shaman (see Miller 2011, pp. 335-37) as a "Lord of Hair," בַּעַל שֵׂעָר, not wearing a garment of haircloth but perhaps a bearskin, or himself hairy as a bear; Brown 1981, p. 391; Kapelrud 1967, p. 92. The shaman Elisha can speak to bears in 2 Kgs 2:24.
[72] Reichert 1977, p. 195.

Babylonian Kish, with the means to attach them to one's face.[73] There is a Late Bronze II mask from the Stelai Shrine at Hazor.[74] Masks have been found in Iron I Palestine at Philistine Temple 200 of Tel Qasile, dated to the 11th century, and from 11th/10th-century Ashdod (Strata X-IX) and 10th-century Tel Ser`a.[75] There are countless examples from the Iron II period (from Shufat, Jerusalem, Beersheba, Akhziv, etc.).[76] There were mask fragment found in the cultic area of Tel Dan from the so-called "Bamah A," which Biran connected with Jeroboam I. Dalia Pakman has shown that the mask was originally fixed to an incense stand found nearby. The mask in question, however, has no eyeholes and was not intended to be worn.[77]

The function of these masks was always unclear.[78] Reichert thought they were used in ritual dances, as seems to have been the case in Cyprus, representing "divine radiation" (*göttlichen Strahlenglanzes*).[79] Those from Hazor, Kition, Enkomi, Korioun, and Sarepta were all found in or near sacred areas.[80] Theriomorphic deer masks, with real antlers attached, are worn for dances by the Yaqui and Mayo people of northern Mexico.[81]

Lucian says that ritual masks were used in the Attis cult at Syrian Hierapolis (*Dea Assyr.*, 15). Herodotus records their use in Egypt (II, 122). A Beset mask is depicted on a female *Sau*, or healer, from a 17th-century BCE tomb near the Ramesseum.[82] Also in the tomb was a box containing medical papyri.[83] A block from a 24th-century BCE tomb from Giza depicts a procession of young dancers, scourged by a youth or a dwarf in a Bes mask,[84] similar to 19th-century BCE painted canvas Bes masks found in a house at Kahun.[85]

---

[73] Carter 1987, p. 362. Similar masks come from later Cyprus; Carter 1987, p. 363. On possible connections to the Akhziv mask, see Carter 1987, p. 364.
[74] A similar mask was found in 11th-century Kition; Carter 1987, p. 366.
[75] Kletter 2007, p. 189.
[76] Kletter 2007, pp. 190, 195. Two antlers and a mask (the nose and part of the eye socket opening next to the bridge of the nose) were found in the 2009 season of excavation of LBIIb Beth Shemesh; Dale Manor, personal communication.
[77] See Pakman 2003, pp. 196-203.
[78] Reichert 1977, p. 195.
[79] Reichert 1977, p. 196. The Cypriote illustrations are also noted by Kletter (2007, p. 195).
[80] Carter 1987, p. 370.
[81] Edson 2009, p. 53.
[82] Pinch 1995, pp. 56-57, fig. 27.
[83] Pinch 1995, pp. 131.
[84] Pinch 1995, pp. 84, 121-22, fig. 63.
[85] Pinch 1995, pp. 122, 132, fig. 71.

Let us turn to the incense altars. Most "biblical archaeologists" automatically relate these to "offering the pleasing odor of incense to the Lord" (Exod 29:25; 29:41; Lev 1:9, 13, 17; 16:12; etc.). The later temple in Jerusalem included an incense altar used for such purposes. Continuity of material evidence for ritual practices does not necessarily reflect a continuity of associated beliefs, however.[86] Ethnographically, they seem best suited for use in "smudging," cleansing places, persons, or objects of negative spiritual energies and inviting benevolent spirits.[87] Raz Kletter and Irit Ziffer have shown that incense was "used in Iron Age cults of the Southern Levant much more commonly than previously believed."[88] Smudging is a key element of shamanic healing.[89]

In Mongolia, each shaman has his (or her[90]) own complex recipe for the burning material.[91] Common burning materials for smudging worldwide include artemisia (wormwood), which was abundant in the Judean Desert, Foothills of Samaria, and Plain of Sharon in the Iron I period, and most importantly juniper, which in Iron I grew in the Foothills of Samaria, the Plain of Sharon, and the Southern Nablus Syncline.[92] Egypt was aware of Palestine as a source of "incense," styrax or mastic incense, as an ostracon from the Ramesseum bears the inscription *ntr sntr ḫ3rw,* "incense from Khor [Syria-Palestine]."[93] There is no need to depend on imported frankincense (*Boswellia sp.*), therefore. Myrrh was also indigenous in the Iron I highlands and extensively marketed in later periods.[94] Juniper (Mong. *arca*) is the essential smudging fuel in Mongolian shamanism for purification of small votive figurines,[95] and in Baloch/Kashmiri shamanism for inducing ecstatic trances.[96]

There is evidence for similar uses of incense in the ancient Near East. Incense was used in Egypt to fumigate the Uraeus of Medinet Habu as a means of purification.[97] When Pi-Ankhi conquered Memphis, he purified

---

[86] Kyriakidis 2007, p. 16; Marcus 2007, p. 67. In fact, much of religious ritual's form is overwhelmingly independent of the changing meanings; McCauley and Lawson 2007, p. 11.
[87] Pflüg 1996, pp. 501, 509; Mullin et al. 2001, pp. 20-22; Portman and Garrett 2006, p. 464.
[88] Kletter and Ziffer 2010, p. 183.
[89] Mandelbaum 1970.
[90] On the importance of female shamans, see Friedman 2001, p. 226.
[91] Pu̇rėv and Pu̇rvėė 2004, 264.
[92] On the importance of these fumigants, see McCampbell (2002, pp. 47, 51, 65, 85). On the occurrence of these plants in Iron I, see Miller 2003.
[93] Nielsen 1986, p. 7.
[94] Gnoli 1997, pp. 413-29.
[95] Pu̇rėv and Pu̇rvėė 2004, p. 267.
[96] Pennacchio et al. 2010, pp. 107-108.
[97] Nielsen 1986, p. 11.

the city by burning incense in it.[98] Papyrus Smith describes smudging with `*ntyw* resin and *sntr* resin incense to cure a woman of delayed menstruation.[99]

In Mesopotamia, the term for incense in general is *qutrinnu*, from the root *qatāru*, which in the D-stem means, "to let go up in smoke."[100] The root seems to be more tied to fumigation than offering,[101] and incense frequently appears in Mesopotamian purification texts.[102] It is unclear if the Hebrew and Ugaritic root *QṬR* (>Ar. *miqṭara,* censer) should be linked to the Akk. *QṬR* (>Ar. *qatara*, to exhale and odor).[103] Juniper (Sum. li gal li gal-la) was commonly used to purify (along with reed and tamarisk, both of which grew in Iron I Israel). Smudging by the "chief purification priest of Eridug" accompanies "cleaning" the temple in Gudea's Cylinders A-B account of the building of Ningirsu's temple (c.2.1.7, line c217.890). Thus, they play an important role in the *mīs pî* ritual for "enlivening" a new statue of a god.[104] Although Dick's translation refers to a "censer of juniper,"[105] the instructions that call for "heaped incense" (Sum. na-de₃ si ga)[106] suggest the "censer" could be an incense stand or bowl (Sum. niĝna; Akk *maksūtu*). So-called "censers," again incense stands, are kept at the head of beds in private homes, as in the Neo-Assyrian (and later) *Maqlu* rituals, asafetida is burned on one by the bed of the sick person.[107] A Neo-Assyrian exorcism ritual describes a censer for juniper in the same position.[108]

However, large statues are not the only items dedicated by juniper smudging. Dick's publication of a Neo-Sumerian text from Nippur CBS 8241 in the University of Pennsylvania Museum provides for purification/dedication of "seven statuettes" (line 24) with "great juniper" (line 4), reed, cedar, and myrtle.[109] Other items purified by *qutāru* include drums and bells.[110]

---

[98] Nielsen 1986, p. 13.
[99] Nielsen 1986, p. 12.
[100] Nielsen 1986, p. 27.
[101] Although this, too, is attested; Thomsen 2001, p. 46.
[102] Banti and Contini 1997, p. 173; Nielsen 1986, p. 32.
[103] Banti and Contini 1997, p. 173; Nielsen 1986, p. 58
[104] E.g., Nineveh Ritual lines 43, 50, 57, 75, 77, 116; Babylonian Ritual line rev. 41.
[105] Dick 1999, e.g., rev.12', TuL #27.
[106] E.g., *ISET* 1 217 Ni 4176; Iddin-Dagan A (*šir-namursaĝa* to Ninsiana) ETCL translation t.2.5.1, lines 195-97.
[107] Tablet IX, lines 121-24; Meier 1937.
[108] *SAA* 10.298, line 10.
[109] Dick 2005, p. 278.
[110] *CAD* 13, 321, citing Namburbi texts.

As in the *Maqlu* ritual, cuneiform texts also describe medicinal use of incense, such as are prescribed for the sick crown prince in *ABL* 570, 11[111] or to treat consuming fever in *CT* 23, 3 (K.2473+2551, 15).[112]

There is another possibility with the incense burners, however. Shamanism always involves altered states of consciousness, and in many cases these are brought on by psychotropic substances.[113] For Native American groups, these were smoked: high-nicotine forms of tobacco.[114]

Incense burned in Iron I Israel would not have been frankincense. It would have included *Artemisia judaica* (wormwood), *Artemisia arborescens* (tree wormwood), *Artemisia herba-alba* (white wormwood), *Juniperus phoenicea* (Phoenician juniper), *Liquidambar orientalis* (Styrax balsam[115]), mastic resin from *Pistacia lentiscus*,[116] *Commiphora myrrha* (myrrh),[117] *Commiphora gileadensis* (balm),[118] broomtree (*Retama raetam*),[119] and labdanum resin from *Cistus creticus* (pink rock-rose).[120]

Wormwood smudging is a key treatment Traditional Chinese Medicine,[121] and Egyptian Bedouin smudge the leaves to ward off evil spirits.[122] Inhaling its smoke causes significant decreases in heart rate, which intensify the longer one inhales.[123] This is accompanied by significant changes in the percentage changes in sequential chamber complexes in the electrocardiogram (ECG).[124] The net effect would be a depressant effect on the body and a stress-reduced tendency toward quiet behavior.[125] Anecdotal evidence from the internet of those who have smoked wormwood denies any hallucinogenic effect, but ascribes to it "extremely vivid dreams ... otherworldly travel, etc. The vividness that it causes can also translate into trance and trance-like half-sleep states, which also helps with channeling."[126] Scientific studies also reported light

---

[111] *CAD* 13, 321.
[112] *CAD* 13, 322.
[113] Whitley 2008, p. 92; Romain 2011, pp. 177-78.
[114] Romain 2011, pp. 179-81.
[115] The source of this is not *Styrax officinalis*, which does not produce an aromatic sap.
[116] Artzy 1994, p. 131; Finkelstein 1985, p. 154.
[117] Quézel 1981, p. 91.
[118] Iluz et al. 2010, p. 516.
[119] Van Zeist 1985, p. 203.
[120] Goffer 1996, p. 242.
[121] Zhao et al. 2011, p. 53.
[122] Osborn 1968, pp. 165-77.
[123] Zhao et al. 2011, p. 54.
[124] Zhao et al. 2011, p. 54.
[125] Zhao et al. 2011, p. 56.
[126] The Road Goes Ever On. Is mugwort simply a hallucinogen or is it poisonous? http://breelandwalker.tumblr.com/post/70272390917/is-mugwort-simply-a-hallucinogen-or-is-it#

euphoria.[127] *Artemisia herba-alba* in particular suppresses arachidonic acid metabolism,[128] which can have major effects on neurons in the brain.[129] The thujones in wormwood inhibit GABA receptor activation so that neurons fire more easily.[130]

With juniper, the leaves are used as incense, the anti-bacterial smoke of which is used even today to repel evil and disease in Mazandaran Province, Iran.[131] Pawnee Skiri Bear Society participants inhale the smoke from juniper's burning twigs ceremonially, and it is said to cure nervousness and nightmares.[132] It was also used in Ghost Dance hand game rituals.[133]

Styrax balsam smudging was the only repellant for "small winged snakes" according to Herodotus (*Histories* 3.107). Styrax balsam or balm – which is unclear – was praised for its medicinal properties by Galen, Pliny (*Natural History*), Celsus (*De Medicina*), Qusta ibn Luqa, Hayyim ben Joseph Vital, and Ibn al-Bayṭār.[134] Experimentally, it has been shown to reduce systemic arterial blood pressure and reduce heart rate.[135] It is usually mixed with Labdanum for burning.[136]

Mastic has been used medicinally since antiquity (Pedanius Dioscorides, *Materia Medica*; Hippocrates; Galen).[137] It has been smudged in Iran to purify the air.[138] Experimentally, its smoke functions as a bronchodilator.[139]

Broomtree smoke contains cytosine, and it has been smoked recreationally for its reported mild intoxicating properties and a heightened awareness of color. Its molecular structure has some similarity to that of nicotine and it has similar pharmacological effects.[140]

(4 February 2015). Archived by WebCite at http://www.webcitation.org/6W6CGH53k; Shroomery; Magic Mushrooms Demystified Message Board. Re: Smoking Wormwood?? http://www.shroomery.org/forums/showflat.php/Number/4258367/fpart/all/vc/1 (4 February 2015). Archived by WebCite at http://www.webcitation.org/6W6ClVEs0.

[127] Wheeler et al 2009, pp. 16-20; Siegel 1976, p. 473.
[128] Juergens et al. 1998, pp. 508–510.
[129] Piomelli 1995.
[130] Höld et al. 2000, pp. 3826–31.
[131] Pirani et al. 2011, pp. 339-40.
[132] Ledford 2012, p. 35.
[133] Ledford 2012, pp. 35-36. Juniper smoke is heavy in deoxypodophyllotoxin, which can cause neuronal cytotoxicity; Carpenter 2012, pp. 695-700; Gao 2011, pp. 680-86.
[134] Iluz et al. 2010, p. 517.
[135] Iluz et al. 2010, pp. 517-18.
[136] Paraschos et al. 2006, pp. 551-59.
[137] Huwez et al. 1946.
[138] Mohagheghzadeh et al. 2010, pp. 577-80.
[139] Mohagheghzadeh et al. 2010; Russo 2011, pp. 1344–64.
[140] Prochaska et al. 2013, p. 5198.

Labdanum resin was used to treat colds, coughs, and rheumatism (Herodotus, *Histories* 3.112; Pedanius Dioscorides, *Materia Medica* 1.128; Pliny, *Natural History*, 12.37).[141] A perusal of the internet finds that those who "smoke it" writing, "It totally messes with intellectual abilities ... It is very very relaxing but not very sedative. In fact it has a stimulant side to it." [142]

When considering the inventory of Israelite "images," especially those found in association with public shrines, no aniconic tendency is evident, although all statuary is markedly small. Humans, dogs, horses (there are no Egyptian or Canaanite horse gods; the nearest are Hittite[143]), bulls, and geese are all represented, with a slight preference for human women. As small as these figurines are, their affinity is to the shaman's "ongons," among which the wolf and goose are common according to the Mongolian ethnographic record.[144] Archaeologically, human women figurines are prevalent in Mongolian shaman graves.[145] Bird and human forms are most common in the closely-related Siberian shamanism, although the wolf or dog is also known.[146] In societies with shamans, "ordinary people as well as shamans carried charms and amulets for protection against spirits, disease, and misfortune," including "fabricated talismans include[ing] small figures carved from wood, ivory, and stone."[147] In Mongolia, reports of religion of the 12th-13th centuries speak not only of the shaman's ongons but also of domestic gods, house-gods[148]

Totemism in Early Israel

But it should also be noted that shamanism is a common feature of totemic societies.[149] If the anthropological literature on shamanism is ambivalent, that on totemism is downright suspect. The origin of the

---

[141] Cf. Gershevitch 1985; Stoerck 1762, p. 14.
[142] Ethnogen-network.com Message Board. Re: Rockroses and Labdanum. http://entheogen-network.com/forums/viewtopic.php?f=10&t=25720 (4 February 2015). Archived by WebCite at http://www.webcitation.org/6W6D2U8c7.
[143] Ivanov 1999, pp. 161-213.
[144] Pu̇rėv, O., and Pu̇rvėė 2004, p. 105.
[145] Aseyev 2006, p. 55.
[146] Balzer 1996, pp. 308-309; 2006, p. 92.
[147] Edson 2009, p. 85.
[148] Heissig 1990, pp. 228, 233.
[149] Pedersen (2001, pp. 418-19) argues that there is no totemism without shamans.

term, drawn from Ojibwa,[150] was an 1869 study by the Scottish ethnologist, John Ferguson McLennan, "The Worship of Plants and Animals."[151] McLennan intended his model to be "an hypothesis only, in the hope that it may be tested by others better qualified for such investigations."[152] He proposed that "Men first worshipped plants; next the heavenly bodies, supposed to be animals."[153] Drawing his evidence from American Indians and Australian Aborigines,[154] he described the relationship of a man and his totem, which was his protector, kindred within a system of matrilineal exogamy, and taboo as food.[155] "The totem was also used as an ensign by the American Indians."[156]

Totemism survived into the rise of scientific anthropological archaeology and the *Kulturgeschichte* thinkers of the 1920s, beginning with Clark Wissler and continuing through James Griffin in the 1950s. A culture was a list of traits, and one such list could be totemism.[157] It was a sort of language that certain societies, ancient or contemporary, might "speak."[158] Malinowski upheld the importance of dietary taboos corresponding to the totem of a clan, derived from the perceived kinship between clan and totem.[159] I should mention that Near Eastern Archaeologists (other than Henri Frankfort), trained as historians using architectural principles, paid little attention to anthropology in neither the *Kulturgeschichte* years nor in the Functionalism (Radcliffe-Brown, William Ritchie) that followed. The death of totemism in anthropology came from Lévi-Strauss in 1963.[160] Lévi-Strauss argued that the term encompassed at least four distinct structural perceptions of societies, which could not be lumped under a single category. Contrary to the "myth" of totemism, the thought of such societies rests upon a rich and complex conceptual structure.[161] The entire concept of totemism was an artifact of Western thinking imposed by anthropology, a projection of Christian separation of man and nature on societies whose thought patterns still functioned in a mythic, timeless

---

[150] Although the Ojibwa are *not* a good example of totemism; Vecsey 1983, p. 78.
[151] For possible earlier origins of the concept in ethnology, see 2000, p. 130.
[152] McLennan 1869-70, p. 408 n.1.
[153] McLennan 1869-70, p. 407.
[154] McLennan 1869-70, p. 409.
[155] McLennan 1869-70, pp. 414, 417.
[156] McLennan 1869-70, pp. 418.
[157] Pedersen 2001, p. 417.
[158] Cf. Malinowski 1984, p. 514.
[159] Malinowski 1948, pp. 44-47.
[160] Bleakley 2000, p. 131.
[161] Bleakley 2000, p. 135.

mode.¹⁶² As a result, discussion of totemism vanished in the 1960s, 70s, and 80s, and by the time biblical archaeologists discovered anthropology, it was a dead concept.¹⁶³

But beginning in the late 1990s, totemism reappeared in anthropological literature, most importantly in the work of Philippe Descola.¹⁶⁴ New totemism can be seen as analogous to ethnicity. Ethnicity is now understood as communal self-definition, a marked opposition between "we" and "other," having its genesis in historical forces and becoming inscribed in culture and the impetus for concrete actions. So, too, totemism is one historically-specific form of such self-classification, collective identity embodied symbolically in markers of contrast between different social groups.¹⁶⁵ Totemism, unlike ethnicity, emerges with the establishment of *symmetrical* relations between structurally similar social groups (even when there are short-term inequalities between them).¹⁶⁶ Thus, totemic social relations are wholly vertical or hierarchical in nature, as opposed to a horizontal, egalitarian animism, as Descola maintained.¹⁶⁷ The symbolic markers of contrast in totemism are "kinships" or ritual relationships between humans and animals.¹⁶⁸Since difference between species are empirically observable, a man who cannot imagine himself to be like other men notes the sort of animals whose differences from his fellow animals are homologous with those that distinguish the man from his fellow men.¹⁶⁹ Occasionally, non-animals, especially plants, function similarly.

The Iban of Borneo have *manang*, who are healers of the body and spirit, never dangerous sorcerers.¹⁷⁰ They are best considered shamans.¹⁷¹ Their business is to combat the spirits that move at night afflicting people, invisible to ordinary individuals,¹⁷² and to retrieve their patients' "lost souls" that have strayed away from the body.¹⁷³ Each Iban shaman has a unique spirit helper with an animal name, distinct from the totem

---

[162] Bleakley 2000, p. 135.
[163] Pedersen 2001, p. 417.
[164] Willerslev and Ulturgasheva 2012, p. 48.
[165] Comaroff 1987, pp. 302-304.
[166] Comaroff 1987, p. 307.
[167] Willersley and Ulturgasheva 2012, pp. 49-50; Pedersen 2011, p. 412.
[168] Bleakley 200, p. 134.
[169] Pedersen 2011, p. 420.
[170] Graham 1987, p. 47.
[171] Graham 1987, p. 11.
[172] Graham 1987, p. 35.
[173] Graham 1987, p. 37; Freeman 1967, p. 316.

of whatever clan the shaman has come from, for Iban shamanism is not hereditary.[174] Moreover, shamanism is not an exclusive vocation in Iban society.[175]

Munda of west-central India have similar shamanism; it is an achieved vocation rather than an inherited ability.[176] The Munda, too, believe in the "stray soul" phenomenon,[177] and – at least among the Birhor, a hunter-gatherer subgroup of the Munda,[178] each shaman also has his spirit-animal.[179]

With the Kpelle of Liberia, the *Zo* medicine men constitute a distinct sodality. As with the Iban, the Kpelle medicine man can come from any clan. But he then joins one of the medicine societies, which functions as a clan of its own.[180] No medicine is practiced except by the medicine societies.[181] But the medicine societies also become hereditary clans. A man becomes a *Zo* by joining one of the societies, but all male members of the patrilineal families of *Zo* members are also *Zo*.[182] The Kpelle medicine man operates as the Iban does, with spirit helpers and spirit adversaries.[183]

Osage medicine men or *Wakon'dagi* were much more dangerous and feared, as they could harm their enemies.[184] The Sauk (now Sac and Fox) had both kinds – the shaman *Sisa'ki'euk* who with animal-spirit helpers combated spirits to heal the sick, and other doctors who could harm one with magic.[185]

The practices of these medicine men regularly involve smudging. For the Birhor, incense was used.[186] The Osage smudged with tobacco,[187] spotted water hemlock, and staghorn sumac,[188] while the Fox used old field balsam.[189] We shall return to this below.

---

[174] Graham 1987, p. 129-30.
[175] Sutlive 1988, 103.
[176] Parkin 1992, p. 83.
[177] Parkin 1992, p. 205.
[178] Parkin 1992, pp. 27-28.
[179] Roy 1925, p. 173.
[180] Bellman 2012, p. 40.
[181] Welmers 1949, p. 221.
[182] Bellman 2012, p. 63.
[183] Bellman 2012, p. 66.
[184] La Flesche 2010, p. 112.
[185] Skinner 1923-25, pp. 54-55.
[186] Roy 1925, p. 174.
[187] Burns 1984, p. 44.
[188] Munson 1981, pp. 233, 238.
[189] Moerman 1979, p. 111; Michelson 1928, p. 95.

Masks are likewise an important part of totemism. For the Sepik River/ Murik Lakes people of northern New Guinea, masks, which are used in ceremonies[190] and handed down from generation to generation, have great power; the mask named Gweim was known to have killed many people.[191] The masks have spirits, which can possess people,[192] or can be communicated with to gain assistance.[193] The Kpelle also inherit totemic masks with ritual functions.[194] Masks form one example of "symbolic property." Clans and their individuals have perceived kin or ritual relationships (e.g., protection) to their totems.[195] For perceptions of the past, this might mean the totem had revealed itself to an ancestor of the clan.[196] This may be manifest in descent trees, in personal names, or in symbolic property held by the clan. For practices of the present, individuals may observe sacred or aesthetic attitudes to the totem animal. Masks bridge both categories, as symbolic property employed in present practices.

Symbolic property is particularly important with Sac and Fox totemism. Fox sacred bundles are owned collectively by the members of a clan.[197] The cloth-bound bundles are handed down from generation to generation, and specific ceremonies belong to each bundle.[198] Moreover, the bundles were laden with power even outside of the rituals.[199] The contents of such bundles, indecorously purchased and ripped open by early 20th-century ethnologists, include small figurines – animal and anthropomorphic – along with jewelry, feather, and fabric.[200] Sepik and Birhor symbolic property includes stones or carved objects that are small enough to be carried around.[201]

Let me return to the small figurines of early Israel. One horse bust from Bethel Phase 1 was found in Room 308 along with a bone pendant with many holes (#1051), a yellow bead (#1070), a carnelian bead (#1076), and a red stone scarab (#1073).[202] The "Astarte Plaque" plaque from Bethel (#104 from Sub6) was found with a carnelian bead #116

[190] Craig 2010, p. 125; Lipset 1997, pp. 135-37.
[191] Craig 1997, pp. 211-12.
[192] Höltker 1975, p. 34.
[193] Höltker 1975, p. 49.
[194] Bellman 1980, p. 61.
[195] Awuah-Nyamekye 2012, p. 5.
[196] Awuah-Nyamekye 2012, p. 5.
[197] Michelson 1930, p. 145.
[198] Michelson 1928, p. 1; Bonvillain 1995, p.24.
[199] As seen in the legends recounted in Jones (1907).
[200] Harrington 1914, pp. 227, 232, 239, pl. 40.
[201] Roy 1925, p. 45.
[202] Albright and Kelso 1968, p. 63 65.

Pittsburgh Theological Seminary #2-0019). These are not random curios. The nearest source of carnelian was the Nubian Desert west of Lake Nasser or from Yemen, but most of the carnelian in antiquity came from western India.[203] The jackal from Ai was found inside the incense burner with a carnelian-and-glass beaded necklace,[204] and next to the burner was the bovine figurine.[205] At Tell Dothan, Level 6, in Area A, the Astarte plaque was found together with a feathered bone wand, a small copper chain, and a carved lion head.[206] Substances like carnelian, only obtained from journeying to the geographical limits of the known world or by exchange with peoples who did so, often have the power to heal or bring fortune in shamanistic societies.[207]

The small figurines of the Iron I highlands were nearly all found either in groups or in mini-hordes with other precious objects. Might we be looking at symbolic property, even sacred bundles?

The flying-man lamp from Dothan is particularly interesting. It is an imitation of a giant clam. Both Maxima Clam (*Tridacna maxima*) and Fluted Giant Clam (*Tridacna squamosal*) are found in the Red Sea. There are no similar species in the Mediterranean. Regardless of whether the inhabitants of Dothan knew where the shell was really found, they had attempted to invoke a far distant land, even a "World Rim," commonly the place where supernatural entities reside. The lamp design itself would have been a statement of shamanic power given that it was modeled after a creature found far outside the boundaries of the Israelite world.[208]

But this is not just a clam shell, it is a flying man. The man is somewhat hidden until the lamp is manipulated in just the right way.[209] If the lamp's underside itself is meant to suggest wings attached to the man's arms, then it is a hybrid creature similar to those of the shamanic Hopewell.[210] The being is flying, like the bird costumes worn by Siberian shamans to travel to the sky world.[211]

Finally, let us turn back to the sacred spaces of early Israel. Recall the sort of "kiva" at Ai and the larger temple at Tirzah. The Mount Ebal altar

---

[203] Insoll and Bhan 2001, p. 495; De Waele and Haerinck 2006, pp. 31-32, 38; Mackay 1933, pp. 143-46.
[204] Gilmour 1995, pp. 172.
[205] Gilmour 1995, pp. 172-73.
[206] Free 1956, pp. 15-16.
[207] Romain 2011, p. 161.
[208] Cf. Romain 2011, p. 51.
[209] Cf. Hopewell examples; Romain 2011, p. 122.
[210] Romain 2011, p. 133.
[211] Romain 2011, p. 194.

is oriented to the compass points. Such cardinal orientation serves to anchor the quadrants of the world whose origin is in the human body and perception, using the sun as a reference point.[212] "Orthogonal pairs of points establish a quadripartite universe, with north-south and east-west situated at right angles to each other. In this system, the east-west line of the sun's rising and setting at the equinoxes is crossed by an orthogonal north-south line, thereby forming a cross – often used as a symbol for the world's four quarters."[213] The large plaza around the altar, then, could have been used like Woodland earthworks for world renewal ceremonies.[214]

SHAMANISM, TOTEMISM, AND THE OLD TESTAMENT

None of this really contradicts anything in the biblical text. That ancient Israel was polytheistic is hardly questionable any more, but, as one colleague put it, "Does the Bible deny it? – I would have thought the Deuteronomists make rather a point of it." In Gen 31:19, Rachel steals some sacred family objects, small enough to conceal in a saddlebag (Gen 31:34), which Laban calls his "gods" (v 30) and the text calls teraphim. Andrew Davis's recent study has shown these can be neither Hoffner's and Albertz's Hittite *tarpiš* divine images,[215] nor van der Toorn's images of dead ancestors.[216] They need not be "household" objects at all, since only in 1 Samuel 19 are they in a house.[217] They are clearly cultic (Judg 17:5; 18:14, 17-18, 20).[218] Flynn concludes that they are mantic in function,[219] but admits that divination may have been added to their function in later anti-teraphim texts,[220] as divinatory usage is most prominent in passages that denounce teraphim (Ezek 21:26; Zech 10:2; 1 Sam 15:23; 2 Kgs 23:29; Hos 3:4).[221] The teraphim in Judges 17 and 18 and even Hos 3:4 are considered Yahwistic,[222] and Genesis 31 is neutral, if not positive, on Rachel's theft.[223]

---

[212] Romain 2011, p. 89.
[213] Romain 2011, p. 89.
[214] Romain 2011, p. 157.
[215] Cf. Albertz and Schmitt 2012, p. 60.
[216] Flynn 2012, pp. 695-96, 698, 701.
[217] Flynn 2012, p. 701.
[218] Flynn 2012, p. 702.
[219] Flynn 2012, p. 711.
[220] Flynn 2012, p. 703.
[221] Flynn 2012, p. 708; LaRocca-Pitts 2001, p. 64.
[222] Cf. Barton 1894, p. 107.
[223] LaRocca-Pitts 2001, p. 30.

Teraphim often appear with the ephod (Judg 17:5; 18:14-20; Hos 3:4), something regularly connected with divination (1 Sam 2:28; Hos 3:4; the latter reference includes the verb "to whore," as in Judges 8:27).²²⁴ In 1 Samuel 14, however, "the" ephod is carried by the priest and brought with the Israelites into battle during their revolt against the Philistines (1 Sam 14:3). In 1 Sam 14:18, Saul is said to be "the man who carried the ephod in Israel." Saul's ephod is not an instrument of idolatry, and there may be no reason to think Gideon's is not Yahwistic somehow.²²⁵ Abiathar carries the ephod before David in 1 Sam 23:6-9; 30:7, and there is nothing amiss with the ephod in Exodus 28-29 and 39.²²⁶ Now the ephod is some sort of a cloth garment in Exodus 28-29, perhaps related to the refer to a rich and costly garment called an *epattu* in old Assyrian texts from Cappadocia.²²⁷ But the occurrence in 1 Kgs 2:26 of the Ark in Abiathar's hands where one would expect the ephod suggests to van der Toorn a portable shrine.²²⁸ I would consider the teraphim to be sacred bundles as described earlier, or perhaps the contents of those bundles. The bundles range in size from equivalent to Rachel's to as large as Michal's, depending on what was in them. The ephod, too, could be the bundles, essentially portable shrines made of fabric, as the text portrays. Galling, followed by Jaroš, considered the teraphim to be masks, which is also possible.²²⁹

Consider the biblical חברים, spell-casters (Deut 18:11; Isa 47:12; Ps 58:5). Postbiblical Jewish tradition made these out as charmers of animals.²³⁰ Traditionally lexicons understood the root as "binding" (cf. Ezek 1:9; Hos 4:7; 2 Chron 20:36; etc.), implying the magical practice of tying knots.²³¹ More recent scholarship has argued for an Akkadian etymology with the basic meaning of "muttering" (cf. Sirach 12:13; Job 16:4).²³² Jeffers considers both understandings to be operating in the biblical example of Psalm 58, "spell-binder, using his power over words to cast spells and therefore binding or tying people to his power."²³³

---

²²⁴ Sharon 2006, p. 93.
²²⁵ Auzou 1966, p. 248.
²²⁶ Sharon 2006, p. 93.
²²⁷ *CAD* 4: 183; Meyers, 1996.
²²⁸ Van der Toorn 1990, p. 213.
²²⁹ Galling 1977, p. 169; Jaroš 1982, p. 71.
²³⁰ Nigosian 2008, p. 77.
²³¹ Meyer and Donner, *HAT*, 2.190; Nigosian 2008, p. 76.
²³² Clines, CDCH, 107; Jeffers 1996, p. 32.
²³³ Jeffers 1996, p. 35.

A final group worth considering as medicine men is the *keššapim*, or wizards (*BDB*, 506; KB³, 469). The etymology is very uncertain,[234] usually related to Assyrian *kassapu*, indicating malevolent magic.[235] But another possible Arabic etymology suggests shredding or cutting, which alongside the Septuagint replacement of *keššapim* with *pharmakos* suggests a compounder of traditional medicines.[236] In the Ugaritic text from Ras Ibn Hani 78/20, the *KSPM* seem to include both people who use plants and herbs to cure and people who do harm like the Osage and Sauk evil medicine men.[237] Ezek 13:18 is quite clear that Israel shared the notion of the "stray soul" with the Iban and Munda: "Woe to the women who sew magic bands[238] upon all wrists, and make veils for the heads of persons of every stature, in the hunt for souls! Will you hunt down souls belonging to my people and keep your own souls alive?"[239]

However, we need not limit ourselves to "illegitimate religion." We sometimes read things that make it appear that the Old Testament represents the "victor's account," the voice of the small but vocal monolatrous, iconoclastic minority that eventually won out. The text itself, however, is not so uniformly "orthodox," as any reading of Psalm 82 shows.[240] Altars described in the Bible have no such orientation, but the four horns required on each altar, otherwise unexplained, suggest the four corners of the world.[241] The Bible describes liturgical uses for many of the fumigants listed above, including myrrh, styrax (Gen 37:25; 43:11), balm, and labdanum (Exod 30:34-38).[242] We have already seen ephod is not always idolatrous.

What about Elijah, described as a "Lord of Hair," בַּעַל שֵׂעָר, not wearing a garment of haircloth but perhaps himself hairy as a bear,[243] given that Elisha can speak to bears in 2 Kgs 2:24?[244] Grabbe notes that, "The Israelite prophets most resembling the traditional shaman are Elijah and Elisha, who control the weather (1 Kgs 17:1; 18:1, 41-45), make

---

[234] Jeffers 1996, p. 65.
[235] *CAD* 8.292; Jeffers 1996, p. 67.
[236] Jeffers 1996, p 66; cf. Mic 5:11; Jeffers 1996, p. 69.
[237] Jeffers 1996, p. 67. For later equivalents in Arab and Palestinian Jewish societies, see Thompson 1908, p. 105-106 and Josephus, *Ant.* 8.2, 5.
[238] Following Ephrem the Syrian and the Hexapla; BDB 492; Clines, *CDCH*, 181.
[239] Thompson 1908, p. 38. For the concept in 19th-century Syrian folklore, see Thompson 1908, p. 37.
[240] Machinist 2005, pp.155-83.
[241] Carroll and Siler 2002, p. 21.
[242] Carroll and Siler 2002, p. 21-25.
[243] Brown 1981, p. 391; Kapelrud 1967, p. 92.
[244] There is human-bear therianthropy in Neolithic Anatolia; Türkcan 2007, p. 260.

miraculous journeys (1 Kgs 18:46), conjure food from nowhere and heal and raise the dead (1 Kgs 17; 2 Kgs 4), and even recover lost objects (2 Kgs 6:1-7)."²⁴⁵ Elijah is "fed by ravens, well known in the shamanistic world as bearer of magic medicine."²⁴⁶

Elisha, too, parts the Jordan (2 Kgs 2), purifies Jericho's spring with salt (2 Kgs 2:19-22), produces a pool for thirsty troops (2 Kgs 3:12-20), purifies poisoned broth (2 Kgs 4:38-41), which is a skill of Mongolian shamans.²⁴⁷ He also causes an axe head to float in the Jordan (2 Kgs 6:1-7) and has Naaman healed in the Jordan (2 Kgs 5:1-14).²⁴⁸ The bones of Elisha even work miracles after his death, like those of a medicine man (2 Kgs 13:21).²⁴⁹

Both Elijah and Elisha are described as איש אלהים (1 Kgs 17:18, 24; 2 Kgs 1:9-13; 2 Kgs 4:1-9, 38-33; 5:26-27; 6:6-10; 8:7-13; etc.), a title Gangloff renders as "paranormal healer." ²⁵⁰ Elisha has this title more than anyone else in the Bible does. Many of the shamanistic activities of Elijah, and even more so Elisha, are not attributed to God at all, as Dolansky has highlighted.²⁵¹

Theological Implications

What are the implications of this for Biblical Theology? On the one hand, theology should not "tether itself to religiohistorical accounts of ancient Israelite religion. To do so, is to mistake how Scripture has historically functioned within Christian theology."²⁵² We should not theologize on the reconstructed history of Israelite religion as if that reconstruction replaced the biblical text as the soul of theology. Biblical scholars have been regularly guilty of this in the past. The scholar reconstructed what *really* happened, and that was then interpreted theologically.²⁵³ On the other hand, the phenomenon of ancient Israelite monotheism cannot

---

²⁴⁵ Grabbe 2010; Cf. 3 Enoch 48D:10, par. 80 for healing.
²⁴⁶ Arnold 1995, p. 139. For ravens in Siberian shamanism, see Balzer 2006, p. 92. For interpretation of Elijah's Mount Horeb experience as a vision quest, see Friesen 2000, p. 103.
²⁴⁷ Heissig 1990, p. 232.
²⁴⁸ Arnold 1995, pp. 141-42.
²⁴⁹ See Balzer 1996, pp. 305-306; Brown 1981, p. 395.
²⁵⁰ Gangloff 1999, pp. 64, 70.
²⁵¹ Dolansky 2008, pp. 68, 70.
²⁵² MacDonald 2010, p. 1077.
²⁵³ Knapp 1989, pp. 123-24, 128; Billings 2010, p. 60; Smith 2001, p. 31. For an example, see Madigan 2009, pp. 1003-1005.

be analyzed in the abstract but must be seen in the light of actual religio-historical contexts.[254] Christianity itself and its creedal tradition are tied to their accounts of the past and that past includes Israel's history, and that history clearly includes its religion.[255]

Let me begin with the observation that the dichotomies of monotheism/polytheism, aniconism/idolatry are ambiguous in most totemic societies. These societies seem to avoid large-scale iconic worship, large statuary and the like, and also show a monolatrous or henotheistic bent. They are not monotheistic in a Judeo-Christian sense, but they also differ markedly from the polytheistic pantheons of the ancient Near East, India, or the classical world.

Let me begin with the Munda. In their religion, while there are many Bongas, spirits, identified with most natural phenomena,[256] there is only one Singbonga, who is the eternal, omnipotent, loving father of his chosen people, the tribe.[257] Singbonga was mistakenly identified by early anthropologists as the sun, but he is not.[258] Properly, Singbonga is the venerated persona of *Haram*.[259] Some toasts and myths interchange the terms Singbonga and *Haram*,[260] and "Any Sarna Munda will tell us that Singbonga is really *Haram*."[261] Everything *Haram*/Singbonga does is for the well-being of humanity, and all animals serve him.[262] He is the omniscient [*leltani'*] creator [*sobena' baikeni'*] of humans and of the entire world.[263] Only Singbonga is worshipped, without images; the Bongas are begrudgingly appeased or placated.[264] There are no myths about the Bongas.[265]

---

[254] Boshoff 2010; Gnuse 1999, pp. 315-36.
[255] Deist 1981, pp. 24, 28. Of course, "We do not believe in a creed: we believe through a creed"; Vann 1962, p. 5. The two extremes just outlined correspond roughly to what Bernard Lonergan called "Theoretical Bias" and "Commonsense Bias" (1957, pp. 175-76).
[256] Adhikary 1984, p. 63.
[257] Barjo 1997, pp. 46-47; Adhikary 1984, p. 64; Ponette 1978, p. 127. His eternal nature is praised in the *Deoñra Hymn*: "In remotest time, you alone existed" [*Nangnangjugujug ure am eskargem taekena*]; Van Exem 1978, p. 85.
[258] Barjo 1997, p. 46; Van Exem 1978, p. 99; Ponette 1978, p. 122: "Not one of them will ever aver that the sun is his god."
[259] Van Exem 1978, p. 115.
[260] Van Exem 1978, p. 97, 99.
[261] Van Exem 1978, p. 115.
[262] Van Exem 1978, p. 94-95.
[263] Van Exem 1978, pp. 83, 85-86; Ponette 1978, p. 123.
[264] Van Exem 1991, p. 243; Ponette 1978, p. 122, 128; Elst, K. The Sarna: a case study in natural religion http://koenraadelst.bharatvani.org/articles/chr/sarna.html (4 February 2015). Archived by WebCite at http://www.webcitation.org/6W6DCWIn7.
[265] Ponette 1978, p. 122.

There is considerably less information on the situation with the other totemic groups we have been describing, and, in some ways, the Munda may be unique. But the Iban, too, make no images of gods, or even temples.[266] The relationship between the Bongas and the one Singbonga is replicated with the Fox Manitou and Gitche Manitou.[267] The Osage consider their high god to reward good deeds and punish sins in Deuteronomic style, and to have a preferential love for the tribe.[268]

I highlight these elements of shamanistic and totemistic cultures to point out that the contrast between early Israelite religion and Christian faith is not as total as we might imagine. We have seen that the biblical text itself considers various shamanic and totemic practices to be at times legitimate, the ephod and teraphim, for example. Belief in spirits of the kinds described for such societies seems to appear in the Hebrew Bible in places without condemnation – e.g., Shedu (Deut 32:17; Ps 106:36), Satyrs (Lev 17:7), Lilith (Isa 34:14), Sons of Reshef (Job 5:7) – as Yehezkel Kaufmann pointed out long ago.[269]

Where should this leave us in terms of biblical theology, which I define not as elucidation of the theology of the biblical text but as contribution to theology that biblical scholarship can provide? I would like to suggest three areas of importance. First, the incidence of shamanism and totemism in early Israel ought to alert us to "the wisdom embedded in indigenous epistemology."[270] The documents of the Second Vatican Council have attuned Catholic theology to this (*Lumen Gentium* 16, 17; *Gaudium et Spes* 22; etc.).[271] This means the new understandings of early Israelite religion and the Bible's relationship to them would be important to the scholarship of missiology. Such work would be largely, however, of value for appreciation of modern indigenous cultures on their own terms, rather than on broader Christian theological terms,[272] and so of limited relevance for theology as a whole.

So a second area of thought might note that "shamanic power" seems to continue to appear in the later biblical tradition.[273] In Tobit 11:5-7,

---

[266] Roth 1896, p. 185.
[267] Michelson, *Notes*, 30-31; Thomas 2007, p. 56.
[268] Wilson 1928, p. 14.
[269] Kaufmann 1960, p. 64.
[270] Fung 2003, p. 39.
[271] I am not thinking here of any sort of Hicks-ean cultural particularity of truths (or deities) or "all paths lead to God." Cf. Hicks (1977, 1981) and discussion in Gavin d'Costa (1991, pp. 66-69).
[272] Fung 2003, p. 40.
[273] Fung 2003, p. 42.

Raphael instructs Tobit in shamanic healing of Tobias's blindness using a fish's gall. In John 9:1-7 (cf. Mark 8:23), Jesus heals another blind man using mud with his spittle (a practice soon forbidden by *M. Sanh.* 10.1) followed by washing in the Pool of Siloam.[274] Why? Why perform the healings in such ways, and can the answer be linked to the shamanism in Israel's past?

The key here is the principle of incarnation.[275] Christianity, as an incarnational faith, has perpetually struggled against forms of Gnostic dualism, and finds itself today continually challenged by the danger of reduction to a philosophy, a set of beliefs, an ideology on the one hand, and a spirituality, an ethereal internal mysticism on the other. The shamanic gene in the faith ought to recall it to the physical, to the corporal embodiedness of its spirituality.[276] This is certainly important for sacramental theology.[277] But it is not only in the sacraments that God "revealed and continues to reveal the divine – yes, God's very self – through the material of human existence."[278] The "Sacramental imagination," like the shamanic (and totemic), "is always one that embraces and uses the world; it does not take us out of the world."[279] And in the case of shamanism, we can be even more specific. The smudging and other material ceremonies are not *themselves* the means of healing; they are ways of engaging with the spiritual world, the stray souls, and so on. So, too, all those things lumped under the inadequate term of "sacramentals," prominent in Orthodox, Catholic, and Anglican traditions but with a tendency to be created anew in Reformed and Evangelical denominations, as well, are themselves prayers. They are prayers embodied in physicality, rather than in audible sound.[280]

Finally, there is a third area of theology for which early Israelite shamanism is important, following on the other two. Such things as "sacramentals," as opposed to sacraments proper, should serve to emphasize every Christian's "own participation in the priesthood of Christ," and not only that of the clergy.[281] Holding on to that notion for a moment, let us return to early Israel. As we have seen, there ought to be links between

---

[274] See Ernst 1981, p. 229. On the authenticity of at least some form of the narrative, in particular the most shamanic elements, see Brown 1966, pp. 378-79.
[275] Fung 2003, p. 43.
[276] Lustiger 1991, p. 286.
[277] Beginning with Rahner 1963, pp. 37-41; continuing through Irwin 2005.
[278] Irwin 2005, pp. 44-45.
[279] Irwin 2014, p. 92.
[280] Rahner and Vorgrimler 1965, p. 418.
[281] Wojtyla (1980, p. 240) building on *Sacrosanctum Concilium,* (79).

the medicine men as a group and totemic clans; entire clans of medicine men, either merely as sodalities or as sodalities that became hereditary. Deut 23:18 refers to some class of clerics called "Dogs."[282] Yet the obvious candidates here are the Levites. The Levites hold the ritual power for Israel.[283] They are the rightful owners of the ephod in Exodus and Samuel, and of the teraphim in Judges 17-18.[284] But as we also see in Judges 17-18, there is some ambiguity about tribal identity: the Levite in Judg 17:7 is from the tribe of Judah. He sojourns in Ephraim and ends up in Dan.

Gunneweg, Ahlstrom, and Van der Toorn have argued that the Levites were a caste drawn from various tribes.[285] This is what I have called a sodality, where non-kin groups are drawn from existing kinship clans forming their own units within society.[286] This identification of the Levites has been developed in more depth by Hutton and Leuchter.[287] They use anthropological evidence to explain in this way the overlapping and conflicting priestly genealogies, the lists of the Levitical cities in Joshua, and Deut 33:9. However, as we have seen for the Kpelle medicine societies, horizontal distinctions like sodalities may over time become asymmetrical and assume hierarchical relationships vis-à-vis kinship groups.[288] This is exactly what happened to the Levites, if Hutton and Leuchter are right, and I believe they are.

Daniel Shaw has made some interesting observations of the practices of Christians of traditionally shamanic cultures.[289] He notes that these "Christians, using their relationship with God, can accomplish for their kin through prayer what non-Christians accomplish through their interaction with the spirits. The concept of interaction is the same – only the power source has shifted."[290] This is not a matter of carryover of *practices*; it is a continuity of explanation: "contacting the superior power source [to] bypass the lesser beings."[291] The reason for this, moreover,

---

[282] Smith 1894, p. 292.
[283] Cf. Harrison 1990, p. 44.
[284] Cf. Michelson, 1930, p. 145.
[285] Gunneweg , 1965, pp. 38-44, 58; Ahlström 1982, pp. 47-48; van der Toorn 1996, pp. 300-305.
[286] Duffy 2010, p. 47.
[287] Hutton, 2009, pp. 223-34; Hutton 2011, pp. 78-81; Leuchter 2012, pp. 479-500; Leuchter 2013, pp. 24-27.
[288] Duffy 2010, p. 47.
[289] Shaw 1981, pp. 359-65.
[290] Shaw 1981, p. 363.
[291] Shaw 1981, p. 364.

is that because of the "priesthood of all believers," every Christian is a shaman.[292]

That the Levitical priesthood is in many ways now the prerogative of each of the baptized is rooted in Revelation 1, 5, and 20, building on Exodus 19:5-6 extending a priesthood to all of Israel. Rev 1:5-6 uses the concrete plural noun "priests," attributing the priestly dignity to each Christian. 1 Peter 2:1-10 grounds the priesthood of the Christian in the priestly role of Christ (vv 4-5). The rhetorical goal of this priesthood, however, is not access to the heavenly realm or priestly dignity but "Spiritual Sacrifices." In other texts, this phrase refers to things as diverse as charity (Phil 4:18, described in Levitical technical terms in Heb 13:16), evangelism (Rom 15:15-16), martyrdom (Phil 2:17; 2 Tim 4:6), unspecified works (Heb 13:16), praise (Heb 13:15), and uses of the body (Heb 12:1).

If all the baptized participate in the priesthood of Christ, as we have seen (cf. *Presbyterorum Ordinis*, 1; *Lumen Gentium*, 10, 34), and if that priesthood is counterpart to the Levitical priesthood (Heb 3:1-5:10), albeit in many ways *unlike* it (Heb 5:11-10:39), then in the light of new understanding of early Israel might we speak of a "shaman totem of all believers?"[293] This is by far my most speculative foray into the theological implications of early Israelite shamanism, and I leave it at this, awaiting the work of theologians with such "raw material."

The religion of early Israel, the 12th and 11th centuries B.C. or the Early Iron Age, as reconstructed by archaeology, can best be understood under the rubrics of shamanism and totemism. This does not, however, set up a reconstruction wholly at odds with the Hebrew Bible. Moreover, there are shamanic and totemic elements that are not condemned as aberrations. Appreciation of these elements can contribute to theology an openness to indigenous wisdom, an emphasis on incarnational sacramentality, and universal priesthood.

ADHIKARY, A. K.
1984   *Society and World View of the Birhor: A Nomadic Hunting and Gathering Community of Orissa*. Calcutta: Anthropological Survey of India.

AHLSTRÖM, G. W.
1982   *Royal Administration and National Religion in Ancient Palestine*. Leiden: Brill.

---

[292] Shaw 1981, p. 365.
[293] Cf. McPartlan 2008, pp. 274-76.

ALBERTZ, R. and SCHMITT, R.
2012 *Family and Household Religion in Ancient Israel and the Levant*. Winona Lake, Ind: Eisenbrauns.

ALLEN, M. W.
1980 *A Synthetic Reconstruction of the Religion of Iron Age Ai and Raddanah*. Unpublished term paper for Southern Baptist Theological Seminary, Louisville.

ANDERSON, E. S. K.
2012 "Signs in Human Hands: A Model for the Intonated Object," in *Beyond Belief: The Archaeology of Religion and Ritual* (Archaeological papers of the American Anthropological Association 21), edited by Y. M. Rowan, pp. 166-179. Hoboken: Wiley.

ARNOLD, P. M.
1995 *Wildmen, Warriors, and Kings*. New York: Crossroad.

ARTZY, M.
1994 "Incense, camels, and Collared Rim Jars," *Oxford Journal of Archaeology* 13: 121-147.

ASEYEV, I. V.
2006 "Ritual Objects," *Archaeology, Ethnology, and Anthropology of Eurasia* 26: 53-60.

AUZOU, G.
1966 *La Force de L'Esprit*. Paris: Éditions de l'Orante.

AVANZINI, A.
1997 *Profumi d'arabia: Atti del convegno*. Roma: "L'Erma" di Bretschneider.

AWUAH-NYAMEKYE, S.
2012 "Totemism, *Akyeneboa* Plant Ethics," *PAN: Philosophy, Activism, Nature* 9: 5-10.

BALZER, M. M.
1996 "Flights of the Sacred: Symbolism and Theory in Siberian Shamanism," *American Anthropologist* 98: 305-318.
2006 "Sustainable Faith? Reconfiguring Shamanic Healing in Siberia," in *Spiritual Transformation and Healing*, edited by J. Koss-Chioino, P. Hefner, pp. 78-100. Lanham, MD: Roman and Littlefield.

BANTI, G. and CONTINI, R.
1997 "Names of Aromata in Semitic and Cushite Languages," in *Profumi d'Arabia*, edited by A. Avanzini, pp. 169-192. Roma: "L'Erma" di Bretschneider.

BARD, K. A.
1992 "Toward an Interpretation of the role of Ideology in the Evolution of Complex Society in Egypt," *Journal of Anthropological Archaeology* 11: 1-24.

BARJO, Y. P.
1997 "The Religious Life of the Sarna Tribes," *Indian Missiological Review* 19.2: 46-47.

BARTON, G. A.
1894 "Native Israelitish Deities," *Oriental Studies* : 86-115.

BARTON, J. and STAVRAKOPOULOU, F.
2010 *Religious Diversity in Ancient Israel and Judah*. London: T & T Clark.

BELLMAN, B. L.
1980 "Masks, Societies, and Secrecy among the Fala Kpelle," *Ethnologische Zeitschrift* 1: 61-78.
2012 *Village of Curers and Assassins* (Approaches to Semiotics 39). Berlin: de Gruyter.

BILLINGS, J. T.
2010 *The Word of God for the People of God: an entryway to the theological interpretation of Scripture*. Grand Rapids, Mich, W.B. Eerdmans Pub. Co.

BLEAKLEY, A.
2000 *The Animalizing Imagination*. New York: St. Martin's Press.

BONVILLAIN, N. and PORTER, F. W.
1995 *The Sac and Fox*. New York, Chelsea House.

BOSHOFF, W.
2010 "Epigraphic sources and Israelite and Judean religion: Did the Histories of Israelite Religions and the Theologies of the Old Testament converge during the last two decades?" paper presented to the International Organization for the Study of the Old Testament (Helsinki, 2010)

BROWN, J. P.
1981 „The Mediterranean Seer and Shamanism," *Zeitschrift für die Alttestamentliche Wissenschaft* 93: 374-400.

BROWN, R. E.
1966 *John I-XII* . Garden City: Doubleday.

BURNS, L. F.
1984 *Osage Indian Customs and Myths*. Tuscaloosa: University of Alabama Press.

CARPENTER, C. D., O'NEILL, T., PICOT, N., JOHNSON, J. A., ROBICHAUD, G. A., WEBSTER, D., and GRAY, C. A.
2012 "Anti-mycobacterial natural products from the Canadian medicinal plant *Juniperus communis*," *Journal of Ethnopharmacology* 143: 695-700.

CARROLL J. L. and SILER, E. M.
2002 "Let My Prayer Be Set Before Thee: The Burning of Incense in the Temple Cult of Ancient Israel," *Studia Antiqua* 2: 17-32.

CARTER, J. B.
1987 "Masks of Ortheia," *American Journal of Archaeology* 91: 355-383.

CHAMBON, A.
1984 *Tell el-Farah I*. Paris: Editions Recherche sur les Civilisations.

CHARTIER, R.
"Culture as Appropriation," in *Understanding Popular Culture* (New Babylon Studies in Social Sciences 40), edited by S. L. Kaplan, pp. 229-254. Berlin: Mouton.

COMAROFF, J. L.
1987 "Of Totemism and Ethnicity," *Ethnos: Journal of Anthropology* 52:302-304.
COSTA, G. D'
1991 "The New Missionary," *International Bulletin of Missionary Research* 15: 66-69.
CRAIG, B.
2010 "The Masterpieces Exhibition," in *Living Spirits with Fixed Abodes The Masterpieces Exhibition : Papua New Guinea National Museum and Art Gallery,* edited by A. L. Crawford, D. Becker, S. M. Eoe, M. Busse, B. Craig, pp 25-252. Honolulu: University of Hawai'i Press.
CULLEY, E. V.
2008 "Supernatural Metaphors and Belief in the Past: Defining an Archaeology of Religion," in *Belief in the Past: Theoretical Approaches to the Archaeology of Religion,* edited by D. S. Whitley and K. Hays-Gilpin, pp. 67-84. Walnut Creek, CA: Left Coast.
DAVIS, N. Z.
1982 "From 'Popular Religion' to Religious Cultures" in *Reformation Europe,* edited by Ozment, S. E. pp. 312-343. St. Louis: Center for Reformation Research.
DE WAELE, J. A. and HAERINCK, E.
2006 "Etched (carnelian) beads from northeast and southeast Arabia," *Arabian Archaeology and Epigraphy* 17:31-40.
DEIST, F.
1981 "The Problem of History in Old Testament Theology," *Ou-Testamentiese Werkgemeenskap in Suider-Afrika* 24: 23-39.
DEVER, W. G.
1997 "Philology, Theology, and Archaeology," in *Archaeology of Israel* (Journal for the Study of the Old Testament Supplement 237), edited by N. Silberman and D. Small, pp. 290-310. Sheffield: Sheffield Academic Press.
2005 "Archaeology and Ancient Israelite Iconography," in *I Will Speak in Riddles of Ancient Times,* edited by A. Maier and P. de Miroschedji, pp. 461-476. Winona Lake: Eisenbrauns.
DICK, M. B.
2005 "A Neo-Sumerian Ritual Tablet in Philadelphia," *Journal of Near Eastern Studies* 64:271-280.
1999 *Born in Heaven, Made on Earth.* Winona Lake: Eisenbrauns.
DOLANSKY, S.
2008 *Now You See It, Now You Don't: Biblical Perspectives on the Relationship between Magic and Religion.* Winona Lake: Eisenbrauns.
DUBOIS, T. A.
2009 *An Introduction to Shamanism.* Cambridge: Cambridge University Press.
DUFFY, P. R.
2010 *Complexity and Autonomy in Bronze Age Europe.* Unpublished diss. Univerisity of Michigan.

EDSON, G.
2009 *Shamanism*. Jefferson, NC: McFarland & Company.

EMERSON T. E. and PAUKETAT, T. R.
"Historical-processual Archaeology and Culture Making: Unpacking the Southern Cult and Mississippian Religion," in *Belief in the Past: Theoretical Approaches to the Archaeology of Religion*, edited by D. S. Whitley and K. Hays-Gilpin, pp. 1676-188. Walnut Creek, CA: Left Coast.

ERNST, J.
1981 *Das Evangelium nach Markus* (Regensburger Neues Testament). Regensburg: Friedrich Pustet.

FAUST, A.
2005 "Farmsteads in the Foothills of Western Samaria," in *I Will Speak in Riddles of Ancient Times*, edited by A. Maier and P. de Miroschedji, pp. 477-504. Winona Lake: Eisenbrauns.

FINKELSTEIN, I.
1985 *Izbet Sartah* (BAR International Series 299). Oxford: British Archaeological Reports.
1995 "Two Notes on Early Bronze Urbanization and Urbanism," *Tel Aviv* 22: 47-69.

FLETCHER, E.
2001 *Man and Nature: Symbolism of Antlers in the Mesolithic and Neolithic.* Diss., Edinburgh University.

FLYNN, S. W.
2012. "The teraphim in light of Mesopotamian and Egyptian evidence," *Catholic Biblical Quarterly* 74: 694-711.

FOGELIN, L.
2007 "History, Ethnography, and Essentialism," in *The Archaeology of Ritual* (Costen Institute of Archaeology Advanced Seminars 3), edited by E. Kyriakidis, pp. 23-42. Los Angeles: University of California Press.

FREE, J.
1956 "The Fourth Season at Dothan," *Bulletin of the American Schools of Oriental Research* 143: 11-17.

FREEMAN, D.
1967 "Shaman and Incubus," *Psychoanalytic Study of Society* 4: 315-343.

FRIEDMAN, E. J. N.
2001 "Amidst Steppe and Taiga," in *Shamanism in Interdisciplinary Context*, edited by A. Leete and R. Firnhaber, pp. 226-236. Boca Raton: Brown Walker Press.

FRIESEN, J. W.
2000 *Aboriginal Spirituality and Biblical Theology*. Calgary: Detselig.

FUNG, J. M.
2003 "Rethinking Missiology in Relation to Indigenous Peoples' Life-Struggle," *Mission Studies* 20: 29-54.

GALLING, K.
1977 *Biblisches Reallexikon*. Tubingen: Mohr Siebeck.

GANGLOFF, F.
1999 ‚L'homme d'Elohim (nin'MnJ wm)', *Biblische Notizen* 100: 60–70.
GAO, R.
2010 "Pharmacological Effect of Deoxypodophyllotoxin," *Neurotoxology* 6: 680-86
GELB, I. J.
1980 "Comparative Method in the Study of the Society and Economy of the Ancient Near East," *Rocznik Orientalistyczny* 41:32.
GERSHEVITCH, I.
1985 *Cambridge History of Iran: Vol. 2, The Median and Achaemenid Periods*. Cambridge: Cambridge University Press.
GILMOUR, G. H.
1995 *The Archaeology of Cult in the Southern Levant in the Early Iron Age*. Unpublished diss. Oxford University.
GITIN, S.
2002 "The Four-Horned Altar and Sacred Space," in *Sacred Time, Sacred Place*, edited by B. M. Gittlen, pp. 95-123. Winona Lake: Eisenbrauns.
GNOLI, T.
1997 "La Produzione del Balsamo nell'Oasi di Engaddi (Israele)," in *Profumi d'Arabia*, edited by A. Avanzini, pp. 413-430. Roma: "L'Erma" di Bretschneider.
GNUSE, R.
1999 "The emergence of monotheism in ancient Israel: A survey of recent scholarship," *Religion* 29: 315-36.
GOFFER, Z.
1996 *Elsevier's Dictionary of Archaeological Materials and Archaeometry*. Amsterdam: Elsevier.
GRABBE, L.
2010 "Shaman, Preacher, or Spirit Medium? The Israelite Prophet in the Light of Anthropological Models," in *Prophecy and the Prophets in Ancient Israel* (LHBOTS, 531) edited by J. Day, pp. 117-132. New York: T & T Clark.
GRAHAM, P.
1987 *Iban Shamanism*. Canberra: Australian National University.
GUNNEWEG, A. H. G.
1965 *Leviten und Priester* (FRLANT). Gottingen: Vandenhoeck & Ruprecht.
HARAN, M.
1993 "'Incense Altars' – Are They?" in *Biblical archaeology today: proceedings of the Second International Congress on Biblical Archaeology, Jerusalem, June-July 1990*, edited by A. Biram, J. Aviram, and A. Paris-Shadur, pp. 237-247. Jerusalem, Israel Exploration Society.
1995 "Altar-ed States: Incense Theory Goes Up in Smoke," *Bible Review* 11: 30-37, 48.

HARNER, M.
1987 "The Ancient Wisdom in Shamanic Cultures," in *Shamanism*, edited by S. Nicholson, pp. 3-16. Wheaton: Quest Books.

HARRINGTON, M. R.
1914 *Sacred Bundles of the Sac and Fox Indians* (University of Pennsylvania University Museum Anthropological Publications 4.2). Philadelphia: University Museum.

HARRISON, S.
1990 *Stealing people's names: history and politics in a Sepik River cosmology.* Cambridge: Cambridge University Press.

HASTORF, C.
2007 "Archaeological Andean Rituals," in *The Archaeology of Ritual* (Costen Institute of Archaeology Advanced Seminars 3), edited by E. Kyriakidis, pp. 77-107. Los Angeles: University of California Press.

HAWKINS, R. K.
2012 *The Iron Age I Structure on Mt. Ebal.* Winona Lake: Eisenbrauns.

HEISSIG, W.
1990 "New Material on East Mongolian Shamanism," *Asian Folklore Studies* 49:2 pp. 223–233.

HICKS, J.
1981 *An Interpretation of Religion.* London: Macmillan.
1977 *God and the Universe of Faith.* London: Fount.

HÖLD, K. M., SIRISOMA, N. S., IKEDA, T., NARAHASHI, T., CASIDA, J. E.
2000 "Alpha-thujone (the active component of absinthe): gamma-aminobutyric acid type A receptor modulation and metabolic detoxification," *Proceedings of the National Academy of Sciences* 97: 3826–31.

HÖLTKER, G.
1975 *Myths and Legends from Murik Lakes* (French and German Collections of Papua New Guinea Folklore 2). Port Moresby: Institute of Papua New Guinea Studies.

HUTTON, J. M
2009 "The Levitical Diaspora I," in *Exploring the Longue Durée*, edited by J. D. Schloen, pp. 223-34. Winona Lake: Eisenbrauns.
2011 "The Levitical Diaspora II," in *Levites and Priests in Biblical History and Tradition*, edited by J. M. Hutton and M. Leuchter, pp. 78-81. Atlanta: SBL.

HUWEZ, F. U., THIRWELL, D., COCKAYNE, A., and ALA'ALDEEN, D. A.
1946 "Mastic Gum Kills Helicobacter pylori," *New England Journal of Medicine* 26:339.

ILUZ, D., HOFFMAN, M., GILBOA-GARBER, N., and AMAR, Z.
2010 "Medicinal Properties of *Commiphora gileadensis*," *African Journal of Pharmacy and Pharmacology* 4: 516.

INSOLL, T. and BHAN, K.
2001 "Carnelian Mines in Gujarat," *Antiquity* 75: 495.

IVANOV, V. V.
1999 "Comparative Notes on Hurro-Urartian, Northern Caucasian and Indo-European" in *UCLA Indo-European Studies 1*, edited by V. V. Ivanov and B. Vine, pp. 161-213. Los Angeles: University of California.

JAROŠ, K.
1982 *Die Stellung des Elohisten zur Kanaanäischen Religion* (OBO 4). Freiburg: Universitätsverlag.

JEFFERS, A.
1996 *Magic and Divination in Ancient Palestine and Syria* (Studies in the History and Culture of the Ancient Near East 8). Leiden: Brill.

JONES, W.
1907 *Fox Texts*. Leiden: E. J. Brill.

JUERGENS, U. R., STÖBER, M., and VETTER, H.
1998 "Inhibition of Cytokine Production and Arachidonic Acid Metabolism by Eucalyptol (1.8-Cineole) in Human Blood Monocytes in vitro." *European Journal of Medical Research* 3: 508–510.

KAPELRUD, A. S.
"Shamanistic Features in the Old Testament," in *Studies in Shamanism*, edited by C.-M. Edsman, pp. 90-96. Uppsala: Almqvist & Wiksell.

KAUFMANN, Y.
1960 *Religion of Israel*. Chicago: University of Chicago Press.

IRWIN, K. W.
2005 *Models of the Eucharist*. New York: Paulist.
2014 *What we have done and what we have failed to do?* New York: Paulist.

KING, S.
1987 "The Way of the Adventurer," in *Shamanism*, edited by S. Nicholson, pp. 189-203. Wheaton: Quest Books.

KLETTER, R.
2006 "Can a Proto-Israelite Please Stand Up?" in *I Will Speak in Riddles of Ancient Times*, edited by A. M. Maier and P. de Miroschedji, pp. 573-586. Winona Lake: Eisenbrauns.
2007 "To Cast an Image," in *Up to the Gates of Ekron*, edited by S. W. Crawford, A. Ben-Tor, and S. Gitin, pp. 189-207. Jerusalem: Albright Institute for Archaeological Research.

KLETTER, R. and IRIT ZIFFER,
2010 "Incense-Burning Rituals," *Israel Exploration Journal* 60:166-87.

KNAPP, S.
1989 "Collective Memory and the Actual Past," *Representations* 26: 123-24, 128.

KYRIAKIDIS, E.
2007 "Finding Ritual: Calibrating the Evidence," in *The Archaeology of Ritual* (Costen Institute of Archaeology Advanced Seminars 3), edited by E. Kyriakidis, pp. 9-22. Los Angeles: University of California Press.

LA FLESCHE, F.
2010 *Traditions of the Osage*. Albuquerque: University of New Mexico Press.

LaRocca-Pitts, E.
2001 "Of Wood and Stone": The Significance of Israelite Cultic Items in the Bible and its Early Interpreters (HSM 61). Winona Lake: Eisenbrauns.

Ledford, C. R.
2012 "Pawnee Ethnic Botany Plant Listing," *Oklahoma Native Plant Record* 12: 35.

Leuchter, M.
2012 "The Fightin' Mushites," *Vetus Testamentum* 62: 479-500.
2013 *Samuel and the Shaping of Tradition*. Oxford: Oxford University Press.

Lewis-Williams, J. D.
1991 "Wrestling with Analogy," *Proceedings of the Prehistoric Society* 57: 149-162.

Lipset, D.
1997 *Mangrove Man: Dialogics of Culture in the Sepik Estuary* (Cambridge Studies in Social and Cultural Anthropology 106). Cambridge: Cambridge University Press.

Liverani, M.
2005 *Israel's History and the History of Israel* (BibleWorld 8). London: Equinox Books.

Lonergan, B.
1957 *Insight: A Study of Human Understanding*. New York: Longmans, Green & Co.

Lustiger, J. M., Missika, J. L. and Wolton, D.
1991 *Choosing God, Chosen by God: Conversations with Jean-Marie Lustiger*. San Francisco: Ignatius Press.

MacDonald, N.
2010 "Response to "A defense of monotheism" by Patrick Madigan," *Heythrop Journal* 51: 1075-1077.

Machinist, P.
2005 "Once More: Monotheism in Biblical Israel," *Journal of the Interdisciplinary Study of Monotheistic Religions* 1: 155-83.

Mackay, E.
1933 "Decorated Carnelian Beads," *Man* 33: 143-46.

Madigan, P.
2009 "A Defense of Monotheism," *Heythrop Journal* 50: 1003-1005.

Malinowski, B.
1948 *Magic, Science and Religion and Other Essays*. Glencoe, Illinois: The Free Press.
1984 *Argonauts of the Western Pacific*. Long Grove, IL: Waveland. Original edition, London: Routledge, 1922.

Malone, C.
2007 "Ritual, Space and Structure," in *Cult and Context*, edited by D. A. Barrowclough and C. Malone, pp. 23-34. Oxford: Oxbow Books.

MANDELBAUM, D. G.
1970 "Supernatural Curing," paper presented at the annual meeting of the American Anthropological Association. Papers of John T. Hitchcock, Smithsonian Institution National Anthropological Archives.

MARCUS, J.
2007 "Rethinking Ritual," in *The Archaeology of Ritual* (Costen Institute of Archaeology Advanced Seminars 3) edited by E. Kyriakidis, pp. 43-76. Los Angeles: University of California Press.

MARQUET-KRAUSE, J.
1935 "La Deuxième Campagne de Fouilles à Ay," *Syria* 16: 340.

MAZAR, A.
1982 "Bull Site," *Bulletin of the American Schools of Oriental Research* 247: 27-42.
1982 "Cultic Sites from the Period of the Judges in the Northern Samarian Hills," *Eretz Israel* 16: 135-45.
1997 "Appointees' Evening with Guest Scholar," Albright Institute for Archaeological Research, Jerusalem.

MCCAMPBELL, H.
2002 *Sacred Smoke*. Summertown, TN: Native Voices.

MCCAULEY, R. N., LAWSON, E. T.
2007 "Cognition, Religious Ritual, and Archaeology," in *The Archaeology of Ritual* (Costen Institute of Archaeology Advanced Seminars 3) edited by E. Kyriakidis, pp. 209-254. Los Angeles: University of California Press.

MCLENNAN, J. F.
1869-70 "Worship of Plants and Animals," *Fortnightly Review* 6-7:194-216

MCPARTLAN, P.
2008 "Who is the Church?" *Ecclesiology* 4: 274-76.

MEIER, G.
1937 *Die Assyrische Beschwörungsamblung Maqlu* (AfO Beiheft 2). Edited and translated by R. S. Caldwell and M.-H. Hoffmann. Berlin: n.p.

MEYERS, C.
1996 "Ephod (Object)", in *The Anchor Yale Bible Dictionary*, edited by D. N. Freedman, 2:550. New York: Doubleday.

MICHELSON, T.
1930 *Contributions to Fox Ethnology – II* (Smithsonian Institution Bureau of American Ethnology Bulletin 95). Washington, DC: Government Printing Office.
1928 *Notes on the Buffalo-Head Dance of the Thunder Gens of the Fox Indians* (Smithsonian Institution Bureau of American Ethnology Bulletin 87). Washington, DC: Government Printing Office.

MILLER, R. D. II
2011 "Shamanism in Early Israel," *Wiener Zeitschrift für die Kunde des Morgenlandes* 101: 309-42.
2004 "Identifying Earliest Israel," *Bulletin of the American Schools of Oriental Research* 333: 55-68.

2003 "Modeling the Farm in Early Iron Age Israel," in *Life and Culture in the Ancient Near East,* edited by R. E. Averbeck, M. W. Chavalas, and D. B. Weisberg, pp. 289-310. Bethesda, MD: CDL Press.

MOERMAN, D. E.
1979 "Symbols and Selectivity: A Statistical Analysis of Native American Medical Ethnobotany," *Journal of Ethnopharmacology* 1: 111.

MOHAGHEGHZADEH, A., P. FARIDI, and Y. GHASEMI,
2010 "Analysis of Mount Atlas Mastic Smoke," *Fitoterapia* 81: 577-80.

MULLIN, J., LEE, L., HERTWIG, S., and SILVERTHORN, G.
2001 "Native Smudging Ceremony," *Canadian Nurse* 97.9: 20-22.

MUNSON, P. J.
"Contributions to Osage and Lakota Ethnobotany," *Plains Anthropologist* 26 (1981): 233, 238.

NIELSEN, K.
1986 *Incense in Ancient Israel* (VTSup 38). Leiden: E. J. Brill.

NIGOSIAN, S.
2008 *Magic and Divination in the Old Testament.* Brighton: Sussex Academic Press.

NUNN, A.
2006 *Alltag im Alten Orient.* Mainz: Philipp von Zabern.

O'SHEA, J. M.
1984 *Mortuary Variability.* New York: Academic.

OSBORN, D. J.
1968 "Notes on medicinal and other uses of plants in Egypt," *Economic Botany* 22: 165-77.

PAKMAN, D.
2003 "'Mask-like' Face Reliefs on a Painted Stand from the Sacred Precinct at Tel Dan," *Eretz Israel* 27: 196-203.

PARASCHOS, S., MAGIATIS, P. and MITAKOU, S.
2006 "In vitro and in vivo activities of Chios mastic gum extracts and constituents against Helicobacter pylori," *Antimicrobial Agents and Chemotherapy* 51: 551-59.

PARDEE, D.
2002 *Ritual and Cult at Ugarit* (Writings from the Ancient World 10). Atlanta: Society of Biblical Literature.

PARKIN, R.
1992 *The Munda of Central India.* Delhi: Oxford University Press.

PEDERSEN, M. A.
2001 "Totemism, Animism, and North Asian Indigenous Ontologies," *Journal of the Royal Anthropological Institute* 7: 417.

PENNACCHIO, M., JEFFERSON, L., and HAVENS, K.
2010 *Uses and Abuses of Plant-Derived Smoke.* Oxford: Oxford University Press.

PFLÜG, M. A.
1996 "'Pimadaziwin': Contemporary Rituals in Odawa Community," *American Indian Quarterly* 20:489-513.

PINCH, G.
1995 *Magic in Ancient Egypt*. Austin: University of Texas Press.

PIOMELLI, D.
1995 "Arachidonic Acid," in *Psychopharmacology: The Fifth Generation of Progress*, ed. F. E. Bloom and D. J. Kupfer. New York: Raven Press.

PIRANI, A., MOAZZENI, H., MIRINEJAD, S., NAGHIBI, F. and MOSADDEGH, M.
2011 "Ethnobotany of *Juniperus excela* M. Bieb. (Cupressaceae) in Iran," *Ethnobotany Journal* 9: 339-40.

POLANYI, L.
1981 "What Stories can Tell Us About Their Teller's World," *Poetics Today* 2: 97-112.

PONETTE, P.
1978 "The Ethics of the Mundas," in *The Munda World*, edited by P. Ponette, pp.116-134. Ranchi: Catholic Press.

PORTMAN, T. A. A. and GARRETT, M. T.
2006 "Native American Healing Traditions," *International Journal of Disability, Development, and Education* 53: 453-469.

PROCHASKA, J. J. DAS, S. and BENOWITZ, N. L.
2013 "Cytisine, the world's oldest smoking cessation aid," *British Medical Journal* 347: 5198.

PÜRÈV, O., and PÜRVËË G.
2004 *Mongolian Shamanism*. Ulaanbaatar: Admon.

QUÉZEL, P.
1981 "The Study of Plant Groupings in the Countries Surrounding the Mediterranean," in *Mediterranean-Type Shrublands* (Ecosystems of the World 11), edited by F. di Castri, D. W. Goodall, and R. L. Specht, pp. 87-93. Amsterdam: Elsevier.

RAHNER, K.
1963 *The Church and the Sacraments* (Quaestiones Disputatae 9); New York: Herder and Herder.

RAHNER, K. and VORGRIMLER, H., EDS.
1965 *Theological Dictionary*. New York: Herder and Herder.

RAPPOPORT, R. A.
1999 *Ritual and Religion in the Making of Humanity*. Cambridge: Cambridge University Press.

REICHERT, A.
1977 "Kultmaske," in *Biblisches Reallexikon* (BRL 2), edited by K. Galling, p. 195-196. Tubingen: J. C. B. Mohr.

RENFREW, C.
1994 "Archaeology of Religion," in *The Ancient Mind*, edited by C. Renfrew and E. B. W. Zubrow, pp. 47-54. Cambridge: Cambridge University Press.

ROMAIN, W. F.
2011 *Shamans of the Lost World: A Cognitive Approach to the Prehistoric Religion of the Ohio Hopewell.* Lanham, MD: AltaMira.

ROTH, H. L.
1896 *The Natives of Sarawak.* London: Praetorius.

ROY, R. B. S. C.
1925 *The Birhors.* Ranchi : G.E.L. Mission Press.

RUSSO, E. B.
2011 "Taming THC," *British Journal of Pharmacology* 163: 1344–64.

SCHMIDT, B. B.
2013 "The Social Matrix of Early Judean Magic and Divination," in *Beyond Hatti*, edited by B. J. Collins and P. Michalowski, pp. 279-93. Atlanta: Lockwood.

SHARON, D. M.
2006 "Echoes of Gideon's Ephod," *Journal of the Ancient Near Eastern Society* 30: 89-102.

SHAW, R. D.
1981 "Every Person a Shaman," *Missiology* 9: 359-65.

SIEGEL, R. K.
1976 "Herbal Intoxication," *Journal of the American Medical Association* 236: 473-76.

SKINNER, A.
1923-25 "Observations of the Ethnography of the Sauk Indians," *Bulletin of the Public Museum of the City of Milwaukee* 5.1-3: 54-55.

SMITH, M. S.
2001 "Monotheistic Re-Readings of the Biblical God," *Religious Studies Review* 27: 25-31.

SMITH, W. R.
1894 *Lectures on the religion of the Semites.* London, A. & C. Black.

STAGER, L.
1999 "Fortress- Temple at Shechem and the 'House of El, Lord of the Covenant,'" in *Realia Dei*, edited by P. H. Williams, Jr., and T. Hiebert, pp. 228-249. Atlanta: Scholars Press.

STOERCK, A.
1762 *A Second Essay on the Medicinal Nature of Hemlock, etc.* London: J. Nourse.

SUTLIVE, V. H. JR.
1988 *The Iban of Sarawak.* Long Grove, IL: Waveland.

THOMAS, R. M.
2007 *Manitou and God.* Santa Barbara: Greenwood.

THOMPSON, R. C.
1908 *Semitic magic, its origins and development.* London, Luzac & Co.

THOMSEN, M. L.
2001 "Witchcraft and Magic in Ancient Mesopotamia," in *Biblical and Pagan Societies* (Witchcraft and Magic in Europe 1), edited by B. Ankarloo and S. Clark, pp. 1-91. Philadelphia: University of Pennsylvania Press.

THOMSEN, P.
1936/7 "Ai (et-Tell), *Archiv für Orientforschung* 11: 95.

TOORN, K. V. D.,
1990 "The Nature of Biblical Teraphim in the Light of Cuneiform Evidence," in *Catholic Biblical Quarterly* 52:203- 222.
1996 *Family religion in Babylonia, Syria, and Israel: continuity and changes in the forms of religious life.* Leiden, E.J. Brill.

TÜRKCAN, A. U.
2007 "Is it a goddess or a bear?" *Documenta Praehistorica* 34: 260.

VAN BINSBERGEN, W. and WIGGERMANN, F.
1999 "Magic in History," expanded version of "Magic in History" in *Mesopotamian Magic*, ed. T. Abusch and K. van der Toorn (Groningen: Styx, 1999). http://www.shikanda.net/ancient_models/gen3/magic.htm (4 February 2015). Archived by WebCite at http://www.webcitation.org/6W6DHXjze.

VAN EXEM, A.
1978 "Haṛam and Singbonga," in *The Munda World*, edited by P. Ponette, pp. 81-115. Ranchi: Catholic Press.
1991 "The Gospel to the Sarna Tribal," *Bible Bhashyam* 17: 243.

VAN ZEIST, W.
1985 "Past and Present Environments of the Jordan Valley," *Studies in the History and Archaeology of Jordan* 2: 203.

VANN, G.
1962 *Myth, Symbol, and Revelation.* Washington: The Thomist Press.

VAUX, R. DE.
1957 "Les fouilles de Tell el Farah, près Naplouse, Sixième Campagne," *Revue Biblique* 64: 552-80

VECSEY, C.
1983 *Traditional Ojibwa Religion.* Philadelphia: American Philosophical Society.

WELMERS, W. E.
1949 "Secret Medicines, Magic, and Rites of the Kpelle Tribe in Liberia," *Southwestern Journal of Anthropology* 5: 208-243.

WHEELER, J., COPPOCK, B., and CHEN, C.
2009 "Does the burning of moxa (*Artemisia vulgaris*) in Traditional Chinese Medicine constitute a health hazard?" *Acupuncture Medicine* 27: 16-20.

WHITLEY, D. S.
2008 "Cognition, Emotion, and Belief: First Steps in an Archaeology of Religion," in *Belief in the Past: Theoretical Approaches to the Archaeology of Religion*, edited by D. S. Whitley and K. Hays-Gilpin, pp. 85-103. Walnut Creek, CA: Left Coast.

WHITLEY, D. S., HAYS-GILPIN, K.
2008 "Religion Beyond Icon, Burial and Monument," in *Belief in the Past: Theoretical Approaches to the Archaeology of Religion*, edited by D. S. Whitley and K. Hays-Gilpin, pp. 85-103. Walnut Creek, CA: Left Coast.

WILLERSLEV, R. AND ULTURGASHEVA, O.
2012 "Revisiting the Animism versus Totemism Debate," in *Animism in Rainforest and Tundra*, ed. M. Brightman, V. E. Grotti, and O. Ulturgasheva, pp. 48-68. New York: Berghahn.

WILSON, L. E.
1928 "Old Osage Religion is Similar to Ancient Jewish Faith," *The American Indian* 3: 14.

WOJTYLA, K. (JOHN PAUL II)
1980 *Sources of Renewal*. San Francisco: Harper & Row.

ZERTAL, A.
1996 *Manasseh Hill Country Survey*, vol. 2. Haifa: University.

ZEVIT, Z.
2001 *The Religions of Ancient Israel*. London: Continuum.

ZHAO, B., LITSCHER, G., LI, J., WANT, L., CUI, Y., HUANG, C., LIU, P.
2011 "Effects of Moxa (*Artemisia vulgaris*) Smoke Inhalation on Heart Rate and Its Variability," *Chinese Medicine* 2: 53-57.

ZUBROW, E. B. W.
1994 "Cognitive Archaeology Reconsidered," in *Ancient Mind*, ed. Colin Renfrew and E. B. W. Zubrow, 187-190. Cambridge: University.

ZWICKEL, W.
1994 *Tempelkult in Kanaan und Israel*. Tubingen: J. C. B. Mohr.

WHAT WOULD (OR SHOULD) OLD TESTAMENT THEOLOGY LOOK LIKE IF RECENT RECONSTRUCTIONS OF ISRAELITE RELIGION WERE TRUE?

Brent A. Strawn

"But whatever else it is, the Old Testament is a set of religious texts – a witness to faith. Ultimately, to treat it as anything different is to deny the witness, and what caused the texts to be written."[1]

"Out of experience comes literature, and out of religious experience comes religious literature."[2]

"Historical criticism has long posed a major challenge to people with biblical commitments, and for good reason....[T]he reverse is also the case: the Bible poses a major challenge to people with historical-critical commitments."[3]

THE TASK AT HAND

The initial title for this essay was slightly different: "What Would (or Should) Old Testament Theology Look Like *If Everything They Said about Israelite Religion Were True*?" This title raises an immediate question: who are these "they" who are saying things about Israelite religion? In addition to being *anonymous*, "they" can be rather *ominous* (as in "they are out to get me") and it is, regardless of any threatening overtones, *plural*, which means that whatever "they" are saying is not going to be one thing at all but *several different things*, and that would no doubt also hold true for "their" reconstructions of Israelite religion. Paulist Press has a longstanding and successful series entitled *What Are They Saying About...?* which faces the same problem of the "they," but

---

Author's Note: Thanks to several individuals for their feedback: James K. Mead, Patrick D. Miller, R. W. L. Moberly, and J. J. M. Roberts.
[1] Rogerson 2010, p. 195.
[2] Smith 2007, p. 5.
[3] Levenson 1993, p. 126.

at least those treatments are book-length. Given the limitations of space afforded me here, far greater selectivity is in order. "They" is too high a mark to achieve and so I altered the earlier title.

Selectivity means that difficult decisions must be made in any overview of reconstructions of Israelite religion and their bearing on Old Testament Theology.[4] And, despite the crucial caveat that whoever "they" are would no doubt *dis*agree, it is also the case that there is occasionally something called "scholarly consensus," though that is always a moving target and subject to constant revision and (re)construction. There is also such a thing, or rather *things*, as "leading lights" – *persons*, in fact, who are crucial in shaping such consensus. In what follows, then, I take a fascinating essay written by Karel van der Toorn as generally illustrative if not also representative of recent scholarly reconstructions of Israelite religion.[5] While my focus on this one essay is somewhat arbitrary, van der Toorn is without doubt a leading scholar in the field, having written a series of brilliant studies on the religion of ancient Israel and the Near East, as well as on the composition of the Hebrew Bible.[6] Furthermore, this particular essay, in addition to being a highly imaginative and engaging piece, is also, by van der Toorn's own account, "informed by a tiresome amount of reading."[7] Even so, while I take van der Toorn's work as representative and illustrative, one must not forget that he is just one of the "they" who say many different things about Israelite religion and who reconstruct it in various ways.

In what follows, then, I will first summarize van der Toorn's essay before asking what (an) Old Testament Theology would (or should) look like if a reconstruction like his were accurate. In order to round out that answer – or more properly, the lingering questions – I next contemplate how Job (or even a reconstructed *Job) fits into a reconstructed *Israelite religion(s).[8] A conclusion completes the study.

To anticipate my argument, I hope to show that reconstructions of Israelite religion are often rather *un(der)*religious if not *non-* or

---

[4] For now I leave the distinctions between "Israelite religion" and "Old Testament Theology" conveniently *un*defined.
[5] Van der Toorn 2003, pp. 393-410.
[6] I mention here only his significant trilogy: Van der Toorn, 1994, 2006, 2007.
[7] Van der Toorn 2003, p. 409. Note his selected bibliography on 409-10.
[8] In this essay asterisk (*) will precede any hypothetical and/or reconstructed text, tradition, or entity, even if I myself remain agnostic about the nature or contents of such reconstructions, their cogency as such, or even their putative existence. This particular use of the asterisk, regardless, is standard in the field especially in redaction-critical studies.

a-religious – and certainly *un(der)*theological – which leaves so much of the Old Testament's religious/theological literature[9] hard to account for, or, if one is to account for it, that must be done by seeing it as the product of a much later, perhaps hostile but certainly elitist takeover, with all that means for a theology written about that literature. Said theology, that is, would presumably also be elitist if not oppressive to boot.[10] And yet, the stubborn existence of the religious literature that is the Old Testament, on the one hand, and the at-least-partially-speculative nature of reconstructions of Israelite religion, on the other, suggests that, in some details (to say the very least), scholarly takes on Israelite religion are not yet definitive – or exhaustive – and therefore Old Testament Theology remains not only viable but crucial, even for the study and reconstruction of ancient Israelite religion. In the end, then, Old Testament Theology contributes to the study and reconstruction of ancient Israelite religion, even as it retains something of an (semi-)independent status insofar as it is not necessarily beholden to the latter.

What Are "They" Saying About Israelite Religion?
van der Toorn's Imaginative Ethnography

As already noted, it is impossible to summarize what "they" are saying about Israelite religion(s), how "they" are reconstructing it (or, better, *them*),[11] for two primary reasons: first, there is no clear delimitation of who "they" are; and, second, what "they" say, how they reconstruct, is too diverse to homogenize. So not only does space prohibit a full treatment here, so does the very (complex) nature of the researchers and their work. Even so, Karel van der Toorn's 2003 essay, "Nine Months among the Peasants in the Palestinian Highlands: An Anthropological

---

[9] Here too I prefer to leave the niceties of distinguishing between religion and theology to others. I admit to using them somewhat exchangeably in what follows, though I am also comfortable with conceding the point that, in biblical studies at least (this is not always the case in ancient Near Eastern studies, especially Egyptology), "theology" is reserved for higher, second-order reflection that can (but need not) be marked by more comprehensive scope and coverage (incluing, at times, a systematizing tendency). I am also quite happy with a more narrow and etymological definition of "theology" – namely, discourse about God and/or the gods.

[10] Dever (2005) comes to mind at this point, and for more than one reason. See the insightful critique of this kind of position in Johnson (1998, pp. 25-26).

[11] The plural form is becoming increasingly commonplace. Note, e.g., the titles to two recent Israelite religions: Zevit (2001) and Hess (2007).

Perspective on Local Religion in the Early Iron Age," is a useful example of recent scholarly reconstructions of Israelite religion for at least three reasons: (1) It is authored by an expert, (2) depends on extensive research, and (3) is intentionally synthetic. Still further, the essay is particularly engaging since it is written as a fictional first person account.[12]

In the essay, van der Toorn recounts something of "a dream report" in which he speculates on "what it would have been like to spend nine months in an early Israelite village in the highlands."[13] While van der Toorn is clear that this is a fictional account (and so also should his readers be), he also indicates that "it attempts to get as close to the historical reality as the data and imagination allow."[14] It is presented as an account of a "scholar-of-religion-turned-anthropologist" who spends nine months "in a hamlet in the central Hill Country, enough to get at least an idea of the inhabitants' customs and beliefs."[15]

As one might expect on the basis of van der Toorn's other publications, the essay places great emphasis on family and ancestor cult. In his dream report, van der Toorn finds himself in the village of Ramat-Yachin, "Hill of Yachin," which is named after an ancient ancestor, Elyachin. Van der Toorn resides with the family of the village chief, who is named Elḥanan, and immediately stresses the importance of Elḥanan's family unit to the (small) society, to agriculture, and to subsistence living. Also in light of van der Toorn's previous work, it is not surprising to find him paying special attention to women's lived experience, and also to how it differed drastically from that of men.[16]

Despite van der Toorn's intention "to get at least an idea of the inhabitants' customs *and beliefs*" and despite the title of the essay, which speaks of "local *religion*," it is actually quite striking to see how much religion is downplayed in his account:

> I was especially eager to follow up on conversation topics that had to do with their beliefs. *Religion was hardly on the minds of these men, however*. They did not even have a word for it. They did hold certain beliefs about the supernatural, but these were rarely discussed.[17]

---

[12] The only thing comparable is the (quite different) account in Michener (1965). (Thanks to R. W. L. Moberly for reminding me of Michener's book.)
[13] Van der Toorn 2003, p. 393; see also van der Toorn 2003, p. 409.
[14] Van der Toorn 2003, p. 393.
[15] Van der Toorn 2003, p. 393.
[16] See, e.g., van der Toorn 2003, 394-95, and *passim*; further, van der Toorn 1994.
[17] Van der Toorn 2003, p. 395 (my emphasis). The "they don't have a word for x" is a common but ultimately fallacious argument, and is a problem for translation more than it is conceptualization. Ancient Israelites didn't have a word for "poetry" either, but

Van der Toorn repeats this sentiment on more than one occasion. Religion just wasn't very important at Ramat-Yachin, and it certainly wasn't a topic of frequent discussion. Even so, van der Toorn continues,

> [t]here was a common, mostly tacit, understanding that the land they lived on was made and governed by El, a word that simply means "god" but was used as a proper name. *This belief elicited little enthusiasm from my hosts, much less devotion.* The deity they most frequently referred to was Baal, held to be responsible for the growth of the crops and the fertility of the cattle. Baal means "lord," and at first I took it as an epithet of El. The villagers located both of them in the sky, or said they lived on a mountain in the north; when asked about the shape of these gods, they came up with contradictory information: some said they looked like giants, others said they were heavenly bulls. The two seemed indistinguishable, but it turned out that El and Baal were really two separate gods. Baal was the lord, and more particularly, the lord of the village; El was a dim deity by comparison.[18]

This is a fascinating paragraph – a synthesis of a gaggle of controversial points – but, for purposes of the present article, the real bombshell is when van der Toorn writes, almost in passing, "A god named 'Yahweh' was unknown to the villagers, although a visiting divine once mentioned him as the deity worshiped in some settlements to the south."[19] And that's all we hear of Yahweh in the balance of the article and the rest of the nine months spent in Ramat-Yachin: just one mention of Yahweh worship, limited to southern climes, and even there only found in a few ("some") villages!

There are other religious factoids that van der Toorn details: for example, the villagers had images – both of Baal and of their ancestors – and one could pray to such images but one didn't have to do so since "Baal could also hear you from the sky."[20] "In general," however, "the men were not forthcoming with details on their religion." While they admitted that the sun and moon were gods ("everybody knew that"), the villagers

---

they clearly had the art form. Indeed, it more accurate to say that they had *words* for poetry (e.g., שיר in Ps 129:1; or מעשה in Ps 45:1); they just weren't the same as the word "poetry." So also with "religion." Why wouldn't עבודה suffice, or, to take a clue from later rabbinics, הלכה? Other possibilities include various derivatives of שבע, שבד, and ירא. (On the latter root, see, e.g., Moberly [2013, p. 245] and Strawn [2014, pp. 91-134]); Note also Smith (1998, p. 269) who writes, "'Religion' is not a native category. It is not a first person term of self-characterization. It is a category imposed from the ouside on some aspect of native culture" (see also Smith 1998, pp. 281-82). In this perspective, no native language (or culture) has a "word" for "religion."

[18] Van der Toorn 2003, p. 395 (my emphasis).
[19] Van der Toorn 2003, p. 395.
[20] Van der Toorn 2003, p. 396.

weren't clear as to "their particular field of activity, apart from the obvious fact that they were the 'lamps of heaven.'"[21] "In the end," van der Toorn writes, though still early in his article, "I had to resign myself to the idea that the villagers had a religion, but that it was more a religion of action than of speculation."[22] So, in the absence of a "resident religious specialist," van der Toorn restricts the balance of his essay "to a description of the rituals that I witnessed. Their deeper meaning is a matter for others to discover."[23]

Already there is much to chew on here with an eye on Old Testament Theology, but van der Toorn's essay continues on for ten more pages, much of which goes a good bit beyond mere description of ritual.[24] So, for example, he describes gestures of greeting the sun and the moon, though he is quick to qualify this action with an interpretive assessment: "No particular fervor was implied by this practice: it was a matter of recognizing the universe in which the villagers lived." No basis is provided for this assessment, nor any definition of what it would mean – especially in the Iron Age – to "recognize the universe."

The impression one gets, then, is not one of mere description of various religious elements, nor heavy-handed interpretation of them, but, instead, a *disallowing* of certain interpretations, especially of the "speculative" (= theological?) sort. For example:

> Although they used religious phrases ("El be with you" – "And with you, too"), the significance is comparable to our "Good to see you" – "Good to see to [sic] you, too"; an affirmation of membership in the community.[25]

Despite the tabooistic origins of, say, the English word "Goodbye," our modern "Good to see you" is far indeed from a greeting (even if is only that!) that invokes a divine name. It is quite intriguing, then, if somewhat odd that, while van der Toorn downplays religion among the (big) gods – and erases it altogether with reference to Yahweh – he trumps it up

---

[21] Van der Toorn 2003, p. 396.
[22] Van der Toorn 2003, p. 396. The categorization of religions into action vs. speculation – and what each one may or may not entail – is an important issue that is not discussed by van der Toorn. See further below and esp. note 57.
[23] Van der Toorn 2003, p. 396.
[24] For description of ritual as an alternative to (and occasionally an end run around) theological analysis, see Strawn forthcoming.
[25] Van der Toorn 2003, p. 396.

elsewhere, especially in family religion (ancestor cult),[26] in what might be called "folk" religion, and in demonic powers. So, for example,

> Religious songs were rare, although the lyrics did recognize unusual events as acts of God....It was presumed to be dangerous to work in the early afternoon; the sun might strike you or a demon might catch you....Religious topics were rare, as I have noted – with one exception. The men loved to tell each other dreams. Their dreams were perhaps not religious in the strict sense of the term, but many of them involved actors from another world, be they gods, demons, or ghosts. It was as though the excitement of the night had to make up for the dullness of the day. These men enjoyed an intimacy with the other world that one would not expect in a people of so practical a bent of mind. As I came to discover, however, the discussion of dreams was their way of expressing their inner life. You must realize that these people were hardly ever alone, nor would they speak about their feelings – to such an extent that you might believe they simply did not have them....Only asleep were they alone, and dreams were the outlet for their feelings. Feelings of desire, guilt, ambition, jealously, love, and hatred assumed the shape of visitors from beyond, commanding them to do things and involving them in strange adventures.[27]

The latter sentiments, in particular, are not just interpretive, they are psychoanalytic, striking one as particularly Freudian, perhaps even excessively so, but without sufficient theoretical support.[28] It is hard, then, to

---

[26] Note van der Toorn (2003, p. 398) where an informant's reference to "the gods" is equivalent to "speaking about the ancestors."

[27] Van der Toorn 2003, p. 397. On the lack of individuality see also p. 408: "In Ramat-Yachin no one is ever alone; it is a condition the villagers do not know. Introspection, which requires at least mental withdrawal, is foreign to them." Cf. similarly van der Toorn 1996, pp. 3-4, 374. These sentiments sound like Alfred North Whitehead's definition of religion (1969, p. 60): "Religion is solitariness; and if you are never solitary, you are never religious" (cited in Janzen 2012, pp. 211-17, 214 n. 8). As J. J. M. Roberts reminds me, however, it is not hard to be alone, even in a hard-working familial, agricultural environment. Cf. Isaac meditating in the field in Gen 24:63. Communal religious experiences refute the overly simplistic equation of religion and solitariness in Whitehead (and van der Toorn). In point of fact, a vast amount of van der Toorn's conclusions depend on his understanding of individuality (or its lack) in the ancient world (see, e.g., van der Toorn 1996, pp. 115-18). I have no doubt that ancient conceptions of the self differed from modern ones, and that cultural differences, too, are to be reckoned with most seriously. I am unconvinced, however, that there was a total lack of subjectivity, interiority, or introspection in antiquity – "no inner life to speak of" (Van der Toorn 1996, p. 117) – and only group/social role and character with all that this means for religious experience. A far more compelling perspective on the fundamentally individual nature of religious experience is found in Johnson (1998, esp. pp. 46-52).

[28] Of course the nature of the essay as a fictive dream report does not allow for extensive theoretical discussion. That granted, note also the interpretation in van der Toorn (2003, p. 398), where he speculates that a dream reported by a family who lost a young child

not see this part of van der Toorn's analysis – fictive though it may be – as rather reductionistic vis-à-vis religion proper.[29]

Unfortunately this trend continues. The women are reported to have put "a small part of the food in a separate basket....not to be eaten, but to be given to the ancestors, present in the *teraphim*"; but, van der Toorn quickly notes, "this small rite" did not "trigger particular demonstrations of devotion."[30] His later remark that "[t]here is little religious activity" – although said about a particular period in the lunar month – holds true, it would seem, for all of Ramat-Yachin's (non)religious life.

Despite the rather understated or minimalistic presentation of religion in van der Toorn's essay, there is nevertheless – to go back to Freud for a moment – the return of the repressed. So, inexplicably, we learn – beyond the demons that somehow motivate ethics that the gods do not[31] – that "the burning of incense has a religious dimension....it is thought to please the gods."[32] How this is so or which gods are pleased we are not told, presumably because the villagers didn't know either. The "repressed" religion that returns is thus far from what one might designate as "orthodox" – however the latter is defined, whether in (later) biblical or Yahwistic perspectives[33] – and it is certainly not very developed. It is telling, regardless, that it is the less "orthodox" religious aspects (judging from later periods and texts) that are alive and well at Ramat-Yachin. So, for example, "the women think most of the goddesses of fertility and lactation....[T]o the peasant women these goddesses, represented by roughly carved wooden statuettes, are of paramount importance."[34] While "El and Baal are the all-important gods...they are the gods with whom the men are concerned; their territory lies beyond

---

reflected their need "to come to terms with their grief before she [the wife] could conceive again." For Sigmund Freud's classic statement on dreams, see Freud 2010.

[29] Cf. the trenchant critique of "the enlightenment project" offered in Levenson 1993, pp. 106-26. Though Levenson's interlocutors do not include van der Toorn, many of the issues and moves are comparable.

[30] Van der Toorn 2003, p. 399.

[31] Prophylactic actions, if nothing else (see van der Toorn 2003, p. 399); for more on demons and warding them off, see van der Toorn 2003, pp. 402-403. On ethics in Old Babylonian religion, see van der Toorn 1996, pp. 94-118 (cf. further below).

[32] For other examples see van der Toorn (2003, p. 398) who mentions the gods "call[ing]," blessing formulae that are used ("my grandfather, blessed be his memory"), or certain aspects of quotidian life ("the women put an almost religious zeal into" preparing food).

[33] I realise the term is anachronistic, especially in the earliest periods. I use it only heuristically.

[34] Van der Toorn 2003, p. 399.

the house. In the domestic realm, the goddesses prevail."³⁵ The confidence of this statement – recall that no one even knows Yahweh's name at Ramat-Yachin – is remarkable, as is the fact that these goddesses are said to be "[k]nown as Asherah and Astarte"!³⁶ Van der Toorn goes so far as to write that the women's "lives depend on" these goddesses.³⁷

Where there is mention of the male gods, it is invariably Baal. A ceremony unites the men of the village, their ancestors, and Baal.³⁸ There is a greeting or blessing (apparently the same thing; see above) of Baal at the same time.³⁹ What happened to El along the way is unclear. As "a dim deity," perhaps he is already otiose,⁴⁰ though the personal name (PN) of the village chief, "Elḥanan" ("El has shown mercy" or the like) shouldn't be forgotten.⁴¹ Why is he not named "Baalḥanan"?⁴² Maybe "Elḥanan" is just an old trace of a naming tradition that goes as far back as the eponymous founder of the village, "Elyachin" ("El established"). Whatever the case, Baal is clearly the most important deity for Ramat-Yachin – any religious "thought" (if it could even be called such) that rises to some level of expression concerns him. Or demons.⁴³ But the victory for the cloud-rider is a muted one. Even in a ritual held at a *bāmâ* that appears to recognize Baal's fructification of the earth,

> No fervent prayers were spoken, and there was no show of devotion.... the ceremony might strike onlookers as a tepid performance, [but] the participants derived comfort from its regularity....[I]t...strengthened their belief that they lived in a world of order and of mutual goodwill between Baal, the dead, and the living. Such thoughts were never spoken out loud, nor did they need to be. The ritual, performed as a pious duty, spoke for itself to the participants; they did not ask for its meaning, nor did they care to talk about it.⁴⁴

How van der Toorn draws these conclusions when so much goes unspoken and no one cares to discuss the subject is unclear.⁴⁵ But a similar

---

³⁵ Van der Toorn 2003, p. 399.
³⁶ Van der Toorn 2003, p. 399.
³⁷ Van der Toorn 2003, p. 399.
³⁸ Van der Toorn 2003, p. 401; cf. van der Toorn 2003, p. 405.
³⁹ Van der Toorn 2003, p. 402.
⁴⁰ Van der Toorn 2003, p. 395.
⁴¹ For this name in the Bible and epigraphic record, see Fowler (1988, pp. 82, 111, 147, 345) and Zadok (1988, pp. 25, 179, 228, 313-14).
⁴² For this name, see Fowler (1988, pp. 62, 82, 338, 345) and Zadok (1988, pp. 25, 180, 232).
⁴³ Van der Toorn 2003, pp. 402-403.
⁴⁴ Van der Toorn 2003, p. 403.
⁴⁵ One suspects that van der Toorn's dream report is being interfered with at this point by (his) other knowledge bases. It was only fiction after all!

question obtains at a later point in the story when we find Elḥanan giving "something amounting to a speech at a ritual"[46] held at the *bāmâ*. In a voice "higher [pitched] than usual," Elḥanan describes Baal's rejuvenated rule of the land after his sojourn in the world below (with the ancestors), which left "the land a playground for Death, his adversary."[47] "But now," the elder goes on to say,

> Baal had returned and had brought the ancestors with him. He showed his presence in the new wine, reinvigorating all those who drink it. Death had been defeated; Baal reigned supreme. In a few weeks' time he would shower his rains upon them, preparing the fields for a new sowing. The coming year would be even better than the last one: the flocks would multiply, women would hold new children on their laps, and the efforts of the men would bear fruit. As Elḥanan spoke about the future, his words had the quality of an incantation. The audience responded now with shouts, now with whispers.[48]

So, at that rare point when something approaching an extended articulation of religious belief is expressed, it is for Baal. Even more striking than that fact is the observation that the belief that is finally expressed corresponds largely to a Baal mythology known (so far, at least) from the textual record of Late Bronze Age Ugarit, which is removed from isolated Ramat-Yachin by many miles and a goodly number of years. How that religious mythology – preserved, we might recall, by a scribal elite[49] – came to be the religion of these highland village peasants is not clear in the article; perhaps it is not available to anthropological ways of knowing.

For a moment it seems like Yahweh *may* make a comeback at the end of van der Toorn's essay, in the description of a case of illness which is treated by a visiting divine known as "the man of God," who defines the problem not as a physical malady at all but as the result of communal sin – a religious vow left unfulfilled, to be precise.[50] This may be the same divine who knew of Yahweh-worship in parts south, but it needn't be and by the end of the account it is more than clear that he is no card-carrying

---

[46] Van der Toorn 2003, p. 405; van der Toorn 2003, p. 406 calls it a "peroration"!
[47] Van der Toorn 2003, p. 405.
[48] Van der Toorn 2003, p. 406.
[49] Cf. below, and note, for example, the role of the scribe Ilimilku in the mythological texts from Ugarit, and Yanḥamu for the lexical texts from there. See Hess (1999, pp. 499-528, esp. 512) and, further, Juan-Pablo Vita (1999, pp. 455-98, esp. 465, 472-73).
[50] The language of "sin" and religious "vows" that must be fulfilled are additional examples of the return of the repressed (religion).

member of the Yahweh-alone party (see below) because he accepts a statement that the village had "kept the covenant [*nb!*] with Baal [*nb!*] and the ancestors," even as he notes that "[t]he dead are dissatisfied" with their actions, and later deduces that "El would speak" on behalf of the village elders via the drawing of lots.[51] Evidently this "man of God(s)" is an equal opportunity soothsayer with the notable exception, or so it would seem, of Yahweh.

Not only is there a return of the repressed (religion) at various points in van der Toorn's description of Ramat-Yachin, there are also moments where this essay seems to be in some conflict with his earlier work on family religion in Babylonia, Syria, and Israel. We learn there, for instance, that despite diachronic change in Israelite family religion, the latter is actually "the prolongation of a Bronze Age phenomenon into the Iron Age."[52] In this way, especially because family religion in the biblical text "has survived mainly as a substratum,"[53] knowledge of Old Babylonian family religion is absolutely essential. Without it, "it would be very difficult to interpret the few and mostly oblique references to family religion in the Bible."[54] And yet, in some contrast to the down-played role of religious devotion in the Ramat-Yachin essay, van der Toorn is at pains in his larger book to *insist* on the importance of religious belief and practice:

> The vitality of religious beliefs and customs in the context of the family belies Oppenheim's assessment that "the influence of religion on the individual, as well as on the community as a whole, was unimportant in Mesopotamia"....The absence of these [religious themes, specifically the cult of the ancestors and the worship of local patron deities]...promotes a myopic vision of the Old Babylonian reality.[55]

Now, to be sure, van der Toorn's nine months in the village of Ramat-Yachin revealed a good bit of ancestor cult – though it was quite nondescript in the end, and also rather un-ceremonial and not highly meaningful, at least in any descriptive sort of way – but "vitality," "religious beliefs," and "worship," to borrow just three of van der Toorn's terms used above, seem curiously absent in the religion of Ramat-Yachin. One wonders if we too are left with "a myopic vision," only this time of the early Israelite, not Old Babylonian, reality.

---

[51] Van der Toorn 2003, p. 407.
[52] Van der Toorn 1996, p. 375; van der Toorn 1996, p. 4.
[53] Van der Toorn 1996, p. 5.
[54] Van der Toorn 1996, p. 5
[55] Van der Toorn 1996, p. 373, citing Oppenheim 1977, p. 176.

Still further on this point, in his earlier book van der Toorn states that "it is impossible to attain a real understanding of the Babylonians without taking into account what their religion did to them,"[56] but in the essay on Ramat-Yachin one gets the sense that if there even is a "religion" of which to speak (perhaps there isn't),[57] it doesn't seem to have "done" much at all to the villagers – at least not in the same way that it did for the Old Babylonians.[58] Or, one might consider how, in the earlier book, van der Toorn seems more comfortable with the symbolic nature of ritual acts and their cognitive content than he is in the later essay on early Israelite religion:

> To say that solidarity with the ancestors and the neighbourhood preceded its ritual celebration is not quite true. The sentiment of such solidarity does not fully exist until it takes place in certain symbols. Family religion can be seen as the complex of symbols (*a term that covers beliefs and values* as well as certain practices) which give substance to the identity and mutual affinity of its followers.[59]

But beliefs and values evidently do not pertain to Iron Age Israelite Ramat-Yachin – or at least everyone is tight-lipped about them – despite the facts that (1) such beliefs and values obtained for Old Babylonian religion long beforehand; and (2) Iron Age Israel is in some sort of profound continuity with the latter (once again: "a prolongation of a Bronze Age phenomenon into the Iron Age").

One final important point of disjuncture between van der Toorn's earlier work and the later essay deserves mention. It concerns the "personal" nature of "personal devotion." In his earlier monograph on family religion van der Toorn emphasizes the "collective" nature of Babylonian religion: "There was, in a sense, no identity outside the group, just as there was no religion outside the community. Left to himself man would be a non-entity, and his religion a private delusion."[60] Such sentiment mandates that we be very careful with the use of adjectives like "personal" and "individual," though van der Toorn also asserts that they

---

[56] Van der Toorn 1996, p. 373.
[57] Cf. van der Toorn's definition of "religion" (1996, p. 7): "religion refers to the various notions, values and practices involving non-empirical powers." This is certainly not the only, nor an exhaustive, description of religion. See, inter alia, Pals (2015) and Smith (1998, pp. 269-84).
[58] "Historical identity" and "a sense of belonging to a specific place" – two central leitmotifs in van der Toorn (1996) – are very vague indeed when it comes to Ramat-Yachin.
[59] Van der Toorn 1996, p. 374 (my emphasis).
[60] Van der Toorn 1996, p. 374; cf. van der Toorn 1996, pp. 3-4.

"should not be simply dismissed."⁶¹ There was, he writes, "hardly any privacy to family religion. The Near Eastern civilizations were unfamiliar with contemplation or silent prayer; acts of devotion always had a public aspect."⁶² But while the non-private nature of lived experience at Ramat-Yachin *is* strongly emphasized in the essay, the public nature of the religion there is *not*, but seems, again, rather downplayed. Even more to the point I wish to explore here, the diachronic focus of the monograph's attention on Israelite religion leads van der Toorn to speak of a move "*from* family religion *to* personal devotion."⁶³ This movement suggests that something happened to change the old (Babylonian or Babylonian-*ish*) family religion into something more familiar to moderns, something that was marked by personal (eventually individual?) devotion and that was presumably characterized by "beliefs and values."⁶⁴

I will say more about the "something" that happened below; the problem to be noted here is that – from the front (early) side of the development – "beliefs and values" *already characterized early religion* according to van der Toorn. And, from the back (later) side of the development, we end up learning from van der Toorn that this personal devotion is ultimately nothing less than "what might be called a national religion."⁶⁵ It is hard indeed to know what a national religion would look like except something that is thoroughly public and presumably also a good bit more systematized or, to borrow from van der Toorn's language, dogmatized.⁶⁶

Let me be clear that I do not intend an overly pedantic critique by this extended summary and analysis of van der Toorn's essay in light of his earlier work. I find van der Toorn's publications consistently insightful and incisive; there are good reasons that he is a leading light and that his work has helped shape scholarly consensus! And if there are points of disjuncture between the book on family religion and the essay on Ramat-Yachin, there are also obvious points of profound similarity. The latter

---

⁶¹ Van der Toorn 1996, p. 3.
⁶² Van der Toorn 1996, p. 4.
⁶³ Van der Toorn 1996, pp. 6, 375; see further all of Part III, on Israel, which is actually subtitled in this way (van der Toorn 1996, pp. 179-372).
⁶⁴ Van der Toorn 1996, p. 6: "The third and most extensive part of the book has been called 'From Family Religion to Personal Devotion', since it describes the waning of the traditional forms of family religion and the emergence of a religion of personal commitment to beliefs and values that transcend the immediate interests of the family and the local community."
⁶⁵ Van der Toorn 1996, p. 375.
⁶⁶ See van der Toorn 1996, p. 2.

essay could simply not have been written without the earlier monograph on family religion, and the seminal ideas of the book are on repeated display throughout the essay.[67]

Even so, there does seem to be a bit of a pulling back on some things – ideas, terms, and subjects – in the Ramat-Yachin essay vis-à-vis the comparative data amassed in the monograph on family religion.[68] It is hard to judge why that should be the case. Perhaps it is because the essay is explicitly "anthropological" whereas the monograph is not.[69] Maybe there are other reasons as well.

Whatever the case, the upshot of van der Toorn's imaginative essay on what it would be like to spend nine months in an early Israelite village is that the religion therein is of a certain and rather understated sort. "Primitive" is the first descriptor that comes to mind, but "superstitious" and "magical" aren't far behind. That is to be expected, one supposes, in an ancient, primitive (there's that word again) culture-*cum*-religion. But what is not expected – even and perhaps especially among ancient cultures and their religions – is how thoroughly *non-affective* this religion is and how deeply *non-cognitive* to boot.[70] Where there is any developed, though hardly fully-formed, articulation of religious experience and/or belief, it relates to Baal worship, especially as that is known (at least to us now) via the finds at Ugarit and not, pointedly, from any textual remains from ancient Israel/Palestine.[71]

---

[67] See above. Note also that van der Toorn (1996, p. 8) is well aware of potential reductionism: "one should beware not to overrate the explanatory potential of the notion of identity" – and, one might add, history or social scientific categories; "[r]eligion fulfils a variety of functions."

[68] This is not to say that I find the monograph fully satisfying on matters of religion, religious experience, or theology. I do not.

[69] See van der Toorn 1996, pp. 4-6, for its method as historical and comparative.

[70] Cf. van der Toorn 1996, p. 2 (cited more extensively below). For the indispensable neurological connections between emotions and cognition see, *inter alia*, Damasio 1994, 1999. For the fundamental role of conceptual analogy or metaphor in the religious symbol system of "Syro-Canaan," see Wright 2013, pp. 129-150.

[71] This is not to say that the name "Baal" does not appear in the epigraphic record, which it certainly does (see esp. the Samaria ostraca), but there is no extented mythology of Baal available from the soil of ancient Israel/Palestine and there are good reasons to question too-simple an identification of the material from Ugarit with that from "Canaan" let alone "ancient Israel." See Grabbe 1994, pp. 113-22. Still further, if the epigraphic record was to be relied on, Yahweh would certainly have to figure more prominently than he does at Ramat-Yachin. On the PN evidence, see most recently Norin 2013. Note also Tigay 1986; Miller 2000; Fowler, 1988; and Zadok 1988. Or, if the Bible is summoned to fill in gaps about Baal, then it would certainly have to be allowed to fill in gaps on Yahweh as well.

Van der Toorn is no maverick in offering such a reconstruction of ancient Israelite religion even if he is rather unique in offering such a creative presentation of such (a creativity for which he is to be commended, in my opinion). As I indicated earlier, I take his essay as generally representative of something approaching scholarly consensus in reconstructions of Israelite religion, at least of the earliest variety, and at least of late.[72] My criticisms, then, should not be taken as singling him out unfairly. To broaden the net a bit further, for example, I note that Tammi J. Schneider's recent volume on Mesopotamian religion is similarly marked by extreme reticence to say anything about the meaning of various rituals and an aversion to speculate at all about the cognitive content of religious belief.[73]

In the end, though, one wonders if some important elements have been left out in these reconstructions. Perhaps the title of van der Toorn's essay says it all: it is about time spent with "peasants in the Palestinian Highlands," and that description seems fair enough. But the essay also speaks of an "Israelite" village, not an "Israbaalite" one,[74] and the village in question is located in Iron Age Israel/Palestine, *not* in Late Bronze Age Ugarit. Or then again the title announces an "anthropological perspective on local religion" but this approach seems unable to get a good grasp on the local inhabitants' religious "beliefs."[75] Does something as simple as a personal name signify anything of the latter? The PN Elḥanan, after all, means "El/God had mercy," and raises a host of questions: What does "mercy" mean in this construction and how is it an action of El/God? To whom was the mercy shown and when? How so? Is that a "real" and "true" assertion in the user's perspective or simply a piece of traditional tripe? Or then there is the PN of the eponymous ancestor, Elyachin, which means "God established." Here too questions abound: What did El/God establish? And for whom? When and how? Really and

---

[72] There are, as R. W. L. Moberly has reminded me, some very marked differences between these more recent reconstructions and those of, say, the mid-20th century. See further below.

[73] Schneider 2011. Cf. van der Toorn 1996, p. 112: "Devotion must not be confused with fervor. A true [Babylonian] gentleman avoids extremes."

[74] The relationship between "Palestinian" and "Israelite" is never clarified in the essay.

[75] See Levenson 1993, pp. 114-15, for an incisive critique of anthropological ways of knowing that fall short of "native belief." Levenson (1993, p. 115) cites Kolakowski (1992, pp. 15-16): "We need more than [the empirical material of the anthropologist] to assert that when people seak of God or the gods, of invisible forces purposely operating behind empirical facts, of the sacred quality of things, they are in fact, and without knowing it, speaking of something entirely different."

truly? It is hard to imagine even people "of so practical a bent of mind" not having an idea or two about these questions, precisely because, if the PNs aren't simply "traditional" (in the modern conceit), they would seem to be the result of intentional choice.[76] Furthermore, devoid of any religious conceptions, a PN like "Spear" (קין) or "Lion" (אריה) would seemed to have done just fine. Why include a deity name, especially if the deity in question is non-functional, uninspiring, and (apparently) downright unimportant? If good old-fashioned and all-pervasive "primitive superstition" is invoked as the likely reason, the dream report from Ramat-Yachin would indicate that names like Nāṣûr ("Protected") or Māgēn ("Shield") would have made just as much sense, given the reality of the demons (see above), than anything invoking the gods proper. It seems preferable, then, to treat the theophoric names at Ramat-Yachin as van der Toorn himself does in his earlier monograph: "Such names [in the Old Babylonian period] are miniature confessions illuminating the conceptual universe of family religion."[77]

What Would (Should) Old Testament Theology Look Like? A First Probe

With the preceding overview of one, particularly fascinating, reconstruction of Israelite religion in place, we may now turn to a first probe of what (an) Old Testament Theology would (or should) look like in light of it.

1. The first thing one might say is that it is hard to say what (an) Old Testament Theology should look like in light of the reconstruction offered in the Ramat-Yachin essay. The focus there is resolutely on (very) early Israel such that one might easily say that, since there is no Old Testament at that point in time, there can be no such thing as an "Old Testament Theology."[78] Somewhat analogously, in his family religion

---

[76] Not to mention the intimacy they enjoyed with the other world (van der Toorn 2003, p. 397).

[77] Van der Toorn 1996, p. 95.

[78] The question that immediately follows is: when is there an Old Testament such that there can be something called "Old Testament Theology"? Cf. Levenson 1993, p. 37: "The juxtaposition of...various sorts of literature in the same book is a matter of literary context; it becomes a fact of history per se only very late in the period of the Second Temple – long after the original historical contexts of the pentateuchal literature and perhaps also the proverb collections had vanished. The construction of a religion out of all the materials in the Hebrew Bible violates the historian's commitment to seeing the

book van der Toorn writes that certain differentiations (such as the opposition between "popular" and "official" religion) are "of little use when we are dealing with religions that have no dogmatics." And, he continues, "[b]oth the Old Babylonian and Early Israelite religion belong to this class – as do most ancient religions."[79]

Quite apart from the questions of whether (an) Old Testament Theology must be "dogmatic" (a particularly fraught term in the history of doctrine) – or, perhaps better, "systematizing"[80] – or whether ancient religions are capable of such thought,[81] the Israelite religion reconstructed by van der Toorn is one that, despite its obvious dependence on parts of the Bible, seems to bear very little resemblance to much of the religion captured therein. To begin with just the most obvious point of distinction: there is no Yahweh at Ramat-Yachin! And what is a religion (at least in the ancient Near East) if it is not something to do with its gods?[82] Ramat-Yachin has no Yahweh; for the Old Testament, Yahweh is indispensable.[83] So, in the old adage, "Never the twain shall meet"…or so it seems. To put things slightly differently, borrowing words from van der

---

materials in their historical contexts. The result will correspond to the religion of no historical community, except perhaps some parties very late in the period of the Second Temple. The argument that Old Testament theology can maintain both an uncompromisingly historical character and its distinction from the history of Israelite religion is therefore not valid." See further below.

[79] Van der Toorn 1986, p. 2. But contrast Zevit 2003, pp. 223-35, esp. 232: "Insofar as there is no reason to assume that cultic observances at the level of the father's house were less formal, regulated, or tradition-bound than at the poly-tribal level, and because there is no reason to assume any significant difference in formality between the observances of consanguine groups and those of affiliations of unrelated individuals, the digitized dichotomies simply do not apply. Their words lack a social or ideological referent in the culture of ancient Israel. They mislead.

There was no state or elite or official or popular religion in ancient Israel. There was a political body that we may label 'state'; there were social and economic elites; there were sacerdotal and royal officials; there was a populace; and there was the so-called "man in the street." But data do not support the proposition that a particular type of pattern of credo or praxis may be associated with them."

[80] I tend to agree with Rolf P. Knierim (1995, pp. 475-486, 548) that systematizing of some sort is inevitable when it comes to Old Testament Theology. Even someone as emically oriented as Walter Brueggemann (1997) evidences thematizing or systematizing trends. See Strawn (2015, pp. 9-47). R. W. L. Moberly has suggested (personal communication) that "synthesizing" might be a better term.

[81] It is interesting that scholars of ancient Egyptian religion do not evidence problems with the word "theology." Cf. Strawn (forthcoming).

[82] See, *inter alia*, Miller 2000, pp. 1-45. For van der Toorn's definition of religion, see note 57 above.

[83] Note, e.g., Reventlow's (1985, pp. 125-33) notion that Yahweh should be the center (*Mitte*) of Old Testament Theology; cf. also Hasel 1991, pp. 139-71. Gerhard von Rad's famous retort ("what kind of a Jahwe is he?") (1965, p. 415) effectively counters

Toorn, the data "that any reconstruction of local religion....must take into account" are "few" and offer "[t]he dissembled bones of a skeleton, at best. Let these bones live!"[84] But vis-à-vis the Old Testament, one may be pardoned in thinking that these particular bones simply *can't* live – not, at least, in terms of (an) Old Testament Theology. These bones are too far desiccated even for the רוח יהוה (Ezek 37:1-14; notwithstanding Jer 32:17, 27; Matt 19:26; Mark 10:27; Luke 1:37; 18:27), precisely because that spirit is the spirit *of Yahweh*, a persona otherwise unknown! Maybe Baal's spirit would have a better go of things.

2. Now, to be sure, van der Toorn's essay appears to concern only (very) early Israel. It could be seen, that is, as the first chapter in a much longer history of Israelite religion that would develop and unfold through time. While that may well be true, it leads to a second thing that can be said about the interface of the Old Testament and Israelite religion: the disjuncture between early Israelite religion as reconstructed in the Ramat-Yachin essay and the religion and/or theology[85] found in the Old Testament means that to make a reconstruction of Israelite religion such as van der Toorn's fit with, work toward, or otherwise have an impact on (an) Old Testament Theology, one must somehow explain what the Old Testament is and/or how it came to be. That means, in the case at hand, that one must explain why the Old Testament at full stretch looks so drastically different than the dream-report about Ramat-Yachin. What one must do, therefore, is create some sort of diachronic model to explain or justify the rise of the Old Testament and its religion and/or theology since it does not appear to relate – at least not directly – to early Israelite religion.

Van der Toorn offers just such an explanation in his book on family religion and in his more recent book on scribal culture.[86] The gist of the former can be briefly recounted: Since family religion is so profoundly social, social changes of any sort lead directly to religious change. In Israel, the rise of the state brought "the possibility of an identification with the supra-local collectivity of the nation," no longer just that of the family.[87] There is now "a kind of competition between state religion and

---

Reventlow's (and others') quest for a center, but does not challenge the centrality of Yahweh for "Old Testament religion."

[84] Van der Toorn 2003, p. 409.
[85] See note 9 above on "religion" and "theology." In what follows I use both, often with "and/or" to show their possible interrelations as well as their potential distinctions.
[86] See also van der Toorn, 2015.
[87] Van der Toorn 1996, p. 375.

family religion, the former validating a national identity, the latter a local identity."[88] State religion can only win this battle by "the creation of a charter myth that might mobilize a sense of national identity among the population" – the priests and prophets are responsible for that step[89] – and by "an attempt at integrating family religion in the religion of state," which is a task for kings.[90] But the coexistence of family and state religion in Israel "was never harmonious. The two were in constant competition"[91] and the integration of Baal worship, in particular, proved too much for the theological conservatives (where they come from – apart from the south – is curious since, if the Ramat-Yachin reconstruction holds any water, most people – at least early on – were Baalists) who eventually congealed into "the incipient [and famous or infamous, depending on one's perspective] Yahweh-alone movement....the zealots of a strict monolatry of Yahweh."[92] The architects (or culprits) of the demise of old family religion and rise of late state religion were, big surprise, those stodgy Deuteronomists! But not all is lost:

> One may regret the oblivion to which much Ephraimite family religion abroad has been reduced, but one should rejoice over the understanding of the Deuteronomists which a study of the competition between family religion and state religion produces.[93]

It is the Deuteronomists, then, who are ultimately responsible for bringing about "a new religion," though "it must be recognized that they were the exponents of a much wider trend."[94] But whence comes this Deuteronomism, or how it reflects a "wider trend," and who those additional "exponents" might be, is not fully described, simply postulated. And yet, despite its dissatisfyingly hypothetical nature, this sort of postulation seems absolutely necessary in the grand scheme of things, owing its existence mostly, if not exclusively, to the fact that one must explain how one gets to the material presently found in the Old Testament from a reconstruction of Israelite religion that is so drastically different.

---

[88] Van der Toorn 1996, p. 375.
[89] Van der Toorn 1996, pp. 375-76. This is, of course, the exodus myth, even if, as van der Toorn allows, it may depend on some small shred of historical fact. Note that van der Toorn (2003, pp. 402-403) details a practice of anointing a door with blood in Ramat-Yachin but it has nothing to do with the exodus proper, but rather with averting demons that might prowl around the houses of the village.
[90] Van der Toorn 1996, p. 376.
[91] Van der Toorn 1996, p. 376.
[92] Van der Toorn 1996, p. 377. Cf. earlier Smith 1987.
[93] Van der Toorn 1996, p. 378.
[94] Van der Toorn 1996, p. 379.

148   BRENT A. STRAWN

It is a short next step from this sort of historical reconstruction of Israelite-religion-into-Old-Testament-literature to a compositional model that posits that the Hebrew Bible, in the aggregate, is the result of scribal elite circles.[95] How else to explain material that seems so much more "Yahwized" – even if not dogmatized or systematized (though perhaps more "dogmatisable/systematisable")? Average Joe- and Judy-Elḥanan from Ramat-Yachin are not well represented in the pages of the Old Testament, after all. They would not find themselves or their religious experiences therein – of course they wouldn't be able to read the Bible anyway, being illiterate, and there wasn't any Bible to speak of until long after their deaths. Even so, the very little trace that they leave in the pages of Holy Writ seems an ominous indicator that they were victims of more than just the vagaries of history. Elite scribal erasure may be to blame.

Unlike some other, more simple-minded theorists, van der Toorn states clearly (and admirably) that he does not wish to posit a simplistic or "uniform development,"[96] but it is hard to avoid the impression that exactly such a development is common among so many reconstructions of Israelite religion, along with their correlate (non-)bearing on the Old Testament and its religion and/or theology. To put this development rather too simply, one might delineate at least four stages in the argument:

STAGE 1: Radical disjuncture between early Israelite religion and anything later (leads to)

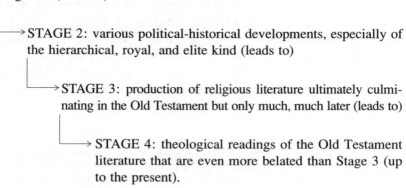

STAGE 2: various political-historical developments, especially of the hierarchical, royal, and elite kind (leads to)

STAGE 3: production of religious literature ultimately culminating in the Old Testament but only much, much later (leads to)

STAGE 4: theological readings of the Old Testament literature that are even more belated than Stage 3 (up to the present).

---

[95] See van der Toorn 2007. Once again, van der Toorn is not alone in this regard and there is a recent spate of books on the composition history of the Hebrew Bible, or its constituent parts, many of which are highly speculative (how could they be otherwise?). For a recent reaction – also not without problems – see Van Seters 2006.

[96] Van der Toorn 1996, p. 377.

WHAT WOULD (OR SHOULD) O.T. THEOLOGY LOOK LIKE?

Once again, if Israelite religion is the kind "on the ground," especially of the average person ("folk religion," to use a problematic term for the moment), especially in earlier periods prior to state "corruption" or "imposition," then the obvious conclusion seems to be, again, that when it comes to Israelite religion of this sort (Stage 1) and Old Testament Theology (Stage 4), never the twain shall meet – despite the intervening stages.[97]

Let me be clear that I do not mean to suggest that all of the above is completely wrong or erroneous somehow. There is no doubt that much of the scholarly consensus depends on good modeling, decent data, and reasonable argumentation. I would not want to challenge, for instance, that few ancient individuals were literate, which means that the vast majority were illiterate (at least by modern standards), leaving *literary production*, at least, in scribal hands and the circles that supported them.[98] All of that seems quite reasonable and decently supported, thanks to the work of people like van der Toorn and others.

I do wish to suggest, however, that much of this kind of model is dissatisfying, not necessarily due to a general lack of explanatory power (though that power may depend on a certain circularity) but because of its *lack* of explanatory power *at certain key junctures*. One such juncture is that *the Old Testament itself* provides some of the key data to build the model – say, Baalistic tendencies that are mentioned in Judges or Kings or the like (cf. also Baalistic PNs in the Samaria ostraca). This is a case of having the proverbial cake and wanting to eat it too. But if the Baalistic tendencies of the Hebrew Bible are legitimate, why shouldn't the Yahwistic ones be as well? Or, at a second, but not unrelated juncture, if the end result that is the Old Testament is (solely) the work of a scribal elite, why is there so much in the Old Testament that simply doesn't seem to fit such "elitism" – that resists it or challenges it?[99]

---

[97] It is worth noting (as R. W. L. Moberly has kindly reminded me), how different this gross distinction between Old Testament Theology and Israelite religion is when compared to works in the early 20th century where Old Testament Theology (at least of a sort) was virtually identified with Israelite religion. See, e.g., the debate between Otto Eissfeldt and Walter Eichrodt reprinted in Ollenburger (2004, pp. 12-29).

[98] Even so, see Routledge (2006, pp. 223-238) for other types of religious literacy that do not depend on reading or writing.

[99] Similar literature is found in the Near East, as well, of course. One thinks of anti-royal oracles in, say, the Mari letters, but while these were no doubt recorded by literate scribes, many do not seem to reflect inner-circle dynamics that support – and certainly not invariably – the royal hierarchy. Whatever the case, note that van der Toorn also attributes Old Babylonian religion, including its theology and ethics (nb!), to the upperclass ("gentility," *awīlūtum*), but also states that "[m]ost Babylonians, it seems, cherished religious

The biggest problem, then, is and remains the existence of the Old Testament itself – especially the burrs it sticks in the saddle of any developmental model that moves seamlessly from something early and almost entirely non-Yahwistic (if not also non- or a-religious) to something that is heavily, if not thoroughly, Yahwistic with its full complement of (admittedly non-uniform) "theological" or "dogmatic" material, all of which would have been unimaginable in the imaginary village of Ramat-Yachin. It should be recalled that, for his part, van der Toorn resists any uniform development, but it seems more common than not for many scholars to assume something very much like it. The development that is postulated is neither wholly unreasonable nor completely unimaginable, but does it have any more claim to reality than the imaginative reconstruction of early Israelite religion at Ramat-Yachin? Is one any less (or more?) speculative than the other? The developmental model needs significant thickening and revision – it must not only resist simplistic uniformity, it must also resist simplistic linearity, and those are only two of the more important qualifications that should be made. Others could be mentioned.[100]

So far, however, all I have offered is an analysis of just a small portion of van der Toorn's work – work that I continue to find insightful, even indispensable, despite the fissures I have identified here and there along the way. I admit that it is easy to conduct this kind of "armchair scholarly analysis"; it is far harder to do the extensive data collection, sifting, and interpretation that van der Toorn and others have done. One may justifiably ask, then, if there are any data to support what are, so far, my rather theoretical observations. Do these latter finally comprise nothing more than a small-minded critique – a gnat bothering a lion? Is there any evidence for an alternative? Obviously I do not have the room here that van der Toorn had to develop his ideas across three book-length studies.

---

notions and ideas very similar to those held by the class of the *awīlū*" (van der Toorn 1996, p. 95) which renders the class distinction somewhat moot. See also note 79 above.

[100] For example, what kind of social mechanism, especially of the elite-political variety, could explain the religiosity one finds in later literature? This is never adequately addressed in my view (see further below). An essay like that of Byrne (2004) attempts such an explanation – though with reference to pillar figures not biblical literature – but in the end I find it unconvincing and reductionistic in terms of lived religious experience. For a similar critique, with reference to Hobbesian and Foucauldian views of power see Levenson (1993, pp. 113-114). It is better, in Levenson's opinion, to pay attention to those ""microrelations" of power' that suffused the society and acquired an enduring literary testament in the Hebrew Bible....[S]cholars...[should] concentrate less on the elites and...show the masses more respect" (1993, p. 114). Cf. also Johnson 1998.

I have only a few pages left, but as a further gesture toward the question(s), if not also the solution(s), of what Old Testament Theology should look like in light of reconstructions of Israelite religion, I wish to turn now to the book of Job.

FITTING JOB INTO *ISRAELITE RELIGION

Job has problems fitting into reconstructions of Israelite religion like the one(s) recounted above for several reasons, but, an excellent entrée into the larger issues is provided by J. J. M. Roberts's classic study, "Job and the Israelite Religious Tradition."[101]

Roberts' essay is rather strongly anti-historical-critical, at least when it comes to Job's intersection with Old Testament Theology. Roberts speaks of "history's *stranglehold* on biblical theology and Old Testament scholarship" that "in general remains unbroken"; of the "persisting theological *tyranny* of history"; the "theological *bias* for history"; and "the *temptation* to historicize."[102] That such "history remains the touchstone of a genuine, normative, biblical theology" is not, in his view, at least vis-à-vis Job, a good thing.[103] This is largely because such an approach must assume an "historical background extraneous to the text of the book" to properly understand or interpret it.[104] More often than not, according to Roberts, this kind of historicizing approach "reduces Job to a mere cipher for Israel, and his theological problem becomes the problem of understanding Israel's national experience" (Job stands for Israel in exile, for example); the book itself, however, presents the theological issue in question as thoroughly "individualistic" in nature.[105]

A further problem identified by Roberts is that historicizing attempts have been unsuccessful in terms of chronology and typology – consider, for example, the individual doctrine of retribution which is sometimes tied to Ezekiel's time with Job consequently following Ezekiel at some later point in history. But it might be contested that such a "doctrine" first appeared with Ezekiel (or in his time) and/or that Ezekiel is the fount for Job's "situated" theology. This chronological-typological

---

[101] Roberts 1977, pp. 107-44, reprinted in idem, Roberts 2002, pp. 110-16. Citations are taken from the latter. See also Janzen 1987, pp. 523-37.
[102] Roberts 2002, pp. 110-11 (my emphases).
[103] Roberts 2002, p. 110.
[104] Roberts 2002, pp. 110-11.
[105] Roberts 2002, p. 111.

reconstruction is just that: a reconstruction – one that seems like a house of cards that Roberts brushes aside with a single, poignant question: "what legitimacy can an interpretive background of history claim in the absence of any clear textual references to that history?"[106] As if "[t]he subjective nature of all...attempts to interpret Job by reference to a particular historical background" weren't enough, Roberts goes on to note "the total lack of consensus in the dating of the book."[107] While the range of possibilities may be more limited now than when he originally penned his essay,[108] Roberts is certainly right that, barring certainty in such matters, "[o]ne cannot use the date of the book...to provide a ready-made background for its interpretation, and lacking this, an historical framework is hard to establish."[109]

In brief, overly-historicised approaches to Job have come up empty.[110] What then? Roberts advocates for "simply stick[ing] to the text," and when one does so,

> the poetic dialogue presents the problem as that of a religious individual who was experiencing what appeared to him as undeserved suffering. There is no hint that the suffering extended beyond his immediate family; indeed 19:13-17 implies that even within his own household Job's agony was his alone.[111]

But of course Job's agony is not, ultimately, just his own:

> A similar theme appears numerous times in Israelite and Mesopotamian individual laments....The same motifs also appear in the narrative portions of the individual thanksgiving song...and several of the Mesopotamian "wisdom" texts often compared to Job actually belong to this genre. Their resemblance to Job stems not from wisdom per se, but from their roots in *the existential experience of rejection, lament, and restoration*.[112]

---

[106] Roberts 2002, p. 111.
[107] Roberts 2002, p. 112.
[108] Roberts delineates a range "as early as the eleventh or tenth centuries and as late as the fourth century," after which he concludes wryly: "In view of this seven-hundred-year discrepancy, it should be obvious that most of the criteria advanced for dating carry little conviction" (2002, 112). For recent discussions of the date of Job, see, e.g., Clines (1989, p. lvii) and Seow (2013, pp. 39-45).
[109] Roberts 2002, p. 113.
[110] Not on all fronts, of course. One thinks of older views on the authorship of Job by Moses or its location in the ancestral period as now permanently debunked, in no small part due to historical considerations (e.g., historical philology).
[111] Roberts 2002, p. 114.
[112] Roberts 2002, pp. 114-15 (my emphasis).

In the end, then, Roberts concludes that "the actual date of the composition of Job is largely irrelevant for its exegesis." He explains:

> If its author stood in a long literary tradition in which basically the same problem had been dealt with before, and if *the human experience necessary for this problem to arise in Israel was independent of any necessary connection to the national history*, it is illegitimate to read that history into the book simply because the book could have come into its present form during an acute national crisis. Not every work written in a period of great upheaval deals with or is strongly influenced by that upheaval, not even when the work could plausibly be interpreted in that fashion.[113]

And so, Roberts concludes, "[t]he historical method has its own peculiar temptation toward eisegesis."[114]

In sum, Roberts argues that Job is something of a "timeless text," and in at least two ways: the first is due to the scholarly inability to fix the text firmly in a time and space that could be definitive for its interpretation (especially for all interpreters); the second is that insofar as Job deals with "the same problem" that "had been dealt with before," one that was not uncommon to "the human experience," especially when considered – via the textual clues – as an individual problem not a theodicy for some national catastrophe, then it can be read, interpreted, and understood independently of 587 BCE – or 722 or 332 or 167, for that matter.

In one sense, then, Roberts cannot "fit" Job into Israelite religion, whatever the historical reconstruction "they" offer (once again, because "they" can't agree), but this does not bother him. Job, in his estimation, doesn't need to be fit into (the history of) Israelite religion due to the book's nature, content, and problem – all of which are somehow "timeless."

To be sure, even "timeless" literature comes into being at a particular point in time at a particular place amidst certain circumstances,[115] all or at least some of which would seem to be important to, if not somehow

---

[113] Roberts 2002, p. 116 (my emphasis). Roberts helpfully refers at this point to J. R. R. Tolkien's *Lord of the Rings* trilogy. Note that this observation gives the lie to the assumption that any and every social change must directly and invariably impact religious change. For sentiments on Job similar to those expressed in Roberts' article, though formulated more briefly, see Moberly (2013, p. 244).

[114] Roberts 2002, p. 116.

[115] Or in the case of composite timeless literature, which has grown through various compositional processes, plural forms are probably in order: particular *points* in time at particular *places*. Job may be one such work, given ongoing questions regarding its compositional unity. See, e.g., Perdue 2008, p. 118. But contrast Clines (1989, p. lviii) and Seow (2013, pp. 26-38).

determinative for, its interpretation. I do not wish to challenge Roberts's main conclusions here, however, so much as put them to slightly different use. If Roberts is right – and I think he is – that Job and other texts like *Ludlul* or *The Babylonian Theodicy* are rooted in "the existential experience of rejection, lament, and restoration,"[116] then that is an important datum for considering the interface between Old Testament Theology and Israelite religion. To be specific: what was missing in the preceding discussion of reconstructions of Israelite religion, at least in the early Iron Age highlands, was, for lack of a better word, any *soul* – that is, real, lived religion that impacted persons in profound and affectual ways.[117] For its part, the book of Job has a good bit of "soul": "the existential experience of rejection, lament, and restoration," as Roberts calls it. This "existential experience" is in Job (so also in *Ludlul* and *The Babylonian Theodicy* et al.) at root religious and theological in so far as it concerns the pious person and his God. And, if Roberts can't fit Job into Israelite religion due to problems pertaining to the insufficiency of diachronic analysis, many recent reconstructions of Israelite religion suffer the same problem – not because of diachrony, but because there seems to be very little room for any religious experience whatsoever in them, and certainly no room for the most profound variety like that attested in Job. Early Israelite religion seems to be little more than subsistence survival, with a dash of primitive "magic" or "superstition." There's no thought in that, and certainly no high thought that would reflect profound wrestling with substantive theological problems – "existential experiences," that is, "of rejection, lament, and restoration" which involve humanity coming face-to-face with what it deems *not* human or *supra*human: namely, the

---

[116] Roberts 2002, p. 115. For *Ludlul* see the sensitive treatment in Moran 2002, pp. 182-200; also Jacobsen 1976, p. 162; 1977, esp. pp. 212-216. For more on texts such as these, see Sparks (2005, pp. 56-83) and, for translations, see *ANET* 589-91, *COS* 1.179:573-75 (*A Man and His God, the "Sumerian Job"*); *ANET* 596-600, *COS* 1.153:486-92 (*Ludlul*); *ANET* 601-604, *COS* 1.154:492-95 (*The Babylonian Theodicy*); *ANET* 600-601, *COS* 1:155:495-96 (*The Dialogue of Pessimism*).

[117] In Johnson's terminology: "religious experience" (1998, *passim*). While benefiting immensely from a reading of Johnson's work at the end of my work on this article, I note that he has a different and more negative view of theology than what I express here (1998, pp. 2-4). My use sees profitable overlap between "theology" and "religion" and "religious experience" (see notes 9 and 85 above). While that is somewhat fuzzy, and Johnson's more consistent terminology might be preferable, it may be that the issues he faces in the study of Christian origins differ from those under examination here. In any event, I do not deem "theology" to be a problem like he does, but see it as a subset of religious experience: faith seeking understanding, as it were, or, in William P. Brown's memorable reformulation, "fear seeking understanding" (2014).

divine. Many reconstructions of early Israelite religion cannot account, then, for a book like Job, or the predicament(s) and issue(s) it raises. At this point, Job is a microcosm of the problem the Old Testament as a whole poses for reconstructions of Israelite religion that were discussed in the previous section. What explains Job in these reconstructions? Where does it come from, especially when it is antedated, in most scholarly reckonings, by ancient Near Eastern materials that address the same issues hundreds of years earlier?

The problem with the non-fit of Job (or *Job)[118] in reconstructions of Israelite religion is two-fold: (1) First, the inability of reconstructions of Israelite religion to account for Job neglects in a rather odd way the fact that these existential-theological-religious issues are attested *outside* Israel, *long before* Israel. Van der Toorn knows this better than most scholars, having written a brilliant treatment of the problem of sin and theodicy in the Hebrew Bible and ancient Near East already as his dissertation.[119] The problem of the non-fit of Job, then, is not because van der Toorn doesn't know of these other ancient Near Eastern texts, their content, or even their "existential" aspects. The problem is that those texts and their concomitant religious experience and theological content are not permitted to function, analogously, in so many reconstructions of ancient Israelite religion.[120] This religious experience is, to crib from Luke Timothy Johnson's work, "what's missing from Israelite religion."[121]

---

[118] The problem persists even in composition-critical approaches that would break the book into its constituent parts or otherwise fillet it into earlier or later pieces. Cf. note 115 above.

[119] See van der Toorn 1985. Note also van der Toorn 1991, pp. 59-75; and van der Toorn 2002, pp. 265-77.

[120] Van der Toorn is certainly not alone at this point. Note, famously, Frank Moore Cross's opinion that "[t]here is a sense in which Job brought the ancient religion of Israel to an end," because the argument of Job "repudiated the God of history" (1973, p. 344). Cf. Roberts 2002, 114: "what F. M. Cross fails to stress is that such a God did not reveal himself to Job's friends either. His friends do not appeal to the sacred history, and they seem as much at home with the god of myth as Job is." Note that Job does not show up in the subject indices of either Zevit (2001) or Hess (2007), its use being confined in those works to small citations of particular verses. Similarly King and Stager 2001, p. 76. Rainer Albertz's work is notable for devoting an extended section to Job (1994, vol. 2, pp. 511-17), but Albertz presents Job as a crisis of personal theology of the upper class. While accounting for Job in one sense, Albertz's treatment falls prey to many of Roberts's criticisms. Cf., similarly, van der Toorn 2002, pp. 265-77, for an account of Job that is strikingly similar to Albertz's, and which is also subject to Roberts's critique.

[121] See Johnson's first chapter, "What's Missing from Christian Origins" (1998, pp. 1-38).

Let me be clear that my point in noting the attestation of these religious/theological aspects in extra-biblical literatures that antedate Israelite instances of the same should not be understood as an argument about influence or dating, the latter of which, at least, would be subject to the same problems Roberts's essay identifies (debate over chronology, mechanisms of influence, and so forth).[122] It is, instead, to simply observe that, if someone in the Kassite period can struggle with these sorts of existential-religious-theological issues,[123] or an Egyptian can do it in *The Dispute of a Man with His Ba*,[124] then certainly Job can. And if Job can — that is, if the author(s) of Job can — then reconstructions of Israelite religion need to become *more biblical* and *more textual* than they have been of late (cf. Roberts's "stick[ing] to the text"), and *far more theological* to boot. The dirt is only going to tell us so much and it won't tell us as much as we need to know if we care about religious experience, affect, and the like. For the latter, we need access to the larger symbolic systems that reflect and shape these aspects of religion, and the textual data, while not comprising a complete picture by any means, are nevertheless crucial for that.[125]

(2) The non-fit of Job faces a second problem because, in the historical and literary reconstruction evidenced in van der Toorn's work, what one encounters in Job can only be the product of a much, much later development. Once again clarity at this point is crucial: I do not wish to challenge developmentalism writ large. Things change, including ideas, and such change often includes thickening, increased precision, and complexity. That is not the only way things develop, however;[126] regardless, we still have to deal with Job-like parallels in the ancient Near Eastern materials that precede Job (whenever Job is to be placed). Again, I am not interested in dating Job early, I only wish to observe the existence of its existential-religious-theological issues in *antecedent* cognate data. So,

---

[122] Roberts (2002, p. 115) cites both *Ludlul* and *The Babylonian Theodicy*, indicating that the latter "must have exercised at least an indirect influence on the biblical work."

[123] For the date, see Moran 2002, pp. 21-29.

[124] See *AEL* 1:163-69; *ANET* 405-407; *LAE* 178-87 for translations.

[125] To be sure, archaeology can get at symbol systems in various ways, perhaps most especially via iconography. See the insightful comments of Othmar Keel and Christoph Uehlinger (1998, pp. 7-13, 393-396). For a recent iconographical attempt to get at emotion-language, see Strawn (2014, pp. 91-134). See Johnson (1998, pp. 39-68) for an approach that is phenomenological.

[126] E.g., languages can simplify, over time, not just become more complicated, even if such simplification is often caused by outside interference of some sort (e.g., linguistic contact, insufficient language acquisition, etc.).

in the positing and articulation of certain developmental schemata – especially of the overly uniform or linear kind – it would seem that many reconstructions of Israelite religion fare no better than classic "Wellhausenianism" when it comes to the finally rather simple-minded idea that complex presentations must be (much) late(r), if not also somehow devolved (an odd development, to be sure!) despite their complexity (so, e.g., for Wellhausen: P long after after J/E).[127] A correlate result (equally problematic it seems) is that the Hebrew Bible becomes the ultimate in late constructivism with its use for understanding Israelite religion deeply problematic at best and perhaps completely irrelevant at worst.

More on this last point – what the Old Testament and its theology is good for in the wake of reconstructions of Israelite religion – in the next section. Before (re)turning to that, however, let me just point out again (cf. above) that Job is not alone in highlighting these sorts of problems that face the interface (or not) of reconstructions of Israelite religion and Old Testament Theology. The Psalms pose the same problem. At least some of them, at least according to some scholars, originate from Iron Age Israel, if not Late Bronze Age "Canaan" – even if we can't be certain about all the details.[128] Or, moving backward, it seems safe to say that not all of the Psalms are Hasmonean! It isn't the date that is the primary point, however, it is *the religious experience* that they represent. Consider but one simple line from Ps 127:2:

> He (i.e., Yahweh) gives sleep to his beloved.

This line seems utterly unexplainable in any depictions of Israelite religion that are insufficiently...well, religious and/or theological.[129] Why would a deity "give" (נתן) sleep to an individual if not out of some sort of care for such a person – a point underscored by calling said person the deity's "beloved" (ידידו)? An intimate term to be sure! And why "sleep" (שנא)?[130] Sleep is fundamental to human health and life; it is also an activity that suggests safety and security. The God depicted in just this

---

[127] Cf. Johnson (1998, p. 182) on how developmental schemata are often ways to avoid dealing with the phenomenon of religious experience.
[128] So (perhaps!), Psalms 29, 68, 104. Others could be added to this list, but all could be seriously debated. Once again, the dating of texts seems an insufficient foundation on which to build.
[129] See Moran (2002, p. 188) for an Old Babylonian text which also captures a great deal of religious affect: "A young man weeps to his god as to a friend."
[130] On the form שנא (rather than שנה), see Goldingay 2008, p. 497 n. 3; Kraus 1993, p. 454.

one line of Psalm 127 apparently feels strongly, even passionately, about human beings, and seems to care for them enough to provide them with something essential for human existence along with the circumstances needed to experience it (cf. Ps 3:5: "I lie down and sleep; I wake again for the LORD sustains me" [NRSV]).[131]

And it doesn't stop with an example like this one from the Psalms – which could be repeated *ad infinitum* – what of the heart language in 1 Sam 2:1; 4:13; and 10:26?[132] Or the love language in Deuteronomy, not all of which need be seen as politicized speech?[133] If one is looking for a rather acerbic religious experience vis-à-vis the Deity, one may perhaps locate that in Qoheleth (though I myself would understand that book somewhat differently), but – and here is further proof of the point – that book is almost universally dated to the Hellenistic period, not the early Iron Age.[134]

CONCLUSION:
WHAT IS THE (*)OLD TESTAMENT GOOD FOR?

It should be clear by now that the preceding section on Job was no detour but actually quite important as it showcased some of the problems involved in relating reconstructions of Israelite religion to Old Testament Theology. This was, of course, also discussed in earlier sections, but considering Job allowed us to see the problems from the other side – a more textual(ized) side rather than an historical or anthropological one. The problems are several, but can be glossed with the question "What is the Old Testament?" or "What is the Old Testament good for?" especially vis-à-vis recent reconstructions of Israelite religion. There is clearly no going back from key insights that have been hard won over decades

---

[131] Cf. Moran (2002, p. 188) for an Old Babylonian exemplar of comparable deity-care: "I am your god, your creator, your refuge. My guards are awake for you, are strong for you. I will open for you a hiding place. Long life will I give you." The god who says this is a personal god, but note the description of Marduk in *Ludlul* I:19-20 as a cow who constantly looks behind for its calf (the worshipper). See also Annus and Lezni 2010, pp., 15, 31; also Moran 2002, p. 194.

[132] 1 Sam 2:1: "Hannah prayed and said, 'My heart exults in the LORD'"; 4:13: "Eli was sitting upon his seat by the road watching, for his heart trembled for the ark of God"; 10:26: "with him [Saul] went warriors whose hearts God had touched" (NRSV).

[133] *Pace* Moran 1963, 77-87. See Lapsley 2003, pp. 350-69.

[134] A notable exception is Choon-Leong Seow, who places Qoheleth in the Persian Period (1997, pp. 11-21).

of painstaking historical research on ancient Israel and its cultural congeners. To the extent that those insights are accurate, they are not only true, they are profoundly helpful; no one would *want* to retreat from them. One of the most important of these insights is that the Old Testament does not provide a direct or unmediated picture of ancient Israelite religion.[135] Things on the ground were far more complicated than what one might otherwise think upon a facile reading of the Old Testament.[136] One aspect of this complexity is precisely religious: religious experience was no doubt more complex and diversified in ancient Israel than what scholars of previous generations envisioned largely because they relied (overmuch) on the Old Testament.[137] In one sense, then, it is no surprise at all that reconstructions of Israelite religion *à la* van der Toorn's dream report about Ramat-Yachin are drastically different than what one finds in the Old Testament. That is to be expected, part of the deal.

Then again, part of the problem in relating studies of Israelite religion and Old Testament Theology is the notorious specter of "the facile reading of the Old Testament." Any such reading – from whichever perspective (and it can come from several sides) – simply will not do, especially when there is a good bit of complexity and diversity present in the pages of the Bible itself, and because at least some of that biblical material is drawn upon and used, even if only selectively, in reconstructions of Israelite religion, especially in those that highlight diversity and difference from the Hebrew Bible and the religion and/or theology it contains or somehow reflects or represents.

This is to say that the Old Testament *itself* is a datum that should – indeed *must* – be considered in reconstructions of Israelite religion. And that means that the religion and/or theology that it contains is also a

---

[135] Cf. Levenson 1993, p. 107: "the basis of religion in biblical times was not a Bible: the religion *in* the Book is not the religion *of* the Book."

[136] See, e.g., Stavrakopoulou and Barton 2010. Note, however, Johnson (1998, p. 21) for the problem in assuming that "each dissected strand of literature adequately represents the ideology of a separate 'community.'"

[137] See, e.g., Ringgren 1966, pp. 4-14; Fohrer 1972, pp. 24-25; Leslie, 1936. Of course this, too, must be qualified. Close attention to the entire Old Testament reveals a large range in terms of religious experience or affect – the difference, for example, between starchy Qoheleth and the rapturous hymns of praise in the Psalter. It is not, then, only historical or archaeological data that produces this kind of differentiated insight, but also attentive reading of the literature. In this way, relying "overmuch" on the Old Testament could actually lead to the very same results as another kind of developmental or diachronic approach. Furthermore, the giants of the previous generation – e.g., Hermann Gunkel, Walther Eichrodt, and Gerhard von Rad – were anything but facile readers.

datum for Israelite religion. Further, the book of Job is a datum, as is the issue(s) that it represents. So also are *Ludlul* and other such texts, along with their comparable issues, data.[138] These too, that is, are, as it were, pieces of historical evidence that are every bit as important and valid as, say, the texts from Ugarit or Baalistic PNs among the Samaria ostraca.[139] But, if one only attends to items such as the latter, what the Old Testament is and what it (re)presents become impossible – virtually unexplainable in terms of origins and content, or explainable only in terms of a certain kind of greatly reduced historicism or ideology. The Old Testament in the aggregate, in this perspective, is good for almost nothing when it comes to reconstructing Israelite religions.[140] If the most un(der) religious presentations of Israelite religion, especially vis-à-vis Yahwism as known from the Hebrew Bible (a diverse phenomenon, let it be again underscored), were true, Old Testament Theology would become ethereal, abstract, even "mythic" (in the fictive sense) – something far removed, if not completely severed, from so much reality in ancient Israel, especially of earlier periods. In such a scenario Old Testament Theology must be(come) something that treats the Old Testament as a product (only) of later elite culture, an ideological product of scribes or priests or kings, that can and perhaps should be mistrusted, not only because it is elite and ideological, but because it is so grossly inaccurate when it comes to the "facts on the ground."[141] Old Testament Theology would need to traffic in the realm of fable, make-believe, fiction, as

---

[138] See Moran (2002, p. 187) for his opinion that in *Ludlul*, the sufferer ("Mesopotamian Everyman") is, "in his hour of deepest desperation…made aware of another and, to him, new reality, the reality of Marduk, and there is revealed to him a new personal religion, the religion of Marduk, a religion that transforms and transcends the religions and problems of the past." Cf. Moran 2002, p. 198: "*Ludlul* seems to be almost the logical extension of Marduk's lordship over creation and history into the domain of individual lives. If he rules the world and all that happens in it, he should rule the individual as well. A sovereignty less pervasive would not be absolute." Cf. Annus and Lezni 2010 p. xxxvi: "Whatever else *Ludlul* is, it is certainly a text that we would intuitively call 'religious' because it praises a deity, Marduk, and commends his veneration."

[139] That is to say that a focus on religious experience and/or theology need not be *a*-historical. See Johnson 1998. Cf. analogously the thoughtful revisioning of historical criticism in F. W. Dobbs-Allsopp (1999, pp. 235-271).

[140] Or, to provide a slightly different angle in light of van der Toorn's reconstruction vis-à-vis Deuteronomism, one could say that Deuteronomy and its exponents changed Israelite religion so drastically that the Old Testament, which is post-Deuteronomy, is of little if no help whatsoever for what was pre-Deuteronomy, simply because the latter has been so drastically and irrevocably altered.

[141] Cf. Dever 2005. It is worth noting that in his most recent book, van der Toorn discusses Job only in passing in a few instances, one of which states "there can be little

something concocted by later religious ideologues – first priests, then scribes, then rulers, until then, even more belatedly, believers (no doubt conservative ideologues themselves) of whatever stripe, whether Jewish or Christian. Old Testament Theology, in this view, could simply be dispensed with – for more than one good reason – as secondary and inferior to the more real and substantive work emerging from historical reconstruction and archaeology, whether the stratification in question is of a tell or of a text. This is the rather sad and dismal picture of what Old Testament Theology would, and perhaps should, look like if recent reconstructions of Israelite religion were accurate.[142]

But, as I have tried to show in this article, not everything "they" say about Israelite religion is true. Consider, for example, Yahweh's servant Job.

ALBERTZ, R.
1994   *A History of Israelite Religion in the Old Testament Period* (Old Testament Library), 2 vols. Louisville: Westminster/John Knox.

ANNUS, A. and LEZNI, A.
2010   *Ludlul bēl nēmeqi: The Standard Babylonian Poem of the Righteous Sufferer* (State Archives of Assyria Cuneiform Texts 7). Helsinki: The Neo-Assyrian Text Corpus Project

BROWN, W. P.
2014   *Wisdom's Wonder: Character, Creation, and Crisis in the Bible's Wisdom Literature*. Grand Rapids: Eerdmans.

BRUEGGEMANN, W.
1997   *Theology of the Old Testament: Testimony, Dispute, Advocacy*. Minneapolis: Fortress Press.

BYRNE, R.
2004   "Lie Back and Think of Judah: The Reproductive Politics of Pillar Figurines," *Near Eastern Archaeology* 67: 137-51.

CLINES, D. J. A.
1989   *Job 1-20* (Word Biblical Commentary 17). Dallas: Word.

CROSS, F. M.
1973   *Canaanite Myth and Hebrew Epic: Essays in the History of the Religion of Israel*. Cambridge: Harvard University Press.

---

doubt that the Book of Job goes back to a scribe as well" (2007, p. 116). Cf. note 120 above on Albertz's and van der Toorn's readings of Job in Israelite religion.

[142] The only alternative of which I am aware would be to take the Old Testament as intentionally polemical *against* much (most?) of Israelite religion and self-consciously so. See, e.g., Wright 1995, pp. 68-90. I deem this approach unsuccessful and unsatisfying as well, in part because – at least in Wright's case – it depends entirely too much on reconstructions of Israelite religion that are not yet certain.

DAMASIO, A. R.
1994 *Decartes' Error: Emotion, Reason, and the Human Brain*. New York: Quill.
1999 *The Feeling of What Happens: Body and Emotion in the Making of Consciousness*. San Diego: Harcourt.

DEVER, WILLIAM G.
2005 *Does God Have a Wife? Archaeology and Folk Religion in Ancient Israel*. Grand Rapids: Eerdmans.

DOBBS-ALLSOPP, F. W.
1999 "Rethinking Historical Criticism," *Biblical Interpretation* 7:235-271.

EICHRODT, W.
2004 "Does Old Testament Theology Still Have Independent Significance within Old Testament Scholarship?" in *Old Testament Theology: Flowering and Future* (Sources for Biblical and Theological Studies 1), edited by B. C. Ollenburger, pp. 21-29. Winona Lake: Eisenbrauns.

EISSFELDT, O.
2004 "The History of Israelite-Jewish Religion and Old Testament Theology," in *Old Testament Theology: Flowering and Future* (Sources for Biblical and Theological Studies 1), edited by B. C. Ollenburger, pp. 12-20. Winona Lake: Eisenbrauns.

FREUD, S.
2010 *The Interpretation of Dreams*. New York: Basic Books.

FOHRER, G.
1972 *History of Israelite Religion*, translated by D. E. Green. Nashville: Abingdon.

FOWLER, J. D.
1988 *Theophoric Personal Names in Ancient Hebrew: A Comparative Study* (Journal for the Study of Old Testament Supplement 49). Sheffield: JSOT Press.

GOLDINGAY, J.
2008 *Psalms*, Vol. 3: *Psalms 90-150*. Grand Rapids: Baker Academic.

GRABBE, L. L.
"'Canaanite': Some Methodological Observations in Relation to Biblical Study," in *Ugarit and the Bible* (UBL 11), edited by G. J. Brooke, A. H. W. Curtis, and J. F. Healey, pp. 113-32. Münster: Ugarit-Verlag.

HASEL, G. F.
1991 *Old Testament Theology: Basic Issues in the Current Debate*. Grand Rapids: Eerdmans.

HESS, R. S.
1999 "The Onomastics of Ugarit," in *Handbook of Ugaritic Studies* (Handbuch der Orientalistik 1/39), edited by W. G. E. Watson and N. Wyatt, pp. 499-528. Leiden: Brill.
2007 *Israelite Religions: An Archaeological and Biblical Survey*. Grand Rapids: Baker Academic.

JACOBSEN, T.
1976 *The Treasures of Darkness: A History of Mesopotamian Religion.* New Haven: Yale University Press.
1977 "Mesopotamia," in *The Intellectual Adventure of Ancient Man: An Essay on Speculative Thought in the Ancient Near East,* edited by H. A. Frankfort, pp. 125-220. Chicago: University of Chicago Press.

JANZEN, J. G.
1987 "The Place of the Book of Job in The History of Israel's Religion," in *Ancient Israelite Religion*, edited by P. D. Miller, P. D. Hanson, and S.D. McBride, pp. 523-37. Minneapolis: Fortress.
2012 "Solidarity and Solitariness in Ancient Israel: The Case of Jeremiah," in *When Prayer Takes Place: Forays into a Biblical World,* edited by B. A. Strawn and P. D. Miller, pp. 211-217. Eugene, OR: Cascade.

JOHNSON, L. T.
1998 *Religious Experience in Earliest Christianity.* Minneapolis: Fortress Press.

KEEL, O. and UEHLINGER, C.
1988 *Gods, Goddesses, and Images of God in Ancient Israel,* translated by T. Trapp. Minneapolis: Fortress Press.

KING, P. J. and STAGER, L. E.
2001 *Life in Biblical Israel* (LAI). Lousville: Westminster John Knox.

KNIERIM, R. P.
1995 *The Task of Old Testament Theology: Substance, Method, and Cases.* Grand Rapids: Eerdmans.

KOLAKOWSKI, L.
1992 *Religion.* New York: Oxford University Press.

KRAUS, H. J.
1993 *Psalms 60-150: A Continental Commentary,* translated by H. C. Oswald. Minneapolis: Fortress.

LAPSLEY, J. E.
2003 "Feeling Our Way: Love for God in Deuteronomy," *Catholic Biblical Quarterly* 65: 350-69.

LESLIE, E.
1936 *Old Testament Religion.* Nashville: Abingdon Press.

LEVENSON, JON D.
1993 *The Hebrew Bible, the Old Testament, and Historical Criticism: Jews and Christians in Biblical Studies.* Louisville: Westminster/John Knox.

MICHENER, JAMES A.
1965 *The Source: A Novel.* New York: Random House.

MILLER, P. D.
2000 *The Religion of Ancient Israel* (LAI). Louisville: Westminster John Knox.

MOBERLY, R. W. L.
2013 *Old Testament Theology: Reading the Hebrew Bible as Christian Scripture.* Grand Rapids: Baker Academic.

Moran, W. L.
1963 "The Ancient Near Eastern Background of the Love of God in Deuteronomy," *Catholic Biblical Quarterly* 25: 77-87.

Moran, W. L.
2002 "The Babylonian Job," in *The Most Magic Word: Essays on Babylonian and Biblical Literature* (CBQMS 35), edited by R. S. Hendel, pp. 182-200. Washington, DC: Catholic Biblical Association.

Norin, S.
2013 *Personennamen und Religion im alten Israel untersucht mit besonderer Berücksichtigung der Namen auf El und Baʻal* (CBOT 60). Winona Lake: Eisenbrauns.

Oppenheim, A. L.
1977 *Ancient Mesopotamia: Portrait of a Dead Civilization.* Chicago: University of Chicago Press.

Pals, D. L.
2015 *Nine Theories of Religion.* 3d edition New York: Oxford University Press.

Perdue, L. G.
2008 *The Sword and the Stylus: An Introduction to Wisdom in the Age of Empires.* Grand Rapids: Eerdmans.

Reventlow H. G.
1985 *Problems of Old Testament Theology in the Twentieth Century.* Philadelphia: Fortress.

Ringgren, H.
1966 *Israelite Religion,* translated by D. E. Green. Philadelphia: Fortress Press

Roberts, J. J. M.
1977 "Job and the Israelite Religious Tradition," *ZAW* 89:107-14
2002 *The Bible and the Ancient Near East: Collected Essays.* Winona Lake: Eisenbrauns.

Rogerson, John W.
2010 *A Theology of the Old Testament: Cultural Memory, Communication, and Being Human.* Minneapolis: Fortress Press.

Routledge, C.
2006 "Parallelism in Popular and Official Religion in Ancient Egypt," in *Text, Artifact, and Image: Revealing Ancient Israelite Religion* (BJS 346), edited by G. Beckman and T. J. Lewis, pp. 223-38. Providence, RI: Brown Judaic Studies.

Schneider, T. J.
2011 *An Introduction to Ancient Mesopotamian Religion.* Grand Rapids: Eerdmans.

Seow, C. L.
1997 *Ecclesiastes: A New Translation with Introduction and Commentary* (AB 18C). New York: Doubleday.
2013 *Job 1-21: Interpretation and Commentary* (Illuminations), Grand Rapids: Eerdmans.

SMITH, J. Z.
1998 "Religion, Religions, Religious," in *Critical Terms for Religious Studies*, edited by M. C. Taylor, pp. 269-84. Chicago: University of Chicago.

SMITH, M. S.
2007 "Recent Study of Israelite Religion in Light of the Ugaritic Texts," in *Ugarit at Seventy-Five*, edited by K. Lawson Younger, pp. 1-26. Winona Lake: Eisenbrauns.

SPARKS, K. L.
2005 *Ancient Texts for the Study of the Hebrew Bible: A Guide to the Background Literature*. Peabody: Hendrickson.

STAVRAKOPOULOU, F., and BARTON, J. EDS.
2010 *Religious Diversity in Ancient Israel and Judah*. London: T & T Clark, 2010.

STRAWN, B. A.
2014 "The Iconography of Fear: *Yir'at YHWH* [יראת יהוה] in Artistic Perspective," in *Image, Text, Exegesis: Iconographic Interpretation and the Hebrew Bible* (LHBOTS, 588), edited by I. J. de Hulster and J. M. LeMon, pp. 91-134. London: Bloomsbury.
2015 "On Walter Brueggemann: (A Personal) Testimony, (Three) Dispute(s), (and On) Advocacy," in *Imagination, Ideology and Inspiration: Echoes of Brueggemann in a New Generation* (Hebrew Bible Monographs, 72), edited by J. Kaplan and R. Williamson, Jr., pp. 9-47. Sheffield: Sheffield Academic Press.
Forthcoming, "The History of Israelite Religion," in *The Cambridge Companion to the Old Testament/Hebrew Bible*, edited by S. B. Chapman and M. A. Sweeney. Cambridge: Cambridge University Press.

TIGAY, J. H.
1986 *You Shall Have No Other Gods: Israelite Religion in the Light of Hebrew Inscriptions* (HSS 31). Atlanta: Scholars Press.

VAN SETERS, JOHN
2006 *The Edited Bible: The Curious History of the "Editor" in Biblical Criticism*. Winona Lake: Eisenbrauns.

VAN DER TOORN, K.
1985 *Sin and Sanction in Israel and Mesopotamia: A Comparative Study* (SSN 22). Assen/Maastricht: Van Gorcum.
1991 "The Ancient Near Eastern Literary Dialogue as a Vehicle of Critical Reflection," in *Dispute Poems and Dialogues in the Ancient and Mediaeval Near East* (OLA 42), edited by G. J. Reinink and H. L. J. Vanstiphout, pp. 59-75. Leuven: Peeters.
1994 *From Her Cradle to Her Grave: The Role of Religion in the Life of the Israelite and Babylonian Woman*, translated by S. J. Denning-Bolle. Sheffield: JSOT.
1996 *Family Religion in Babylonia, Syria and Israel: Continuity and Change in the Forms of Religious Life* (SHCANE 7). Leiden: Brill.
2002 "Sources in Heaven: Revelation as a Scholarly construct in Second Temple Judaism," in *Kein Land für sich allein* (OBO 186), edited by U. Hübner and E. A. Knauf, pp. 265-77. Freiburg: Universitätsverlag.

2003 "Nine Months among the Peasants in the Palestinian Highlands: An Anthropological Perspective on Local Religion in the Early Iron Age," in *Symbiosis, Symbolism, and the Power of the Past: Canaan, Ancient Israel, and Their Neighbors from the Late Bronze Age through Roman Palaestina: Proceedings of the Centennial Symposium W. F. Albright Institute of Archaeological Research and American Schools of Oriental Research, Jerusalem, May 29-31, 2000,* edited by W.G. Dever and S. Gifin, pp. 393-410. Winona Lake: Eisenbrauns.

2007 *Scribal Culture and the Making of the Hebrew Bible.* Cambridge: Harvard University Press.

2015. "Scribes and Scribalism," in *The Oxford Encyclopedia of the Bible and Law*, 2 vols., edited by B. A. Strawn, 2: 278-85. Oxford: Oxford University Press.

VITA, J. P.
1999 "The Society of Ugarit," in *Handbook of Ugaritic Studies* (Handbuch der Orientalistik 1/39), edited by W. G. E. Watson and N. Wyatt, pp. 455-98. Leiden: Brill.

VON RAD, G.
1965 *Old Testament Theology*, Vol. 2: *The Theology of Israel's Prophetic Traditions*, translated by D. M. G. Stalker; San Francisco: Harper and Row.

WHITEHEAD, A. N.
1969 *Religion in the Making.* New York: World.

WRIGHT, D. P.
2013 "Syro-Canaanite Religions," in *The Cambridge History of Religions in the Ancient World*, Vol. 1: *From the Bronze Age to the Hellenistic Age*, edited by M. R. Salzman and M. A. Sweeney, pp.129-50. Cambridge: Cambridge University Press.

WRIGHT, J. W.
1995 "Toward a Holiness Hermeneutic: The Old Testament against Israelite Religion," *Wesleyan Theological Journal* 30: 68-90.

ZADOK, R.
1988 *The Pre-Hellenistic Israelite Anthroponymy and Prosopography* (Orientalia Lovaniensia analecta, 28). Leuven: Peeters.

ZEVIT, Z.
2001 *The Religions of Ancient Israel: A Synthesis of Parallactic Approaches.* London: Continuum.

ZEVIT, Z.
2003 "False Dichotomies in Descriptions of Israelite Religion: A Problem, Its Origin, and a Proposed Solution," in in *Symbiosis, Symbolism, and the Power of the Past: Canaan, Ancient Israel, and Their Neighbors from the Late Bronze Age through Roman Palaestina: Proceedings of the Centennial Symposium W. F. Albright Institute of Archaeological Research and American Schools of Oriental Research, Jerusalem, May 29-31, 2000,* edited by W.G. Dever and S. Gifin, pp. 225-35. Winona Lake: Eisenbrauns.

Contributions to Biblical Exegesis and Theology

1. J.A. Loader, *A Tale of Two Cities, Sodom and Gomorrah in the Old Testament, early Jewish and early Christian Traditions*, Kampen, 1990
2. P.W. Van der Horst, *Ancient Jewish Epitaphs. An Introductory Survey of a Millennium of Jewish Funerary Epigraphy (300 BCE-700 CE)*, Kampen, 1991
3. E. Talstra, *Solomon's Prayer. Synchrony and Diachrony in the Composition of 1 Kings 8, 14-61*, Kampen, 1993
4. R. Stahl, *Von Weltengagement zu Weltüberwindung: Theologische Positionen im Danielbuch*, Kampen, 1994
5. J.N. Bremmer, *Sacred History and Sacred Texts in early Judaism. A Symposium in Honour of A.S. van der Woude*, Kampen, 1992
6. K. Larkin, *The Eschatology of Second Zechariah: A Study of the Formation of a Mantological Wisdom Anthology*, Kampen, 1994
7. B. Aland, *New Testament Textual Criticism, Exegesis and Church History: A Discussion of Methods*, Kampen, 1994
8. P.W. Van der Horst, *Hellenism-Judaism-Christianity: Essays on their Interaction*, Kampen, Second Enlarged Edition, 1998
9. C. Houtman, *Der Pentateuch: die Geschichte seiner Erforschung neben einer Auswertung*, Kampen, 1994
10. J. Van Seters, *The Life of Moses. The Yahwist as Historian in Exodus-Numbers*, Kampen, 1994
11. Tj. Baarda, *Essays on the Diatessaron*, Kampen, 1994
12. Gert J. Steyn, *Septuagint Quotations in the Context of the Petrine and Pauline Speeches of the Acta Apostolorum*, Kampen, 1995
13. D.V. Edelman, *The Triumph of Elohim, From Yahwisms to Judaisms*, Kampen, 1995
14. J.E. Revell, *The Designation of the Individual. Expressive Usage in Biblical Narrative*, Kampen, 1996
15. M. Menken, *Old Testament Quotations in the Fourth Gospel*, Kampen, 1996
16. V. Koperski, *The Knowledge of Christ Jesus my Lord. The High Christology of Philippians 3:7-11*, Kampen, 1996
17. M.C. De Boer, *Johannine Perspectives on the Death of Jesus*, Kampen, 1996
18. R.D. Anderson, *Ancient Rhetorical Theory and Paul*, Revised edition, Leuven, 1998
19. L.C. Jonker, *Exclusivity and Variety, Perspectives on Multi-dimensional Exegesis*, Kampen, 1996
20. L.V. Rutgers, *The Hidden Heritage of Diaspora Judaism*, Leuven, 1998
21. K. van der Toorn (ed.), *The Image and the Book*, Leuven, 1998
22. L.V. Rutgers, P.W. van der Horst (eds.), *The Use of Sacred Books in the Ancient World*, Leuven, 1998
23. E.R. Ekblad Jr., *Isaiah's Servant Poems According to the Septuagint. An Exegetical and Theological Study*, Leuven, 1999
24. R.D. Anderson Jr., *Glossary of Greek Rhetorical Terms*, Leuven, 2000
25. T. Stordalen, *Echoes of Eden*, Leuven, 2000
26. H. Lalleman-de Winkel, *Jeremiah in Prophetic Tradition*, Leuven, 2000
27. J.F.M. Smit, *About the Idol Offerings. Rhetoric, Social Context and Theology of Paul's Discourse in First Corinthians 8:1-11:1*, Leuven, 2000
28. T.J. Horner, *Listening to Trypho. Justin Martyr's Dialogue Reconsidered*, Leuven, 2001
29. D.G. Powers, *Salvation through Participation. An Examination of the Notion of the Believers' Corporate Unity with Christ in Early Christian Soteriology*, Leuven, 2001
30. J.S. Kloppenborg, P. Hoffmann, J.M. Robinson, M.C. Moreland (eds.), *The Sayings Gospel Q in Greek and English with Parallels from the Gospels of Mark and Thomas*, Leuven, 2001

31. M.K. Birge, *The Language of Belonging. A Rhetorical Analysis of Kinship Language in First Corinthians*, Leuven, 2004
32. P.W. van der Horst, *Japheth in the Tents of Shem. Studies on Jewish Hellenism in Antiquity*, Leuven, 2002
33. P.W. van der Horst, M.J.J. Menken, J.F.M. Smit, G. van Oyen (eds.), *Persuasion and Dissuasion in Early Christianity, Ancient Judaism, and Hellenism*, Leuven, 2003
34. L.J. Lietaert Peerbolte, *Paul the Missionary*, Leuven, 2003
35. L.M. Teugels, *Bible and midrash. The Story of 'The Wooing of Rebekah'* (Gen. 24), Leuven, 2004
36. H.W. Shin, *Textual Criticism and the Synoptic Problem in Historical Jesus Research. The Search for Valid Criteria*, Leuven, 2004
37. A. Volgers, C. Zamagni (eds.), *Erotapokriseis. Early Christian Question-and-Answer Literature in Context*, Leuven, 2004
38. L.E. Galloway, *Freedom in the Gospel. Paul's Exemplum in 1 Cor 9 in Conversation with the Discourses of Epictetus and Philo*, Leuven, 2004
39. C. Houtman, K. Spronk, *Ein Held des Glaubens? Rezeptionsgeschichtliche Studien zu den Simson-Erzählungen*, Leuven, 2004
40. H. Kahana, Esther. *Juxtaposition of the Septuagint Translation with the Hebrew Text*, Leuven, 2005
41. V.A. Pizzuto, *A Cosmic Leap of Faith. An Authorial, Structural, and Theological Investigation of the Cosmic Christology in Col 1:15-20*, Leuven, 2005
42. B.J. Koet, *Dreams and Scripture in Luke-Acts. Collected Essays*, Leuven, 2006
43. P.C Beentjes. *"Happy the One Who Meditates on Wisdom"* (SIR. 14,20). *Collected Essays on the Book of Ben Sira*, Leuven, 2006
44. R. Roukema, L.J. Lietaert Peerbolte, K. Spronk, J.W. Wesselius (eds.), *The Interpretation of Exodus. Studies in Honour of Cornelis Houtman*, Leuven, 2006
45. G. van Oyen, T. Shepherd (eds.), *The Trial and Death of Jesus. Essays on the Passion Narrative in Mark*, Leuven, 2006
46. B. Thettayil, *In Spirit and Truth. An Exegetical Study of John 4:19-26 and a Theological Investigation of the Replacement Theme in the Fourth Gospel*, Leuven, 2007
47. T.A.W. van der Louw, *Transformations in the Septuagint. Towards an Interaction of Septuagint Studies and Translation Studies*, Leuven, 2007
48. W. Hilbrands, *Heilige oder Hure? Die Rezeptionsgeschichte von Juda und Tamar (Genesis 38) von der Antike bis zur Reformationszeit*, Leuven, 2007
49. J. Joosten, P.J. Tomson (eds.), *Voces Biblicae. Septuagint Greek and its Significance for the New Testament*, Leuven, 2007
50. A. Aejmelaeus, *On the Trail of the Septuagint Translators. Collected Essays*, Leuven, 2007
51. S. Janse, *"You are My Son". The Reception History of Psalm 2 in Early Judaism and the Early Church*, Leuven, 2009
52. K. De Troyer, A. Lange, L.L. Schulte (eds.), *Prophecy after the Prophets? The Contribution of the Dead Sea Scrolls to the Understanding of Biblical and Extra-Biblical Prophecy*, Leuven, 2009
53. C.M. Tuckett (ed.), *Feasts and Festivals*, Leuven, 2009
54. M. Labahn, O. Lehtipuu (eds.), *Anthropology in the New Testament and its Ancient Context*, Leuven, 2010
55. A. van der Kooij, M. van der Meer (eds.), *The Old Greek of Isaiah: Issues and Perspectives*, Leuven, 2010
56. J. Smith, *Translated Hallelujehs. A Linguistic and Exegetical Commentary on Select Septuagint Psalms*, Leuven, 2011
57. N. Dávid, A. Lange (eds.), *Qumran and the Bible. Studying the Jewish and Christian Scriptures in Light of the Dead Sea Scrolls*, Leuven, 2010

58. J. Chanikuzhy, *Jesus, the Eschatological Temple. An Exegetical Study of Jn 2,13-22 in the Light of the Pre 70 C.E. Eschatological Temple Hopes and the Synoptic Temple Action*, Leuven, 2011
59. H. Wenzel, *Reading Zechariah with Zechariah 1:1–6 as the Introduction to the Entire Book*, Leuven, 2011
60. M. Labahn, O. Lehtipuu (eds.), *Imagery in the Booky of Revelation*, Leuven, 2011
61. K. De Troyer, A. Lange, J.S. Adcock (eds.), *The Qumran Legal Texts between the Hebrew Bible and Its Interpretation*, Leuven, 2011
62. B. Lang, *Buch der Kriege – Buch des Himmels. Kleine Schriften zur Exegese und Theologie*, Leuven, 2011
63. H.-J. Inkelaar, *Conflict over Wisdom. The Theme of 1 Corinthians 1-4 Rooted in Scripture*, Leuven, 2011
64. K.-J. Lee, *The Authority and Authorization of Torah in the Persion Period*, Leuven, 2011
65. K.M. Rochester, *Prophetic Ministry in Jeremiah and Ezekiel*, Leuven, 2012
66. T. Law, A. Salvesen (eds.), *Greek Scripture and the Rabbis*, Leuven, 2012
67. K. Finsterbusch, A. Lange (eds.), *What is Bible?*, Leuven, 2012
68. J. Cook, A. van der Kooij, *Law, Prophets, and Wisdom. On the Provenance of Translators and their Books in the Septuagint Version*, Leuven, 2012
69. P.N. De Andrado, *The Akedah Servant Complex. The Soteriological Linkage of Genesis 22 and Isaiah 53 in Ancient Jewish and Early Christian Writings*, Leuven, 2013
70. F. Shaw, *The Earliest Non-Mystical Jewish Use of Iαω*, Leuven, 2014
71. E. Blachman, *The Transformation of Tamar (Genesis 38) in the History of Jewish Interpretation*, Leuven, 2013
72. K. De Troyer, T. Law, M. Liljeström (eds.), *In the Footsteps of Sherlock Holmes. Studies in the Biblical Text in Honour of Anneli Aejmelaeus*, Leuven, 2014
73. T. Do, *Re-thinking the Death of Jesus. An Exegetical and Theological Study of Hilasmos and Agape in 1 John 2:1-2 and 4:7-10*, Leuven, 2014
74. T. Miller, *Three Versions of Esther. Their Relationship to Anti-Semitic and Feminist Critique of the Story*, Leuven, 2014
75. E.B. Tracy, *See Me! Hear Me! Divine/Human Relational Dialogue in Genesis*, Leuven, 2015
76. J.D. Findlay, *From Prophet to Priest. The Characterization of Aaron in the Pentateuch*, Leuven, forthcoming
77. M.J.J. Menken, *Studies in John's Gospel and Epistles. Collected Essays*, Leuven, 2015
78. L.L. Schulte, *My Shepherd, though You Do not Know Me. The Persian Royal Propaganda Model in the Nehemiah Memoir*, Leuven, 2016
79. S.E. Humble, *A Divine Round Trip. The Literary and Christological Function of the Descent/Ascent Leitmotif in the Gospel of John*, Leuven, 2016